NATO ASI Series

Advanced Science Institutes Series

A series presenting the results of activities sponsored by the NATO Science Committee, which aims at the dissemination of advanced scientific and technological knowledge, with a view to strengthening links between scientific communities.

The Series is published by an international board of publishers in conjunction with the NATO Scientific Affairs Division

A	Life Sciences	Plenum Publishing Corporation
B	Physics	London and New York
C	Mathematical and Physical Sciences	Kluwer Academic Publishers Dordrecht, Boston and London
D	Behavioural and Social Sciences	
E	Applied Sciences	
F	Computer and Systems Sciences	Springer-Verlag Berlin Heidelberg New York
G	Ecological Sciences	London Paris Tokyo Hong Kong
H	Cell Biology	Barcelona Budapest
I	Global Environmental Change	

NATO-PCO DATABASE

The electronic index to the NATO ASI Series provides full bibliographical references (with keywords and/or abstracts) to more than 30000 contributions from international scientists published in all sections of the NATO ASI Series. Access to the NATO-PCO DATABASE compiled by the NATO Publication Coordination Office is possible in two ways:

- via online FILE 128 (NATO-PCO DATABASE) hosted by ESRIN, Via Galileo Galilei, I-00044 Frascati, Italy.

- via CD-ROM "NATO Science & Technology Disk" with user-friendly retrieval software in English, French and German (© WTV GmbH and DATAWARE Technologies Inc. 1992).

The CD-ROM can be ordered through any member of the Board of Publishers or through NATO-PCO, Overijse, Belgium.

Series F: Computer and Systems Sciences Vol. 113

The ASI Series Books Published as a Result of
Activities of the Special Programme on
ADVANCED EDUCATIONAL TECHNOLOGY

This book contains the proceedings of a NATO Advanced Research Workshop held within the activities of the NATO Special Programme on Advanced Educational Technology, running from 1988 to 1993 under the auspices of the NATO Science Committee.

The books published so far as a result of the activities of the Special Programme are as follows (further details are given at the end of this volume):

Vol. F 67: Designing Hypermedia for Learning. 1990.
Vol. F 76: Multimedia Interface Design in Education. 1992.
Vol. F 78: Integrating Advanced Technology into Technology Education. 1991.
Vol. F 80: Intelligent Tutoring Systems for Foreign Language Learning. 1992.
Vol. F 81: Cognitive Tools for Learning. 1992.
Vol. F 84: Computer-Based Learning Environments and Problem Solving. 1992.
Vol. F 85: Adaptive Learning Environments: Foundations and Frontiers. 1992.
Vol. F 86: Intelligent Learning Environments and Knowledge Acquisition in Physics. 1992.
Vol. F 87: Cognitive Modelling and Interactive Environments in Language Learning. 1992.
Vol. F 89: Mathematical Problem Solving and New Information Technologies. 1992.
Vol. F 90: Collaborative Learning Through Computer Conferencing. 1992.
Vol. F 91: New Directions for Intelligent Tutoring Systems. 1992.
Vol. F 92: Hypermedia Courseware: Structures of Communication and Intelligent Help. 1992.
Vol. F 93: Interactive Multimedia Learning Environments. 1992.
Vol. F 95: Comprehensive System Design: A New Educational Technology. 1993.
Vol. F 96: New Directions in Educational Technology. 1992.
Vol. F 97: Advanced Models of Cognition for Medical Training and Practice. 1992.
Vol. F104: Instructional Models in Computer-Based Learning Environments. 1992.
Vol. F105: Designing Environments for Constructive Learning. 1993.
Vol. F107: Advanced Educational Technology for Mathematics and Science. 1993.
Vol. F109: Advanced Educational Technology in Technology Education. 1993.
Vol. F111: Cognitive Models and Intelligent Environments for Learning Programming. 1993.
Vol. F112: Item Banking: Interactive Testing and Self-Assessment. 1993.
Vol. F113: Interactive Learning Technology for the Deaf. 1993.
Vol. F115: Learning Electricity and Electronics with Advanced Educational Technology. 1993.
Vol. F116: Control Technology in Elementary Education. 1993.
Vol. F117: Intelligent Learning Environments: The Case of Geometry. 1993.

Interactive Learning Technology for the Deaf

Edited by

Ben A. G. Elsendoorn
Instituut voor Doven (Institute for the Deaf/IvD)
Theerestraat 42, 5271 GD Sint-Michielsgestel
The Netherlands

Frans Coninx
Instituut voor Doven (Institute for the Deaf/IvD)
Theerestraat 42, 5271 GD Sint-Michielsgestel
The Netherlands
and
Universität zu Köln, Heilpädagogische Fakultät
Klosterstrasse 79b, D-50931 Köln, Germany

With the assistance of
Annelies Brekelmans

Springer-Verlag
Berlin Heidelberg NewYork London Paris Tokyo
Hong Kong Barcelona Budapest
Published in cooperation with NATO Scientific Affairs Division

Proceedings of the NATO Advanced Research Workshop on Interactive
Learning Technology for the Deaf, held in Sint-Michielsgestel, The
Netherlands, June 4-7, 1991

CR Subject Classification (1991): K.3.1, J.3, J.5, K.4.2

ISBN 3-540-57150-7 Springer-Verlag Berlin Heidelberg New York
ISBN 0-387-57150-7 Springer-Verlag New York Berlin Heidelberg

This work is subject to copyright. All rights are reserved, whether the whole or part of the material is
concerned, specifically the rights of translation, reprinting, reuse of illustrations, recitation, broadcast-
ing, reproduction on microfilms or in any other way, and storage in data banks. Duplication of this
publication or parts thereof is permitted only under the provisions of the German Copyright Law of
September 9, 1965, in its current version, and permission for use must always be obtained from
Springer-Verlag. Violations are liable for prosecution under the German Copyright Law.

© Springer-Verlag Berlin Heidelberg 1993
Printed in Germany

Typesetting: Camera-ready by authors
45/3140 - 5 4 3 2 1 0 - Printed on acid-free paper

*Dedicated to the memory of
Ronald Elsendoorn
(1959-1991)*

Preface

This book is the final result of the NATO Advanced Research Workshop 'Interactive Learning Technology for the Deaf', which was held between June 4 - 7, 1991, in Sint-Michielsgestel, the Netherlands. The scientific organizing committee consisted of Frans Coninx (director), Ben Elsendoorn, Richard Foulds and Christopher Jones.

The idea for this workshop originated from the observation that interactive learning technology seemed to be very promising in that it might help improve education of deaf children, but also from the given fact that general achievements in helping deaf children to acquire language could still be improved.
    Before this workshop, results on research in the areas of (sign) language acquistion and education of deaf children, improvement of speech production and listening skills, as well as the use of interactive learning technology, could be gathered in journals and at congresses. However, no meeting was ever organised where experts from these different fields were present at the same time.
    The aim of the workshop was to bring together experts in the fields of deaf education as well as interactive learning technology, to construct a multi-disciplinary platform where ideas and research results could be discussed from various angles and which would serve as a jumping-board for future collaboration. We thought it essential that specialists from various directions in deaf education - i.e. bilingual, oral, and Total Communication (TC) approaches - were present, to contribute to the multi-displinary character of the workshop.

Many of the workshop presentations have been collected in this volume. The book closely follows the division into sections, which was also the outline, of the workshop.
    We asked our speakers (authors) to concentrate on three topics:

- The acquisition of (written) language. In all approaches, be they oral,

bilingual or TC, the development of literacy is a major educational goal.
- The development of oral communication skills. This part of the workshop addresses the use of training devices aimed at improving speech production and speech reading, as well as the use of residual hearing to support both of these skills.
- Sign language and manual communication. In this area it will be necessary to develop interactive learning devices which can be employed by both deaf and hearing persons wanting to acquire sign language.

A number of questions can be posed that are relevant to each of these topics:

- How to find or define the optimal compromise between introducing and adapting new interactive systems and teaching strategies on the one hand and existing practice in education on the other? The development and implementation of innovative learning technology will only be successful if it can become an integral part of current educational approaches and teaching strategies.
- How to prevent that introducing new learning technology will merely be a replacement of existing techniques instead of an improvement? Careful and gradual implementation and conscientious research into the effectiveness of the new technology seem to offer a likely solution.
- What new technology could be beneficial to mainstreamed deaf children as well? During the developmental phase of new interactive systems care should be taken that these will be easy to transport, user-friendly and self-explanatory, and, if possible, obtainable at relatively low prices.

Not all of these questions are addressed in great detail in the various contributions collected in this book. However, we feel that they are important issues to keep in mind when working in this field of interactive learning technology for deaf and hard-of-hearing persons.

We are indebted to the NATO program committee for Advanced Educational Technology who decided to fund this workshop, and to the Instituut voor Doven (Institute for the Deaf/IvD) who co-sponsored it.

Thanks are also due to the other two members of the workshop's Organizing Committee: Dr. Richard Foulds, A.I. DuPont Institute, University of Wilmington, Delaware, USA, and Christopher Jones, at the time connected to the Scottish Interactive Technology Centre, Edinburgh, UK, and presently vice president of Teletec International Ltd., Milton Keynes, England, who both supplied the right names and the right connections for workshop participants.

The assistance of Ing. Rob de Haan in attending to all technology before and during the workshop is gratefully acknowledged. His conscientiousness and enthusiasm resulted in perfect functioning of all interactive systems that were presented during the speakers' presentations, but also at the interactive evenings, when participants could more informally discuss these systems and become acquainted with them.

Annelies Brekelmans embodied what interactive systems should be like in the future: friendly, patient, flexible, efficient, never-tiring and providing correct information and feedback at all critical points of the interactive process that is called 'Organizing a workshop'. She also played a substantial part in the preparation of the book you are now holding. Not only did she prepare and lay-out the manuscript, but also frequently pointed out illogical ways of reasoning or omissions in the manuscripts. It is therefore only right for her name to be printed on the title page of this volume.

Ben Elsendoorn, Frans Coninx
Sint-Michielsgestel, June 1993

Contents

Introduction

Design and Evaluation of Interactive Instruction as a
Communicative Dialogue 3
D.G. Bouwhuis

Language: Storage and Retrieval Systems

The Use of an Individual Word-Base in a Classroom Environment ... 21
M. van den Meiracker

Multimodality: a Theoretical Argument for Multimedia
Interactive Learning 31
F. Loncke

Deaf Children Learning in a Multimedial Environment 43
*C. Caselli, S. Corazza, V. Volterra, G. Lombardi, B. Pennacchi,
S. Rampelli*

A Multimodality and Multimedia Approach to Language,
Discourse, and Literacy Development 55
P.M. Prinz, K.E. Nelson, F. Loncke, G. Geysels, C. Willems

Linguistic and Educational Principles of the Computer
Aided Language Learning Software A.D.A.M. & E.V.E. 71
L.K. Engels

Grammar in a Visual Mode: an Alternative for Hearing-
Impaired Children? 81
H. Veenker

Oral Communication

Computer Interactive Techniques in Training and Evaluation
of Communication Skills 95
H. Levitt, K. Youdelman, J.J. Dempsey

Design and Evaluation of Interactive Training Programs for
Speech Reading and Hearing Skills (ISEG) for Children and
Adolescents with a Profound Hearing Impairment 105
F.J. IJsseldijk, B.A.G. Elsendoorn

ALLAO - an Interactive Videodisc for Teaching Lipreading 121
I. Guilliams

Voice and Intonation - Analysis, Presentation and Training 137
A. Fourcin, E. Abberton, V. Ball

Teaching Intonation to Deaf Persons through Visual Displays 151
G.W.G. Spaai

Conceptual and Technical Considerations in Developing
Visual Aids for Speech Training 165
D.J. Povel, N. Arends

Sprach - Farbbild - Transformation (SFT): the Conversion of
Sound to Coloured Light as a Visual Aid in Speech Therapy 175
P. Nolte, R. Printzen, G. Esser

The Development and Application of the IBM SpeechViewer 187
F. Destombes

Sign Language and Manual Communication

Multimedia Dictionary of American Sign Language 199
S. Wilcox, W.C. Stokoe

A Computer Dictionary for Subject Specific Signs 215
S. Prillwitz, R. Schulmeister

Machine Recognition of Human Gestures 231
S. Peters, R. Foulds

A Multi-Media System for the Teaching of Sign Language 239
B. Woll, P. Smith

Glossary for the Deaf - A Laservision Sign Language Dictionary ... 249
O. Eriksen

Interactive Introduction of the Logical Bases of a
Communication System 259
F. Lowenthal

Contributors 281

Subject Index 283

Introduction

Design and Evaluation of Interactive Instruction as a Communicative Dialogue

D.G.Bouwhuis
Institute for Perception Research/IPO, P.O.Box 513, 5600 MB Eindhoven, the Netherlands

Abstract. Throughout history hearing people have been puzzled about the difficulty to communicate with deaf people; a puzzlement perhaps strengthened by the fact that hearing is only one of the human sensory faculties. Apparently loss of hearing affects human communication far more than any other sensory impairment.

On analyzing the communication process in more detail one finds that it is made possible by a large number of conditions that all have to be satisfied in order to proceed successfully. It appears to be inherently uncertain, it requires a great deal of redundancy, and makes use of an, often implicit, protocol. On closer analysis it turns out that the process of manual signing embodies the same communicative principles as spoken communication; even if a number of features are different as a consequence of the visual display. Inasmuch as the development of sign language seems to parallel that of spoken language in many ways, sign language qualifies undoubtedly as a language in its own right.

Interactive instruction can be considered to be a special kind of communication with dialogue rules that are in many ways different from those in other types of person-to-person communication. Some of these are beneficial for interactive instructional systems, but a persistent problem is still how to obtain informative feedback, and how to deal with it in the ongoing interaction. One example is the question of how to provide spoken instances of letters in words, or words in a text for hearing impaired or deaf children when they try learning to read. Alphabetic script has many problems for those who do not have the same audible representation of language as hearing people.

Current insight in communication processes suggests that one should abstain from strong statements on education for deaf people and concentrate instead on evaluation of the intelligibility and comprehensibility of the instructional dialogue.

Design and Evaluation of Interactive Instruction as a Communicative Dialogue

Around 1535 the friar Bernardino de Minaya made his way from South American Peru to pope Paul III in Rome to vindicate his belief that Indians were more than parrots, had a soul and could not be enslaved at will (Josephy, 1961). The pope, who was a renowned political schemer and had rather more grandchildren than a pope really should have, needed little time to release the papal edict Sublimis Deus, which, accompanied by a range of briefs, outlawed slavery completely and stated in full that Indians were persons, endowed with a soul, and had the same rights as all other human beings. Apparently, such had not been acknowledged by European colonists. They considered them to be inferior beings, no more than animals, to which harsh and inhuman treatment could be inflicted at will.

This attitude towards the South American Indians after the Columbus sailings reminds one of another fate; that of deaf people before the eighteenth century. Deaf persons were considered as "dumb" or imbecilic and not recognized as persons under the law: "...they were limited to the most menial work and their economic situation was often desperate." (Perlmutter, 1991).

Indeed, there is a striking similarity in the way the Indians of those early days and deaf people behaved in the eyes (and ears) of the ruling classes. It is useful to consider why this was the case.

First, there are differences in habits and culture, and such differences make not only behaviour incomprehensible, but behaviour also may seem outright mindless. Moreover, any attempt at language communication, either by speech or gesture, will fail in the face of the inability of the partners to understand the language that is entirely foreign to them. Indian languages have been found to be rather different from Western languages which will certainly have impeded effective communication (Carroll & Casagrande, 1958). It is also remarkable that only fairly recently evidence has been found for a highly sophisticated writing system in Mesoamerica dating from around 150 A.D. (Morell, 1991). Clearly, the writing system was not seen as such by the followers of Cortez and practically everyone after them.

Similarly, the sign language of deaf people is at first sight completely incomprehensible to hearing people using oral language; Sacks (1990) relates the astonishment of Abbé de l'Epée who, wanting to bring deaf people the word of God, discovered that the deaf community in Paris already had a language; a signed language. But also Sacks himself appears to be continuously amazed by the powers of the signed language and insists that it is not only different, but also requires different neural architectures; and that it does not follow the structures of spoken languages. Indeed, sign language seems to many so alien that, citing Perlmutter again: "Many educators viewed signing as an imprecise, defective mode of communication. After the International Congress of Educators of the Deaf in Milan in 1880, sign was officially banned from schools for the deaf, first in Europe and then in the United States".

These few observations suffice at demonstrating how quickly a lack of understanding may give rise to an inability to communicate, and that, in turn, to inferring fragmentary thinking or even a complete lack thereof from the part of the misguided outsider. It is, therefore, of major interest to explore the role and use of communicative systems like speech, writing, graphics and gestures in human behaviour, especially when implementing interactive environments. And this will be even more challenging for people who can make only a limited use, or not at all, of one important perceptual mode: hearing.

Communication

Uncertainty versus Redundancy. One of the more intriguing properties of communication between two partners is that no partner can ever be sure that the information he or she transmits will be received successfully and understood correctly. Inasmuch as this is a principal difficulty, this can be termed the *uncertainty principle* of communication. This state of affairs is complicated even more by the fact that also the answer to the original message cannot be guaranteed to be received successfully and understood correctly by the original sender. The uncertainty, therefore, is mutual and the proper description should be the *recursive uncertainty principle*.

The interesting consequence of recursive uncertainty is that it provides the basis for communication theory. If all information that was broadcast would ultimately be received with certainty and interpreted correctly, communication could be described by a passive dispersal model, in which no feedback would be necessary. This is the case for scents released by animals and used for signaling to partners or competitors. Pheromone dispersal by male moths is an example of such a process; the released pheromone will ultimately be picked up by a female moth and always be interpreted correctly. But there is no behavioral feedback that would lead to different ways of dispersal during the lifetime of the male. Communication theory is not needed by moths. In many situations, however, the uncertainty in human communication is very low, and communication can proceed successfully even if there are slight mismatches from time to time, that can be glossed over by either of the partners. Speakers employ various means to ensure intelligibility and interpretability of their messages. They adjust the loudness of the speech and its rate, but also choose words and phrases that are likely to be understood by the listener. Inherent properties of spoken language also support recognizability and comprehensibility. The speech signal is redundant on almost all levels of observation. Segments of phonemes have a duration, spectral composition and loudness that enables them to be easily resolved by the hearing system; the identity of the speech sounds is codetermined by the words they form, syntax provides redundancy on the phrase level. Prosodic features may still add expressive power to the sentence. Speakers can and will repeat utterances in part or in whole, but can also paraphrase or provide additional context if this is asked for by the listener.

Much of the redundancy of the lower levels of the speech signal may be said to be provided by syntax, by which we understand compositional and structural rules that are satisfied in the composite whole.

Dialogue Control. If redundancy does not suffice for whatever reason, speakers have to resort to feedback. Much of this feedback has the form of *dialogue control acts* (Bunt, 1989). Dialogue control acts do not transmit any information as part of the message but are only concerned with the state of transmission of information. Examples are: "What did you say?", "I don't understand." "Is that true?" In spoken dialogues up to 50% of all utterances may consist of dialogue control acts (Bunt, 1989), which means that almost as much time is spent on the *process* of message transfer as on message transfer *per se*. It is therefore that we distinguish in a dialogue *content* and *protocol*, where content is the information to be transferred, and protocol the ways in which this is performed. Traditionally, linguistics has been concentrating on how content is represented in language and on the structure of single sentences. This is clearly related only to the content aspect of sentences occurring in dialogues; the specific nature and role of dialogue control utterances has only recently become clear (Taylor, Néel & Bouwhuis, 1989). Inasmuch as dialogue control utterances relate more to style of communication than to content they are bound to be very much dependent on culture and situation. Stating that dialogue control is part of a protocol alludes to conventions in diplomatic exchanges. If people of different cultures have to negotiate effectively without violating traditional rules of behaviour, they act according to an agreed protocol. Though official protocol looks artificial and inefficient, it is in fact a highly effective way of dealing with critical transactions.

Apart from the distinction between message content and dialogue control, a number of requirements must be met before effective communication can take place. Language is only an empty hull, serving as the carrier of information and the transfer of meaning; so any speaker must assume that the things that language represent are also part of the representational world of the listener. Communication presupposes world knowledge from the part of both partners, and specifically shared world knowledge. On the protocol side of communication there must be shared knowledge of protocol rules. Indeed, even from a linguistic point of view it is very hard to distinguish between a content bearing message and dialogue control. Interesting examples are provided by Beun (1989) who showed that many a question in a dialogue can have a declarative form, like "The bus leaves at eleven?" This may also be construed as an inform message; but in response to a bus-timetable inquiry it may be a repetition of the information, that enables a correction from the information provider when incorrect. Beun showed that declarative questions have a special function in a dialogue; they present feedback, enable correction, and give the impression that the speaker is relatively sure that the information is correct.

However, if one did not know the declarative utterance was a question, it would have to be seen as a information message. The use of these dialogue conventions is clearly pitted against the recursive uncertainty principle mentioned in the previous paragraph.

Also other problems result from the interplay between content messages and protocol. An important one is the indirect request. In Western languages at least, people rarely express directly what they want, but phrase their request in an indirect way, involving the potential preparedness on behalf of the listener, like in the request: "Can you tell me the time?" This is almost a dialogue control act and the literal interpretation of this indirect request is a yes-no question. But interpreting it that way violates principles of cooperation. The analysis by Bunt (1989) shows how complex the dialogue becomes in the case of an indirect request. If A asks B whether he can tell A the time, then:

- A thinks that B knows the time
- B thinks that A does not know the time
- B thinks that A thinks that B knows the time
- B thinks that A wants to know the time.

Consequently, B will try to tell A the time, which takes precedence over the formally correct answer which would be 'yes', but which would not be very cooperative. Interestingly, if B did not know the time, he would have to answer 'no', and still be cooperative.

Analyses like these posit that rule-governed dialogues are driven by intentions, which is the basic tenet of formal semantics. Other theorists, e.g. Schegloff (1968) state that dialogues are rather governed by conventions, because intentions are all but impossible to track in the ongoing dialogue, and partners seem rather to conform to conventions of spoken exchange. In this respect the continuous interaction and turn taking in the dialogue has also been described as a game of cooperation (Airenti, Bara & Colombetti, 1989).

Basic Preconditions. The issues raised by these special dialogue properties demonstrate the importance of cooperation in both partners participating in any dialogue. This brings us to a last point in the description of dialogues:

felicity conditions. Felicity conditions are not very formally defined, but give a global view on minimal requirements for successful transactions. One is that the speaker must know that the request can in principle be satisfied by the hearer; another that the speaker is serious in his intentions. In fact, these felicity conditions do also apply on several levels of the communicative exchange, and then may be termed the *complementarity principle*. This holds, among others, that the speaker knows that the hearer can hear and understand, while the hearer knows and expects that the speaker will speak.

These observations concerning successful communication make clear that communication proficiency will take considerable time to learn, and that it develops in close interaction between the individual personality and the social environment. This extensive experience causes communication to be considered as a routine activity that is not principally difficult or critically dependent on many subtle conditions. That is, until communication breaks down; at which point usually consternation arises. Why? The concept of complementarity, mentioned before, has to be taken in a deeper sense here. A frequently used term is *cooperation*, but in the present context we prefer the terms *preparedness* and *commitment*.

It may be seen as surprising that right from the start of any dialogue the listener is *prepared* to listen, to understand and to engage in the dialogue. This is such a powerful property that even if the person addressed does not want to engage in the initiated dialogue, he will make this perfectly clear in the context of that same dialogue, that will proceed much differently than the originator had expected. But if the dialogue is cooperative both partners show a particular *commitment* to

- understand the utterances from the other speaker and to ask questions, clarification,
- repetition and convey approval, belief, or agreement and so on, but also to
- choose words and language that are optimally comprehensible,
- repeat or paraphrase utterances for better understanding and
- answer questions about what has been stated.

Speakers seem not to be content with their participation in a dialogue until they have made sure that the hearer has indeed captured even the finer points of what has been brought across. Not rarely multimodal communication is employed to amplify the meaning of a message, in the form of gestures, facial expressions, body posture or drawings. Truth value of messages is often supported by reference to witnesses, the existence of written or published proof, pictures, photographs or other spokesmen. This commitment is a typical property of human communication; if computers were to send each other messages then (if they could), they probably could not care less about the effect the messages have on the state of the other. In a more formal sense: communicating partners aim at a common, or a shared knowledge state, and in doing so they, mostly unwittingly, combat the recursive uncertainty principle. In attempting to obtain successful transfer of information to the other partner the informer has to engage in what we call here *channel procurement*. This consists of the establishment of a communication channel by which the information can be transferred most effectively, and one that also enables monitoring as to the continuity of the channel. The communication channel exists only when, through it, information arrives at the other partner. Not only the sending partner, but also the receiving partner is able to cancel the channel at any moment. The continuity of the channel is then, apparently, mostly determined by feedback. This brings us back to the defining principle of communication, that can exist only if there is complementary turn-taking by the partners providing the feedback, on the basis of which the dialogue process can be continued successfully. Communication exists only when the loop connecting tenuously both partners can be closed.

Signed Communication

It is fascinating to see how the basic principles of communication are being maintained in the highly successful process of manual signing. As an example we will use here the process of transcription signing where a hearing signer translates the spoken utterances of a speaker to a deaf person. This situation is complicated by the fact that while the speaker is addressing the audience, the deaf viewer may be inclined for various reasons to watch the speaker, but has to obtain the bulk of the information from the signer. But it can be observed that during signing the signer and the viewer look each other straight in the eyes. The shapes, the gestures and the movements of the hands generally leave the face and especially the region around the eyes free. Nevertheless, the face may frequently be employed as a referent for the gestures, like in indicating the acts of thinking, speaking, eating etc. that are easily comprehensible in many different sign languages. Facial expression is commonly used to emphasize and amplify the meaning of the utterance. Some signers refer to facial expression as being similar to intonation in spoken language. Facial expression, predominantly conveyed by the mouth, may also be employed for giving morphological information and in some sign languages modifiers. So, it is really the hands that provide the greater part of the semantic information during signing. The centroid of the signing space is located approximately over the lower facial region; mouth or chin and frequently even lower, like the chest. Most of the time the signs are made in the space around and below the head, and may get as far and as low as the elbows. Yet, all the time the viewer and signer look straight at each others' eyes. Only rarely short eye saccades are made in the direction of extreme locations of signs.

From a visual point of view this seems not optimally suited to accurate visual information processing that suffers already considerably only a few degrees of visual angle from the fixation point (Bouma, 1970). This is further worsened by the presence of other visual stimuli, visual clutter, producing additional interference.

There are, however, two favourable variables involved as well. First, movement is much more conspicuous than static visual stimulation, so dynamic gestures are much easier to recognize in the peripheral regions of the visual field than static shapes. Second, the hands span a relatively large area within the visual field, up to $10°$ of visual angle, which may be further amplified by movement. This sheer size can compensate reduced recognizability. From these considerations it can be deduced that only global properties of signs and their locations can be information-bearing, not any detailed and tiny movements. This is why signs may show a great variety in realizations while still being completely unambiguous (Meier, 1991). This state of affairs then makes it possible that viewers do not have to fixate the gesturing hands directly.

But there is still another reason why viewers and signers fixate each others' eyes. Looking at each others' eyes indicates the current existence of a communication channel. It is remarkable to observe that either partner gets noticeably annoyed when the other averts his or her gaze to anything else than the eyes. Averting the gaze is apparently interpreted as breaking the communication channel so that no information or feedback can be transferred anymore. Eye-to-eye fixation, therefore, serves as a means of continuously monitoring the state of the communication and feedback channel, while it still can procure sufficient semantic information from the gesturing hands in the periphery of the visual field. If the sign reader looks away from the signer's eyes, the marked annoyance of the signer reflects the commitment of the latter to the process of information transfer. Despite the fact that the sign reader may obtain a better view of the signs in looking away, it also gives the impression of temporarily cancelling the channel. It is interesting to note that facial expression of the sign reader is much livelier than that of listeners to speech. This can be compared to those dialogue control acts that convey acknowledgement of what has been communicated. As this kind of feedback cannot be orally presented, facial expression has to be particularly informative.

This visual channel property is much less obvious in spoken communication, owing to the different nature of the visual and auditory signals and systems. Auditory signals travel freely in space and ears are always open to hear. In contrast, optical signals are highly directional and can be easily blocked. Eyes can see sharply only in a very limited area of the total visual field, and can be closed as well. So, whereas auditory signals may in many cases supposed to be heard by default, this is not so for visual signals. Additional certainty is needed for visual communication.

Language Development

It is well known by now that there are certain time periods that are determining for language and communication skills; especially the first five years of age seem to be of immense importance for effective maturation (Piaget & Inhelder, 1966; Lane, 1984; Meier, 1991). Yet, there is sufficient evidence that a much longer time is needed for acquiring good communicative skills (Bouwhuis, 1992). Reading is a good example, where it is commonly found that youngsters of 10-12 years of age are markedly slower than adults in naming individual words (appr. 100 ms) and make more errors in naming them (about 10% -20% more). The existence of childrens' books, as well as books for other age brackets testifies that not every book is suitable for every reader. Speech intelligibility scores reach a peak between 20 and 30 years of age.

The time frame in which various aspects of language develop seems similar for spoken language and for signed language. Meier (1991) shows that this holds for vocabulary, word order and morphology. Anecdotal evidence has it that signs can be earlier acquired than words, even after some weeks, but consistent use is generally observed at 12 months. Meier (1991) cites a number of investigations to show that indeed sign language fully qualifies as a language, even if its referential system is different in many ways. Though many signs are "iconic" there are many others which are not, and qualify as what we tend to regard as words of an abstract language.

What may strike us in observing users of sign language is that delayed learning of it shows many features of delayed learning of a spoken language. A frequent complaint of teachers and researchers of deaf people is that their own signing is spastic and does not come close to the smoothness and expressiveness of the "native" signers. This may give rise to the feeling that the "other" does not belong to the group that the observer belongs to. Indeed, the depreciatory attitude towards deaf people in even recent times bears testimony to this; on the other hand, as a group, deaf people may be both more isolated and socially cohesive than any other group with a sensory deprivation. One is tempted to state that communication makes culture, and not participating in that culture excludes a person from it.

Instruction

Instruction is a rather special kind of communication, that differs in a number of ways from a normal dialogue between two people. Nevertheless the basic premises that hold for communication, do so for instruction as well. In an instructional process it is additionally understood that there is an expert and a novice, and it is quite sure to either of the partners who is who. As a result the initiative relies practically always with the teacher, who is the expert, while the novice, the pupil, is automatically supposed to do whatever the teacher demands (Bouwhuis, 1991). In principle, this makes the design of an automatic interactive instructional system much easier than, say, an interactive information system for an unpredictable interrogator.

From early age onwards, teaching seems to proceed rather by example; by trial and error, and much less by corrective feedback. Consequently, learning in a more formal setting, with repetitive study and drill sessions, has to be learned just as any other form of communication. There is, however, also an important distinction in kind of learning. These different kinds of learning lead to *skills* on the one hand and to *declarative knowledge* on the other. Declarative knowledge consists of structured facts, and these facts may be acquired in a single presentation. That is; on being told that an object A has property b, the hearer may be expected to remember this fact from that moment on. The hearer does not necessarily need any training to understand that fact, or to remember it. This is very different from acquiring a skill, like walking, swimming or in the field of language: pronunciation. One can be told to an arbitrarily detailed degree how to walk or swim, or how to pronounce words; but that same activity will only be acquired after a long range of trials and errors, even if the performer knows exactly how it should be done in a declarative sense. It is obvious that the acquisition of declarative knowledge is a process well suited to be conducted efficiently in formal training. On the other hand, skill acquisition requires a lot of teaching investment and time, progress is slow and activities centre on uninteresting details, all of which is unattractive in school settings. Yet, many daily life activities cannot successfully be performed eventually without overtraining and rote learning, like reading, writing and arithmetic. Interestingly, the subjective feeling of experienced people performing such activities is that the process at hand is natural, automatic and needs no explanation. Such a feeling may not only be misleading in teaching endeavours but also be outright damaging for educational success.

Learning to Read

Reading is one of the typical activities that can be described entirely in a declarative fashion, and yet cannot be performed until after exhaustive training. Children cannot read as well as adults long after they know how it has to be done. Its difficulty is exemplified by proficient readers who try to learn a foreign language with a different script. While Cyrillic and Greek seem not impossible to master to the extent that these are alphabetic scripts with some similarity with our letters, the difficulties are soaring with Hebrew and Arabic, and greater even with Chinese, Japanese or Thai. Apparently, having learned to read one language effectively, does not generalize easily to languages with a different script or symbol systems. But also a system like the alphabetic script is far from trivial, how automatically and spontaneously it may be deployed by proficient readers. Research carried out by psychologists of the Université Libre de Bruxelles has shown that illiterates have a different conception of speech sounds than literate people (Morais, Cary, Alegria & Bertelson, 1979; Morais, Cary & Alegria, 1986). Illiterates are unable to swap the initial letter of a word for another, e.g. making *fat* from *cat*. They seem not to have an idea of single discrete sounds that we know as phonemes, let alone letters. The best performance that only a few illiterates can attain, is to rhyme at the end of words, which is usually seen as highly artful and provokes great admiration. The way in which literate readers look at and listen to words of the language is very much influenced by their ability to read alphabetic script.

In order to understand the inherent difficulties of script better, it is useful to consider that script is a double code. Writing is actually a notational form for the *sounds* people make when referring to specific objects. Writing depends not on the objects it refers to but to the spoken name of the object. In a hearing world the sounds of the words, referring to things and concepts, are shared knowledge. Sound is the back-up mechanism for learning new codes for the words and objects in the world. Reading methods that pay attention to letters or phonics employ the sound-symbol relation as the basis for initial reading. It seems that after the alphabetic principle has been mastered, reading may proceed without articulatory coding, overt or covert (Bradshaw, 1975). So adult reading may be considered to be wholly graphically based. The graphical form of a printed word is sufficient to evoke recognition of the concept the word is representing, without the intermediary sound pattern. It is a logical wish that such should be the ideal information carrier for non-hearing people, while at the same time one has to acknowledge that the route leading to it is all but inaccessible. Many critical surveys have demonstrated that deaf people are generally poor to very poor readers. It seems quite likely that the lack of an auditory basis of letters, and the convoluted rules of pronunciation of words, are impenetrable barriers for proper understanding of the visual word units. That the printed word can indeed be considered as a learnable visual code is demonstrated by some, relatively rare, deaf people who can read quite well. They usually refer to their reading ability as being based on a personal kind of discovery, which is sometimes claimed by some hearing children[1] as well.

In early reading instruction effective communication between teacher and deaf pupils is hampered by the limitation or even *absence of shared knowledge*; the sound of spoken words, of letters and of printed words. Consequently, the uncertainty principle prevails but cannot effectively be overcome by feedback. So, basic requirements for successful communication are not met and information transfer, learning and skill acquisition will suffer or become impossible.

Interestingly, before 1800, many children attending school in the Netherlands were not able to read, during the first few years and frequently not even after leaving school (de Booij, 1977) while they had received extensive training in identifying letters. The most likely explanation is that overtraining on letters in a number of different type faces (print, handwriting, newspaper print, Bible etc.) makes letters into independent units that resist blending in a word with a different pronunciation pattern. The development of letters as units, then, impedes the abstraction step necessary to form words. Something similar can be occasionally observed in deaf children who, while struggling at trying to read a word or sentence are "mouthing" the letters of words, i.e. making the articulatory movements that correspond to these letters. Frequently these movements are imitated from the teacher who, desperate to convey the nature of letters and words, employs all available means to clarify their status. Such a coding, unreliable as it may be, seems a particularly fragile means of representation, that in principle could be counterproductive. Note that in such a case script is almost a triple code, visual; auditory and articulatory, of which the auditory code will usually be the weakest, or practically absent.

Inasmuch as reading problems are rather frequent in hearing children, for the treatment of which there is hardly any reliable theory to go by, it seems unlikely that reading theory will have much to offer for the reading education of deaf children in the foreseeable future.

Interactive Instruction

Both the analysis of communication processes and that of the process of

---

[1] Churchill claimed that, being an extremely refractory pupil, he invented reading by himself.

learning to read indicate that the design of interactive instructional programs for deaf children is a challenging endeavour indeed. For interactive systems the discipline of information ergonomics has produced a number of guidelines for interface design, the most important of which are:

- all available options for user action should be clear at every stage of the interaction
- the results of the user actions to be taken should be known
- it should be clear to the user how the current stage was arrived
- what the potential next stages are
- how the user can go back to a previous stage
- there should be adequate feedback for every user action
- the user can at any time correct his or her actions
- whenever feasible the system should correct low-level user errors (graceful error correction).

Of these guidelines the nature of the feedback to be provided in different situations has not been systematically explored; mainly because it is probably very task specific. In general, however, and certainly for public systems, user behaviour will be expected to be largely error-free and correct actions need only simple and straightforward feedback. In learning situations this is not the case. And it turns out that it is much harder to decide what adequate feedback is, when errors are made. Optimal feedback is that which departs from the cause of the error, and so what is required is a diagnostic system that identifies the source of the error and bases the feedback on this source. But here again the designer is running into problems of shared worlds. Frequently, and certainly in the case of sensory deficits, it is hard to know what the world experienced by the user is. The default option of the designer is that the shared world is that of him- or herself. But that is the default option of the user as well. The mismatches that may arise at the sensory interface of a system may, therefore, be strongly impeding factors for a successful communication to arise.

Taking into account that successful training systems can be made provided the communicative aspects are taken into account in a systematic way in the design (Spaai & Ellermann, 1990), a useful amount of skill development may yet be expected to be gained in the case of sensory deficits. It seems clear that such interactive instructional systems should train the abilities that are supported by an environment with a clear and unambiguous representation for hearing-impaired and deaf children. One point of departure here could be the Reflective Maternal Method, devised by Van Uden at the Instituut voor Doven at Sint-Michielsgestel. In general, however, what needs to be validated is the representational value of variables involved in the training program for deaf children. For the time being it seems that such is only feasible for relatively simple variables, and simple tasks, since as much, or even more, research has to be spent on perception, representation and action as on the design of the instructional program itself. Superimposed coding schemes, like we encountered in letter representation (graphemic - auditory - articulatory) will probably be rather refractory in such research.

Conversely, Fourcin and his associates (Faulkner, Ball & Fourcin, 1990; Faulkner, Fourcin & Moore, 1990) have shown that for hearing-impaired people direct perceptual support can be very productive in attaining good learning results and remediation. In this respect the study of Spaai (this issue), who tries to improve intonation of hearing-impaired children by means of direct visual feedback, is also relevant. In addition, this study points at a real difficulty in providing visual feedback. If the feedback is incorrect, e.g. due to freak properties of the signal, what is the pupil to understand, or to improve? Such occurrences serve as important guidelines on how to fit instructional programs to their users.

References

Airenti, G., Bara B.G. & Colombetti, M. (1989). Knowledge for Communication, In: M.M. Taylor, F. Néel & D.G. Bouwhuis (eds) *The Structure of Multimodal Dialogue*. Amsterdam: North-Holland.

Beun, R.J. (1989). Declarative Question Acts: Two Experiments on Identification, In: M.M. Taylor, F. Néel & D.G. Bouwhuis (eds), *The Structure of Multimodal Dialogue*. Amsterdam: North-Holland.

Booij, E.P. de (1977). *58 miljoen Nederlanders en de lagere school* (Fifty eight million Dutchmen and the elementary school). Amsterdam: Amsterdam Boek b.v.

Bouma, H. (1970). Interaction Effects in Parafoveal Letter Recognition. *Nature, 226*, 177-178.

Bouwhuis, D.G. (1991). Speech Technology in Interactive Instruction. In: R. Bennett, A. Syrdal & B. Greenspan (eds), *Speech Technology*. Amsterdam: Elsevier.

Bouwhuis, D.G. (1992). Aging, perceptual and cognitive functioning and interactive equipment. In: H. Bouma & J. Graafmans (eds), *Gerontechnology*. Amsterdam: IOS Press.

Bradshaw, J. (1975). Three interrelated problems in reading. *Memory and Cognition, 3*, 123-134.

Bunt, H.C. (1989). Information Dialogues as Communicative Action in Relation to partner Modelling and Information Processing. In: M.M. Taylor, F. Néel & D.G. Bouwhuis (eds), *The Structure of Multimodal Dialogue*. Amsterdam: North-Holland.

Carroll, J.B. & Casagrande, J.B. (1958). The function of language classification in behavior. In: E.E. Maccoby, T.M. Newcomb & E.L. Hartley (eds), *Readings in Social Psychology*. New York: Holt.

Faulkner, A., Ball, V. & Fourcin, A.J. (1990). Compound speech pattern information as an aid to lipreading. Speech, Hearing and Language, University College London, Dept. of Phonetics and Linguistics, *Working Progress, 4*, 65-80.

Faulkner, A., Fourcin, A.J. & Moore, B.C.J. (1990). Psychoacoustic aspects of speech pattern coding for the deaf. *Acta Otolaryngologica, Suppl. 469*, 172-180.

Josephy Jr., A.M. (ed.) (1961). *Book of Indians*. New York: American Heritage.

Lane, H. (1984). *When the Mind Hears*. Harmondsworth: Penguin.

Meier, D. (1991). Language acquisition by deaf children. *Science, 79*, 60-70.

Morais, J., Cary, L., Alegria, J. & Bertelson, P. (1979). Does awareness of speech as a sequence of phones arise spontaneously? *Cognition, 7*, 323-331.

Morais, J., Cary, L. & Alegria, J. (1986). Literacy training and speech segmentation. *Cognition, 24*, 45-64.

Morell, V. (1991). New light on Writing in the Americas. *Science, 251*, 268-270.

Perlmutter, D.M. (1991). The Language of the Deaf. *The New York Review of Books, 38*, 63-70.

Piaget, J. & Inhelder, B. (1966). *The psychology of the child*. London: Routledge & Kegan Paul.

Sacks, O. (1990). *Seeing Voices: A Journey into the World of the Deaf*. Berkeley: University of California Press.

Schegloff, E.A. (1968). Sequencing in conversational openings. *American Anthropologist, 70*, 1075-1095.

Spaai, G.W.G. (1992). Teaching intonation to the deaf through visual displays. In: B.A.G. Elsendoorn & F. Coninx, (eds), *Interactive Learning Technology for the Deaf*. NATO ASI Series F, Vol.113. Berlin: Springer. (This volume)

Spaai, G.W.G. & Ellermann, H.H. (1990). Learning to read with the help of speech feedback: an evaluation of computerized reading exercises for initial readers. In: J.M. Pieters, P.R.J. Simons & L. de Leeuw (eds), *Research on Computer-Based Instruction*, Amsterdam/Lisse: Swets & Zeitlinger BV.

Taylor, M.M., Néel, F. & Bouwhuis, D.G. (eds) (1989). *The Structure of Multimodal Dialogue*. Amsterdam: North-Holland.

Language: Storage and Retrieval Systems

The Use of an Individual Word-Base in a Classroom Environment

Maud van den Meiracker
Andersen Consulting/ECC, Postbus 3881, 7500 DW Enschede, the Netherlands

Abstract. The Institute for the Deaf in Sint-Michielsgestel applies the so-called maternal reflective method in language learning. Words are learned from classroom conversations in meaningful contexts. These words are stored on so-called word cards, together with context sentences and additional word information. In this way, each pupil builds his own vocabulary-bank, consisting of word cards. A software program has been implemented which allows the teacher and/or pupil to make word cards in a standardized and easy way. Each pupil has its own word-base which serves as a personal and accessible dictionary. At the same time, the teacher is provided with a tool to closely manage the vocabulary development of the pupils.
This software strongly supports sound classroom practice.

Vocabulary Acquisition

Nobody learns his mother-tongue in a formal way. We do not learn words and their meanings from a dictionary or language book. We have learned our mother-tongue from discourse with our mother, from 'conversations' with our direct environment. Only in meaningful conversational situations did we learn our basic vocabulary.

Similar strategies are being used in the Institute for the Deaf in Sint-Michielsgestel in the Netherlands. It is called the maternal reflective method. This reflective method tries to combine the normal colloquial language from early childhood with the teaching of the rules or laws of grammatical behaviour.

The classroom conversation plays a crucial role. The importance of an active involvement by the deaf child in the language acquisition process underlies this educational practice. The form of contact between a mother and her baby is the type of contact which is taken as a model in teaching deaf children to communicate, including the teaching of language.

The conversation is the perfect situation to exercise the correct form of language and the correct usage. All too often the value of spontaneous conversation seems to have been forgotten in education and training. The emphasis is on instruction, which in most cases means teaching words or making children look for answers to questions of which the teacher already knows the answer (van Hagen, 1991).

Language is probably the most complex system of rules a person ever learns. Yet, the task of learning the bulk of these rules is accomplished readily by most children in an astonishingly short period of time, approximately before the age of four. Most young children learn words by hearing them. The child sees an object and hears the name that belongs to the object. This image is remembered and receives the function of a prototype. New experiences are being compared and if experiences grow it becomes more and more clear which characteristics belong to this prototype. In this way, new words are better remembered because they can be placed in a context. So words are never learned in isolation, but as labels of concepts which are embedded in the total network that indicates somebody's knowledge of the world.

In this way normal hearing children add an enormous number of words to their vocabulary each year. By the time they enter school at age 4 or 5 they have a vocabulary of at least 1000 words, a solid basis to learn more and more.

For hearing impaired and deaf children, the situation is less rosy. By the time they go to a special school, often at age 3-4, we see an enormous delay in vocabulary acquisition in spoken language. The basis is too weak to start with the teaching of regular school subjects; vocabulary acquisition will receive a lot of attention.

If we follow the verbal intelligence development of deaf students, we see that the scores on the subtest vocabulary are always the lowest subetst scores. The gap with the other subtest scores only becomes bigger over time (IJsseldijk, 1989).

To acquire the basic vocabulary for Dutch, consisting of 3600 words and 15000 meanings, a deaf child will have to learn 2 new words and 5 new meanings of a word every day in primary school (van Uden, 1977).

An example of a relative simple words with many meanings is the word home. The Webster dictionary gives the following meanings:

- a place where one lives
- the physical structure (house)
- one's close family and one's self (house and home)
- an environment or haven of shelter of happiness and love
- any valued place, original habitation, or emotional attachement regarded as a refuge or place of origin
- the place where one was born or spent his early childhood as a town, state

or country
- the native habitat of a plant, animal or the like
- the place where something is discovered, founded or developed
  (And this is good old Boston, the home of the bean and the cod)
- a headquarters or base of operations from which activities are coordinated; home base
- a goal or place of safety towards which players of a game progress (baseball)
- an institution where people are cared for (a nursing home)
- (verb) to be guided to a target automatically
- to go or return home
- make yourself at home
- a home game
- the arrow struck home.

Of course, other aspects of language cannot be neglected, the development of vocabulary as the most important part of semantics cannot be separated from other aspects of language development (syntax and phonology). This interdependency, however, is limited. The domain of syntax and phonology is restricted to a certain (big) set of rules. This is not the case with semantics, since a language can always be enriched with new meanings and phrases (think for example about all the new words we have learned when we started to become interested in information technology).

Vocabulary development is not a closed system but strongly linked to the total emotional and cognitive development of the deaf child. This is not so much the case with the development of syntax and phonology. Acquisition of the basics of syntax and phonology is nearly complete by four or five years of age.

It should not be surprising that vocabulary acquisition is an important aspect in the didactic process of teaching language to deaf children. The deaf student's language is often not correct and imcomplete. The teacher adds additional information and records the words and the contexts on a word card, a so-called vocabulary card. Gradually, the number of vocabulary cards increases, more and more words are learnt and more and more different meanings of the words.

The starting point is always the utterance of the deaf student in the class conversation lessons. No formal text books are being used to build up the vocabulary. Words have to mean something to the child and this will motivate him to learn more about the word and its meaning. Additional word information is added over time.

Since vocabulary acquisition obviously is so crucial for the language acquisition of deaf students, it is important to monitor the vocabulary acquisition of the students by registering which words are being learned, the total number of words, the kind of words, the meanings of words, etc. In practice it means that new words and new meanings of words are

recorded on the word cards.
Some problems which are connected to this practice are:

- lack of uniformity in filling in the cards among teachers,
- time consuming practice since cards have to be made for each individual pupil,
- if the number of cards grows, and that is of course what you hope, it becomes increasingly difficult to extract the important information.

For these reasons, a computer program was developed to manage the vocabulary acquisition of language impaired students. This software is called VOCARD (VOCAbulary CARDs). The content of the software is closely linked to the already existing educational practice at the Institute for the Deaf in Sint-Michielsgestel. Hence, the software in itself is not necessarily innovative.

Description of VOCARD

The software can be devided into two parts:

- teacher environment
- wordbank environment

The functions of the software will be discussed shortly.

Teacher Environment

The functionality of the teacher environment consists of:

Password Administration. To change the password for accessing the teacher environment. Only teachers are allowed to access the teacher environment.

Pupil Administration. To add and delete pupils who are allowed to use VOCARD and to assign the functional level. Once the student has been entered in the program, he can log in with his own name and get access to his own wordbase.

Project Administration. To add and delete projects which serve as collective categories to link words to. In this way a semantic network can be build up around a word. It is possible to serach for words which are linked to a certain project.

Word Category Administration. To change the labels of word categories. This enables each teacher (school) to use the labels which are familiar to their pupils. Some schools use the formal dictionary labels like 'verb', 'noun', etc.; other schools use less formal, often more pupil-friendly labels, for example 'do-word' instead of verb.

Pupil Results. To get an overview of all the words and word categories (amount and percentages) which are in each individual pupil's wordbank as well as the word categories, in any given time period. This is an important function since it enables the teacher to have, at any given time, a quick and accurate overview of the vocabulary development of the individual pupils.

Functional Level Administration. To determine different functional levels, i.c. the number of functions which are available for each level. This makes it possible to adjust the program to the language and developmental level of the pupil. It also includes an option to choose a regular or big font. Each pupil will be assigned a functional level in the pupil administration.

Wordbank Environment

The wordbank environment consists of the word cards. Each pupil has access to those cards which have been assigned to him by the teacher and the cards he has made himself. Similar to the traditional classroom situation, each pupil has his own personalized wordbank.

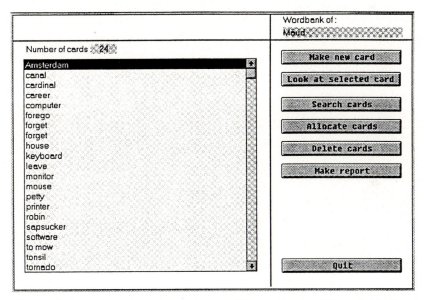

Figure 1. Overview of wordcards in a pupil's wordbank with available functions.

The functionality of this part of VOCARD consists of:

Make New Word Cards. The teacher/pupil is prompted to fill in a word and a context sentence. Words are never entered in isolation but always in combination with a context sentence which clarifies the meaning of the word. The date of entry is automatically recorded.
The word card is the central element of the wordbank environment.
Each word card consists on the minimum of a word and a context sentence and the date of entry. Additional information can be added in a standardized way. The main categories are: word info; project; sentences and pictures.

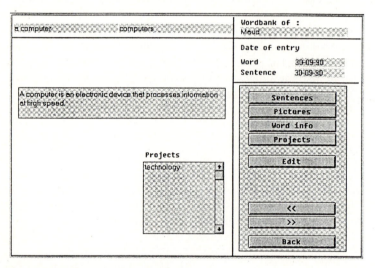

Figure 2. The electronic word card.

Word Info. The following information can be filled in:

- Information for the pronunciation
- Syllables
- Word label. The label can be chosen from a list. Depending on the choice, additional information can be added in a new field, such as:
  - verb conjugation
  - gender of article
  - diminuative
  - conjugation of adjectives

Project. Words can be linked to one or more projects from the project list which has been drawn up by the teacher in the teacher environment.

Sentences. Additional context sentences can be entered with an indication of the specific characteristic of the context sentence (proverb, use of synonym, etc.).

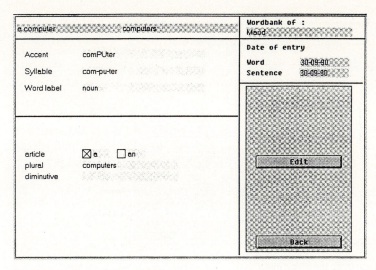

Figure 3. Electronic word info card.

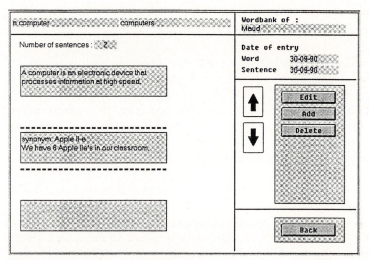

Figure 4. Electronic word sentences card.

Pictures. The word can also be linked to a picture from the picture database. With all the information entered on a wordcard the following functions are available to 'manipulate' the wordbase. It is up to the teacher to decide which functions a pupil is allowed to use. In the teacher environment the teacher can allocate a functional level to each student, specifying the available function.

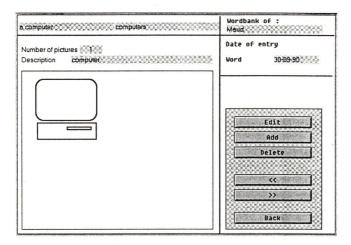

Figure 5. Electronic picture card.

View Existing Word Cards. A word from the wordbank can be selected and the connecting wordcard can be looked at.

Delete Word Cards. To delete words and all connecting information from the wordbank.

Allocate Word Cards. A word card and all connecting information can be allocated to any pupil who has access to the wordbank. This is a very time saving function. The teacher only has to make one card and can allocate this card to all the individual wordbanks of the pupils.

Search Word Cards. There are several options to search for cards in the wordbank.
One of the most interesting options is to search for words which are linked to a certain project. A quick overview can be given of all the words which 'belong' to, for example, the project 'vacation' or 'computer', etc.
Another interesting option is to search for words which have been entered in a certain time period, like last week, last month, etc.

Make Report. A report can be generated showing (printing) all words, word categories and context sentences which have been entered in a certain time period or which are linked to a certain period.
Every week such a report can be printed and used for home-work assignments and use in other classes.

Classroom Use

In order to make good use of the software, it is strongly recommended to have at least one computer in the classroom permanently.
The minimum hardware requirements are:

- AT computer with 2 MB RAM and a hard disk of 20 MB
- VGA color screen
- Mouse
- Dot matrix printer
- A run-time version DBMS OMNIS 5

The teacher will start with the installation of the software. The next step is to enter the pupils' names and at least their functional level in the student administration. Only registered pupils will be able to use the software. The standard terminology of the word categories will have to be checked and, if necessary, adjusted. Meaningful 'projects' need to be entered in order to link words in a later stage.

Both teacher and pupils can make word cards. This will depend on the age and language level of the pupils. The program is easy to use by pupils.

Each week a report can be printed, listing all the words, word categories and sentences which have been entered that week. This report can be used in other classes and at home to practice.

At any given moment the teacher can quickly create an overview of the vocabulary development of the pupils in his class. Group reports and individual reports can be easily generated with an overview of the total number of words, classified within the categories, within a certain time frame. This information should serve the teacher in developing and checking the educational goals for the pupils.

The structured way of data-entry will facilitate the educational value of the word cards. The easy and quick way of data-entry will encourage the teacher to use the program and be more involved with the undoubtly important aspect of language development: vocabulary acquisition. The personalized wordbank will stimulate pupils to look up words which they have encountered before but are no longer in active memory. In the long run, this will have a positive impact on their vocabulary development.

At present additional software is in preparation consisting of an exercise program to practice the words and context sentences which have been entered in the wordbase in the form of 'flash words' and 'flash sentences'. With this software the teacher can quickly put together an exercise consisting of a selection of words from the pupil's wordbank. The word (with or without the context sentence) will be presented to the pupil for a couple of seconds after which the pupil is prompted to type the word (or sentence) from visual memory.

```
Wordbank report

Teacher     Maud
Date        19-03-92
Period      none

Word label codes:    1-  verb           6-  prep.
                     2-  noun           7-  conj.
                     3-  adj.           8-  ref.
                     4-  adv.           9-  int.
                     5-  num.          10-  excl.

                     N- number of cards
                     P- percentage
```

Student name		Word labels										total
		1	2	3	4	5	6	7	8	9	10	
Jane	A	3	5	1								12
	P	25	42	8								
John	A	4	11	1								22
	P	18	50	5								
Maud	A	5	11	1								24
	P	21	46	4								
Paul	A	3	9									16
	P	19	56									

Figure 6. Summarized class report.

Acknowledgments

This project was subsidized by a grant from the Ministry of Education as part of the national PRINT project.

References

Hagen van, T. (1991). *The conversation*. International course on the education of the deaf. Sint-Michielsgestel: Instituut voor Doven.

Uden van, A. (1977). *A world of language for deaf children*. Amsterdam: Swets & Zeitlinger.

IJsseldijk, F. (1989). De ontwikkeling van de woordenschat bij dove leerlingen. *Van Horen Zeggen, 30, 1*.

Multimodality: a Theoretical Argument for Multimedia Interactive Learning

Filip Loncke
Department of Deaf Education Research, Sint-Gregoriusinstituut, Jules Destréelaan 67,
9219 Gentbrugge, Belgium
Research Department, IRSA, Brussels
Neurolinguistics Dpt, University of Brussels

Abstract. Linguistic modality is a central issue in the structuring of communication input in deaf children and henceforth a basic issue concerning setting up an educational philosophy for deaf children. In this paper we want to address the issue of underlying implicit assumptions concerning modality and especially multimodality in educational techniques for deaf children. The introduction and the use of multimedia appears to open possibilities to influence in a rather direct way psycholinguistic strategies in the deaf child.

Introduction

Multimedia is mostly described as an highly productive learning tool which assures increased learning results. For deaf children, multimedia can possibly be much more, because of the striking parallels with psycholinguistic processing. More than is the case for hearing children, in deaf children language acquisition is characterised by its multimodal nature. For deaf children, sign, speech, fingerspelling, writing and even non-linguistic (e.g. pictural) information can contain clues that enable them to decode a linguistic utterance. Although little is known about the precise strategies deaf people follow in processing multimodal information, it is supposed to be based on combining the information from different modalities. Strategic use of multimodal information would probably contain switching from one modality to another, comparing information from two modalities, etc. in order to extract the most likely meaning of the message. Multimedia offers a rough simulation of interconnected modalities. If the different media are used to represent modalities, then it could be seen as a projection of the way modalities are treated by the individual. This can open the way to investigate processes involved in multimodality as well as the direct stimulation of specific multimodal strategies.

Multimodality as a Central Phenomenon

Multimodality can be defined as the use of several modalities for structuring internal mental information.

Roughly spoken, human beings have a preference for two modality channels: the visual modality channel and the auditory modality channel. Each modality channel has its preferred way of processing information. For example, in visual information processing we see a tendency to structure information units within spatial groups. Operations can occur within and between groups. In sign language part of the syntax is based on establishing groups of information and performing operations and setting relations between them (Loncke, 1990b. Between modality channels, language can be represented through repesentational modalities.

In this paper we will focus on five modalities: speech, Cued Speech, AKA., sign and fingerspelling.

Cued Speech is a system that is devised to facilitate lipreading/speechreading by handconfigurations and handmovements containing minimal information in order to disambiguate the visual information of the speaking mouth and face (Cornett, 1975).

AKA (Wouts, 1987) stands for Alphabet des Kinèmes Assistés: it is a manual speech supporting system in which the handconfigurations and the movements are supposed to be neuromotorically associated with speech articulation.

Sign as a representational modality is mainly used in two ways: in educational settings sign is most used in systems following the same lexical order as spoken language, allowing to some degree the simultaneous production of speech and sign. This stands in contrast with the way sign is used in sign languages, which have historically emerged within deaf communities as the result of deaf people exploring linguistic use of the visual modality. Quite naturally, this has lead to languages with proper syntactical structures, made to be processed and understood through vision (Fischer & Siple, 1990).

Fingerspelling is a term for using a hand alphabet as a communication system. Hand alphabets consist of hand configurations representing printed letters. Fingerspelling is a kind of writing in the air (Périer, 1987).

If an individual receives information of the language he is acquiring through more than one of these modalities, then his acquisition is likely to be built on multimodal processing. In the following, we will discuss some aspects of multimodality:

- the level of representation of spoken language in the various modalities
- support of the acquisition of the spoken language/ the possibility to use the system in simultaneous communication
- the compatibility with oral skills

- user's 'comfort'
- processability.

The Level of Representation of Spoken Language in the Various Modalities

If learning and acquisition of the structures of spoken language is considered as one of the main goals of using several modalities, then it should be checked whether the different modalities cover the spoken language in a consistent way. The rationale for the use of non-speech modalities relies in the assumption that they render the spoken message more 'readable' to the deaf student. However, the information provided by these modalities is mostly not as complete as the spoken information itself. Therefore, very often -in 'bimodal' educational systems- the idea is that speech and the other modalities function in some complementary way.

However, the value of information of the non-speech modality is different depending upon the systems used. A system is a way of systematic encoding spoken language into a non-speech (visual) modality.

In case of Cued Speech or AKA, the help is essentially a cue at the phonemic or subphonemic level. This implies that the system does not provide a direct help at the lexical, semantic or syntactical level. Using Cued Speech appears to be most adequate in situations where phonological coding constitutes the weakest point in the acquisition and learning of the spoken language (Périer, 1987).

In case of sign systems, the added information is mostly on the lexical level. In most systems, signs are borrowed from an existing sign language of a deaf community. They are used in a non-sign language way, i.e. as lexical elements -words- of the spoken language. This technique facilitates bimodal communication. However, there is no implicit nor structural relationship between the word and the sign: only the fact that they might cover a similar semantic field establishes the relationship between both.

However, the use of such a signed system might have a serious drawback: as the signs are generally 'borrowed' from an existing sign language, it is highly probable that the deaf child has to use the same set of signs in two different ways: as elements of a spoken language and as elements of sign language (each with their own morphosyntactical combinatorial rules). In bimodal communication signs are used simultaneously with words and in the word order of the spoken language. In sign language - the language most deaf children are bound to explore from the very moment on they are exposed to other deaf persons (mostly peers) using signing - the signs are used following structural rules, originating in the direct linguistic ordering of visual communication.

Fingerspelling, another modality, makes reference to written language rather than to spoken language. The use of fingerspelling is part of a long tradition in deaf education in which written language is used as a primary modality for acquiring language. Fingerspelling does not constitute a direct representation of spoken language. Representation is rather indirect by a graphemic code which is intermediary between the spoken phoneme (the unit of articulation) and the grapheme. Table 1 states the levels of spoken (sign) language representation.

Table 1: Levels of spoken/sign language for each of the representational modalities.

Representational modality	Level of representation and referential language (SpL= spoken language, SL= sign language)	
Cued Speech	phoneme	SpL
AKA	sub-phoneme	SpL
Sign system	lexical element	SpL/SL
	morpheme	SpL
Fingerspelling	grapheme	SpL

Support of the Acquisition of the Spoken Language/ the Possibility to Use the System in Simultaneous Communication.

The use of non-speech modalities often implies that they can give a support to the acquisition of spoken language or of the directly spoken message. Two types of positive effects can be assumed using non-speech modalities.

The first effect presupposes that the non-speech system offers a direct stimulation of the linguistic capacities in the child, which promotes the mental development of syntactical structures, lexical networks etc. This linguistic awareness functions then as a referential base underscoring the acquisition of a second language. This is the point of view of educators in favour of bilingual education. Sign language functions then as a first and referential language - easy accessible for deaf children. The acquisition of the less accessible language - the spoken language - will be smoothed through knowledge and mastery of sign language.

The support given by other modalities is supposed to reside in direct and simultaneous association with speech. The use of those systems is based on the hypothesis that speech decoding is possible for deaf children if a simultaneous visual element offers key information. A second hypothesis says that decoding will be helped and communication will be smoothed, but also that the child will acquire useful psycholinguistic strategies such as predicting occurrence of words, recognizing word/sign clusters etc. The possibility to use the representational system simultaneously with speech is reflected in Table 2.

A form of using simultaneity outside of direct communication is the use of bimodal reading based on textbooks where written words are combined with some graphic drawing of the sign and/or a drawing of a referential meaning of the word/sign. The possibility of associating printed words with sign drawings as a core element in teaching deaf children to read is a core element in some initial reading curricula for deaf children (Loncke, 1989, 1990a): it is based precisely on the idea that children find clues to decode the printed words code by relying on the graphic references to the sign.

Table 2. Simultaneous use of representational modality and speech.

Representational modality	Simultaneous use with speech
Cued Speech	+
AKA	+
Sign	+/-
Fingerspelling	+

The Compatibility with Oral Skills

The use of non-speech modalities has often been conditional upon its non detrimental effect on oral skills. This issue has always been part of the debate between proponents and opponents of using non-speech modalities in educating deaf children. Opponents mostly rely on an ecologically motivated either-or reasoning: the more the child invests in one exclusive modality during the early development, the better this modality will be developed. Spreading psycholinguistic investment over more than one modality will weaken the strength of development of the weakest-to-learn modality: speech and speech-related skills (auditory functioning and speechreading/ lipreading). Based on these premises, several educators tend to avoid as much as possible more systematic use of signing.

Within another line of reasoning, using signs should not automatically considered to be detrimental for the development of oral skills. A key principle within this view says that signs are authentic elements in the psycholinguistic internal processor of most deaf children - they will inevitably play a structuring role in developing output skills for language - such as speech. The authenticity for sign in a vast group of profoundly deaf children comes from the observation that visual-gestural language happens to be the most spontaneous and creative outcome of the core language capacity in young deaf children (Loncke, 1990b; Supalla, 1991). This phenomenon has been explained on the basis of enhanced linguistic nativisation development (Gee & Goodhart, 1988).

A second principle of this line of reasoning is that language - information processing is always based on audio-visual input, not only in deaf people. Also in hearing people, visual information from the speaking face can influence and alter what is actually perceived. In deaf people, linguistic information processing will inevitably tend to include more non-speech related language-related information. This non-linguistic information will be encountered by a language-oriented mental device and will thus preferably be processed in language-like ways - a phenomenon very close to nativisation. In order to give opportunities to oral development - without much intruding of sign - some educators of the deaf have proposed to use so-called body language. This would satisfy in a way the need for visual referencing supporting the spoken message - avoiding the assumed detrimental effect of signing (Van Uden, 1980). However, evidence points in the direction that deaf children might operate linguistically upon those non-linguistic information - transforming it to basic and protolinguistic structures (Mylander & Goldin-Meadow, 1991).

However, the main reason for assuming a basic compatibility between using signs and developing speech skills is linked to the linguistic strength that a deaf child can possibly develop if acquisition of language in the sign modality is sufficiently encouraged. Under such circumstances, the development of oral skills could be facilitated if its structuring is supported by internal linguistic structures and by the child's linguistic awareness. Having an enhanced access to linguistic structures, the deaf child will be more likely to use psycholinguistic strategies in speech and speech recognition - such as looking for semantic relationship, morfosyntactical agreement, syntactical grouping (constituents), predicting, etc. In other words, the child able to work with signing, would adopt more top-down directed strategies in his approaches to speech and speechreading.

The effect of the sign modality on the child's performance in speech and speechreading will be dependent upon several factors:

- the child's own linguistic and eupractic abilities (1), and
- the type of communication code input and its consistency (2).

(1) *The child's own linguistic and eupractic endowment:* the individual child's ability to reflect on sign linguistic structures and his ability to compare, contrast and generalize these towards spoken language structures. In bilingual education programs for deaf children one of the main

goals is to make the child aware of the structures he is spontaneously using and discovering in the visual-gestural modality in order to understand better the structures of spoken language. However, performance in speech and speechreading will be most of all dependent on specific psychoperceptual and psychomotor skills - sometimes termed as the eupraxia of speech (Caplan, 1987). In educating speech and speechreading skills, the results of training will be highly influenced by the individual's performance on such subtle abilities as successive visual memory, rhythmical structuring, etc. (Van Uden, 1983). It is evident that these skills are only minimally under the direct influence of training by the educator.

(2) *The type of communication code input and its consistency.* Very often, the educators' policy is described as a matter of choices, among which the choice for one communication type or style is one of the most prevalent. However, there are important indications that this issue is put in a rather misleading way when it is merely considered as a matter of choices for the educator (see Hoiting & Loncke, 1990): deaf children are exposed to a whole range of communication input, varying from more sign language-like via some use of simultaneous speech-sign input to spoken only input. However, it seems clear that within this mixed input, still varying degrees of consistency can occur. This consistency can be linked to persons and to situations: the child will associate and build up an habit of well-structured communication style in response to a well-structured style of communication from a specific person or within a specific situation. Well-structured patterns of communication imply a well-structured strategy of using one or multiple modalities in relation to each other.

User's 'Comfort'

Within deaf education modalities can be combined in various degrees. Although multimodality is primarily a matter of processing information, it is highly dependent upon the choice(s) for communication style in educational philosophies which modalities will be selected to be used in educational settings. In several critical studies perceptual and neuromotor restrictions in combining modalities have been debated (see e.g. Fischer, Evan Metz, e.a., 1991). Combining modalities requires some ability to identify the basic nature of the elements to be combined: the correspondence between the two modalities can reside at the lexical, the phonological or the morphological level. For example, it is necessary to be able to identify in a high speed the phonemic characteristics of the sounds while speaking. For simultaneous sign-and-speech communication a fast identification of the corresponding lexical items in the sign and the word lexicon is necessary. There is virtually no research concerning the level (phonemic, lexical) at which an individual can monitor two modalities in the most fluent way (Alegria e.a., 1990).

Processability

Choices of modalities and their combinations are often put in terms of organizing the communication input to the child and its feasibility. Although this issue has shown limitations in producing elements in several modalities (signs - words - fingerspelling - etc.) the ultimate question ought to be how the user is processing this input. If language acquisition is one of the main goals of deaf education, how will acquisition processes be influenced by multimodality? In traditional unilingual approaches in deaf education, unimodality (the use of speech in oralism) is implicitly assumed to guarantee the most adequate language processing strategies. Simultaneously using non-speech associated modalities would possibly lead to a decrease of developmental investment in oral skills. On the other hand, simultaneous communication has been introduced in schools, based on the hypothesis that no such mechanism is active. In its turn, it is not very clear either how a deaf child manages to process the simultaneously presented information. Is a person able to follow both modalities and extract the same amount of information from both? This is not very likely given the fact that the deaf child has obvious problems in processing speech. The child might follow mainly one modality and only rely on the other modality for information checking etc. The child might also switch strategies for parts of the messages: relying on speech for some segments, focusing on signing for other segments and combining speech and sign information for other segments.

There is still another problem with the processing of sign and speech simultaneously. This problem is due to the fact that deaf children are in a process of acquiring two languages at the same time: a spoken language and a sign language. A peculiar aspect of this condition is that both languages are dramatically different as well as tightly interlinked. The difference between the two types of language is due to the fact that sign languages are structured in a linguistic way for visual-gestural processing: this condition yields some very specific characteristics and mechanisms for the language (Loncke, 1990b). The typical way linguistic categories such as morphology, phonology, syntax are structured in sign language has been amply documented in linguistic accounts of sign languages (see e.g. Fischer & Siple, 1990). The linkage is the result of the fact that deaf children mostly acquire the two languages in atypical conditions: sign language is only seldom a consistent and well established part of the language input while spoken language is hard to access for the obvious sensory reasons. In educational praxis both types are often brought together to support language acquisition, e.g. in the already mentioned simultaneous communication. The exposure to some kind of signing almost inevitably leads to the deaf child's exploration of typical ways for structuring linguistic information in the visual - gestural modality.

When signing is used in simultaneous communication, the child has to process signs as if they belong to structures of a spoken language. At other occasions, the child processes signs as belonging to other systems, i.e. typical sign language systems with their own structures. This leaves us with the central question which strategies the child will adopt to sort out two basic types of information: Language Connecting Information (LCI) and Language Distinctive Information (LDI).

Language Connecting Information is all sorts of information containing parallel data where referential use is able to make one language support the other: e.g. a word and a sign can have similar semantic referential meaning. By associating the word with the sign, the word will become more accessible to the child. Also, structural resemblance such as flectionality and similarity in order principles can function as Language Connecting Information.

Language Distinctive Information is the opposite: differences in structure and build-up of the elements, information which tells the user that this is another language. Language Distinctive Information is apparent in the lexicon as well as in structural differences. Modality could be considered as Language Distinctive Information for distinguishing sign language from spoken language. However, if signs are used in structures of spoken language, as is the common praxis in simultaneous communication, the distinctiveness in modality may be masked.

The problem of blurring the distinction between the two languages is not limited to modality, it is also apparent in the lexicon itself. The reason is that it is common practice to use signs of the sign language in the structures of the spoken language. If deaf children are developing proficiency and competence in spoken and in sign language, it will be important that they build up internally two different (and in some ways contrasting) linguistic systems. One central part of this internal linguistic system will be the mental lexicon. If the same signs are used as lexical items as well within spoken language structures (for simultaneous communication) as within sign language structures (for sign language communication) the child might have difficulties in contrasting the lexicons of the two languages. Exactly the same lexical elements -the same signs- will be used within totally different morphosyntactical systems. For example, in sign language a sign is likely to be executed in different ways due to the morphosyntactical flectional operations in the context: the movement and the place of execution of the sign will differ. To express the same idea in simultaneous communication, the sign will be mostly executed in the so called 'frozen', non-flectional form.

These uncertainties about possible conflicting processes in the child are at the basis of critics toward the praxis of simultaneous communication as the standard communication input toward deaf children. There is a growing tendency among educators that some kind of educational bilingualism should be institutionalized: using and recognizing sign languages as the fully accessible first languages for the deaf children, allowing them to acquire linguistic knowledge and abilities to acquire or learn a spoken language (in spoken and/or written form), in some ways comparable to the learning of a second spoken language by hearing persons. The bilingual idea certainly has a few very strong points: it stresses the strength of the most accessible language in which the child is most likely to develop good linguistic and communicative skills. Secondly, it is also a basis for avoiding mixing of structurally conflicting systems such as a spoken language and signing (as is the case in simultaneous communication).

Nevertheless, in its implementation the bilingual philosophy is confronted with issues which are basically very similar to the problems of simultaneous communication: which types of mental strategies are deaf children supposed to develop? In acquiring two languages, will the two languages be kept separated or will there be some referencing to each other - as is the case in simultaneous communication? If no explicit referencing to sign language is done, then there is no strong reason to believe that the child will use his linguistic knowledge of sign language in a explicit way to learn the spoken language. A solution for this problem might be a didactical system of contrasting the two languages while keeping each one in its pure form. These techniques imply a didactical emphasis on LDI. Bouvet (1982) has used this principle in her teaching of deaf children.

Multimodality through Multimedia

Multimedia offers quite interesting possibilities for language education in deaf children. There are interesting developments which allow linking data bases of sign pictures or sign video sequences, data bases of written/spoken words and data bases of pictures or film sequences of actions. If these linked data bases are controlled with a syntax program, the user of the system can explore the system in several directions. He can work at the lexical level and compare the lexical items in different modalities, like consulting a translation dictionary. He can explore a sentence in print and see what it looks like when the words are given in sign. In that case, he stays within the same (spoken - written) language and uses two modalities to represent it.

The user can also explore a sentence - or a whole paragraph - within one language (written, e.g.) and compare it to the sentence in the other language (sign language). Therefore, it is necessary that the multimedia system is operated by a strong syntactical program which distinguishes between sign language and spoken language. Here, switching modalities (sign and written) correspond with switching from one language to the other.

These two types of explorations require two different psycholinguistic strategies in the user. In the former, the user is encouraged to work at the lexical level: to obtain congruence between modalities, the morpho-syntactical information of lexical elements of sign language (e.g. the flectional modifications) are stripped off. The addition of the sign modality helps the child to understand the written sentence on a word-for-word assembly basis. In the latter, the user can only work at the sentence level. A direct matching between lexical elements in both modalities is no real help. For each sentence, the user is encouraged to stay within the syntactical system of sign language when he is working in the sign modality, and within the syntactical system of spoken/written language when he is working in the written modality.

This example illustrates how the set-up of multimedia influences the type of strategies the user will adopt. It is also clear that it opens up possibilities to exploit maximally the advantages of multimodality through multimedia: i.e. aiming at a functional integration of semantic and syntactical information in order to allow the user to follow linguistic encoding and decoding strategies. This integration is important when it comes to LCI. On the other hand, for LDI it will be more crucial to forward information to the user which allows him to compare structures from the two languages in a contrasting way.

The use of multimedia in educational settings should take into account the strategies the deaf child is going to adopt. A critical inspection of these strategies is necessary.

References

Bouvet, D. (1982). *La Parole de l' Enfant Sourd Collection 'Fil Rouge'*. Paris: Presses Universitaires de France.
Alegria, J., Lechat, J. & Leybaert, J. (1990). Role of Cued Speech in the Identification of Words by the Deaf Child: Theory and Preliminary Data. *The Cued Speech Journal, 4,* 10-23.
Caplan, D. (1987). *Neurolinguistic and Linguistic Aphasiology.* Cambridge: Cambridge University Press.
Cornett, O. (1975). What is Cued Speech? *Gallaudet Today, 5,* 28-30.
Fischer, S. & Siple, P. (1990). *Theoretical Issues in Sign Language Research Vol 1. Linguistics.* Chicago: University of Chicago Press.
Fischer, S., Evan Metz, D., Brown, P. & Caccamise, F. (1991). The Effects of Bimodal Communication on the Intelligibility of Sign and Speech. In: P. Siple & S.D. Fischer (eds), *Theoretical Isusses in Sign Language Research. Vol 2: Psychology.* Chicago: University of Chicago Press.

Gee, W.P. & Goodhart, W. (1988). American Sign Language and the human biological capacity for language. In: M. Strong (ed.), *Language Learning and Deafness.* Cambridge: Cambridge University Press.

Hoiting, N. & Loncke, F. (1990). Models of acquisition and processing of multilingual and multimodal information. In: S. Prillwitz & T. Vollhaber (eds), *Current trends in European Sign Language Research. Proceedings of the third European Congress on Sign Language Research. Hamburg July 26 - 29, 1989.* Hamburg: Signum Press.

Loncke, F. (1989). El lenguaje por senar y la lectura en ninos sordos. La Lectura EE.SS.UU. *Logopedia y Psicologia del Lenguaje.* Salamanca: Universidad Pontificia.

Loncke, F. (1990a). Sign language and reading in young deaf children. In: M. Spoelders (ed.), *Literacy Acquisition.* Lier: Van In and C & C, 147 - 159.

Loncke, F. (1990b). *Modaliteitsinvloed op Taalstructuur en Taalverwerving in Gebarencommunicatie.* Unpublished Ph.D. dissertation. Department of Neurolinguistics. Free University of Brussels.

Mylander, C. & Goldin-Meadow, S. (1991). Home Sign Sytems in Deaf Children: The Development of Morphology without a Conventional Language Model. In: P. Siple & S.D. Fischer (eds), *Theoretical Isusses in Sign Language Research. Vol 2: Psychology.* Chicago: University of Chicago Press.

Nelson, K., Loncke F. & Camarata, S. (1992). Integrating Research on Deafness and Development. In: M. Marshark & D. Clark (eds), *Psychological Perspectives on Deafness.* Hillsdale, NJ: Lawrence Erlbaum and Associates.

Périer, O. (1987). L'Enfant à Audition Déficiente. Aspects médicaux, éducatifs, sociologiques et psychologiques. *Acta Oto-Rhino-Laryngologica Belgica, 41,* 125-420.

Prinz, P.M., Nelson, K.E., Loncke, F., Geysels, G. & Willems C. (1992). A multimodality and multimedia approach to language, discourse, and literacy development. This volume.

Supalla, S. (1991). Manually Coded English: the modality question in Signed Language Development. In: P. Siple & S.D. Fischer (eds), *Theoretical Isusses in Sign Language Research. Vol 2: Psychology.* Chicago: University of Chicago Press.

Uden, A. van (1980). Das gehörlose Kind - Fragen seiner Entwicklung und Förderung. *Hörgeschädigte Pädagogik. Beiheft 5.* Heidelberg: Julius Groos Verlag.

Uden, A. van (1983). *Diagnostic testing of deaf children: the syndrome of dyspraxia.* Lisse: Swets & Zeitlinger.

Wouts, W. (1987). *A.K.A. Alphabet des Kinèmes Assistés.* Namur: Pro Surdis.

Deaf Children Learning in a Multimedial Environment

Cristina Caselli[1], Serena Corazza[1], Virginia Volterra[1], Giuseppe Lombardi[2], Barbara Pennacchi[2] and Silvia Rampelli[2]
[1] Istituto di Psicologia CNR, Rome, Italy
[2] Olivetti Ricerca

Abstract. The multimedia application we are going to describe has been realized through a special collaborative agreement between the Institute of Psychology of the Italian Research Council (CNR) and the Olivetti Systems and Networks. This project has been supported by the CNR's Targeted Project "Prevention and Control of Disease's Factors" (FATMA) - Subproject "Stress".

The goals of this collaboration, called "ALTED" (Advanced Learning Technology for the Education of the Deaf), are in particular:

- To show that multimedia applications can be usefully adapted in order to teach young children, whereas most of the applications previously introduced in Italy are addressed to young people and adults.
- To realize multimedia applications addressed to the deaf, for whom multimedia cannot be considered as an optional but as an indispensable instrument which affords them immediate, visual and full access to the same information their hearing peers usually receive at the school (which would be almost impossible to obtain through the lip-reading and/or the use of the residual hearing).

According to these general goals, "The animals of the Savannah" is aimed at the creation of a bilingual learning environment for deaf children. At present, a bilingual approach for deaf children (Kyle, 1987) is unavailable in the Italian school system for various reasons.

Introduction

In Italy it has been thought for a long time that access to education should necessarily follow the acoustic-vocal approach. It was considered essential that deaf children first learned articulation and lip-reading and only then would they be able to gain access to any form of education, especially in the written form. Pre-lingual deaf children, even those benefiting from early diagnosis and speech therapy, take years to learn to lip-read and/or exploit any residual hearing. It was not realized that this process would necessarily mean that the deaf child would enter the educational system at a late stage and only partially (Conrad, 1979).

Sign language was long considered in Italy as a partial communication system that was inferior to vocal language (Mottez, 1979). As a result of this attitude, sign language is still not used in educational and school environments and is still in practice separate from the spoken, and especially written, language (Battacchi & Montanini, 1991). Only over the last two decades has linguistic and psycholinguistic research ranked sign language on a par with any other language (Klima & Bellugi, 1979; Stokoe & Volterra, 1985; Volterra, 1987).

It is now believed that a child who already possesses the conceptual tools pertaining to a language he has acquired in a way natural for him, in this case the Sign Language, has a considerable advantage when it comes to learning another language (signed or spoken and written), and this is indeed an important prerequisite for a normal developmental process. For this reason, in recent years a bilingual model of education has been proposed in numerous countries (Belgium, Denmark, France, UK, Holland, USA and Sweden), in which deaf children make a parallel use of both languages, Sign Language and written and spoken language. Although theoretically and practically it is useful and consistent with reference to the recent findings on language acquisition processes and to the possibility of a real insertion of deaf people in the society without wiping out their cultural identity, this model is actually hard to implement in Italy. Sign Language is still not enough well-known and accepted, so it is still hard to introduce it in hearing families and schools.

In this perspective, our application is a first attempt to realize a bilingual learning environment through multimedial technology. The positive results of the use of new technologies in deaf children's education have been reported by various researchers (Caselli, Franchi, Rampelli, Volterra & Zingarini, 1989; Conte & De Mola, 1989; Conte & Chiappini, 1990; Conte, Pagliari Rampelli & Volterra, 1991; Maragna 1990; Rampelli, 1990).

Our application has been very much influenced by the interactive videodisc produced by Hanson and Padden (1990), offering a combination of ASL and written English. The main difference is the presence in our application of two other sources of information in addition to Italian Sign Language (LIS) and Italian written text: the filmed event and the graphic explanations (drawings, maps, schemes, etc.). Italian deaf children, for the most, have very little knowledge of LIS and our application has been designed also to improve their Sign Language competence.

A recent research (Donin, Doehring & Browns, 1991) on text comprehension and reading achievements in orally educated hearing-impaired children gives evidence that comprehension of a text is affected mainly by the background knowledge and the familiarity with the contents of the text. And all of those elements are generally poorer in orally educated deaf children than in hearing children of the same age.

Our application is aimed, then, at offering the deaf children also the possibility to acquire a wider background knowledge and a better familiarity with text contents.

The Application

The application involves setting up a multimedia learning environment in which different paths may be followed independently. Exploration of the environment offered by the computer stimulates the user to use and integrate four sources of information: film, written text, comment in LIS, graphic explanation. The information provided in the various forms is only partially equivalent, and retains some differences of content and form, which depend on the specific modality of presentation.

The four modalities are all visual but two are linguistic, while the other two are not. The two linguistic modalities, Italian Sign Language and written Italian, offer the same contents, but respect the grammatical, syntactic and morphological rules of the specific languages.

The choice of the topic, the animals of the Savannah, was determined from the outset by the availability of existing video material for the use of which permission was available. Experiments of three months' duration were then carried out with a group of deaf children in order to ascertain whether the theme identified by us actually aroused their interest. Out of the limited range of possible themes, we selected the "Animals of the Savannah" because of their biological appeal and the undeniable fascination they have for both children and adults. They are large awe-inspiring creatures of which the child perhaps already has some experience through fairy stories and books, and for which he has no direct referent. Furthermore, the Savannah links all these animals to a common environment and thus allows the actual concept of environment to be introduced, together with the relations on which it depends for its survival (as well as a possible development of the food chain, ecological equilibrium, etc.).

Regarding the equipment, the hardware-software components of the system are as follows:
Hardware:

- PC Olivetti M386/25
- Videologic Card DVA 4000
- Sony LDP-3600D Videodisc player

Software:

- Toolbook by Asymetrix
- Olivetti IM-AGE Authoring Toolset
- Olivetti MCL (Media Control Library)

Organization of the Pathway

The pathway is organized as follows:

- The Savannah environment is presented;
- Ten animals are introduced as a group and more specifically the lion, the hyena, the vulture, the elephant, the zebra, the giraffe, the gazelle, the rhinoceros, the ostrich and the baboon;
- For each animal three types of information are available: physical characteristics, feeding habits and special living habits.

The child enters the application guided by a lion mascot that will accompany him along the entire pathway and give him the instructions he needs in order to proceed.

The lion introduces the first film presenting the Savannah environment. As soon as the film sequence has finished the child is presented with a menu (see Figures 1 and 2) which gives him access to the following environments: written text, LIS, graphic-based explanations, notebook.

The same menu will reappear at various stages of the journey along the pathway. The choice of the proposed levels of complexity is dependent on the users. The lower level is determined by the need to be able to read, insofar as the procedures governing navigation through the application are given only in written form. We have thus assumed that we are dealing with deaf children in the third, fourth and fifth elementary grades, possibly extending up as far as the middle school [scuola media] (about written competence of deaf children of this age, see: Devescovi, Caselli, Volterra & Rampelli, in press; Taeschner, Cevescovi & Volterra, 1988).

After some consideration on the various degrees of freedom of potential pathways, we came to the conclusion that it was necessary to set limits to the opening of this hypertext. We have thus chosen a pathway which offers some degree of structure and some degree of freedom:

- Procedure texts must be read and understood in order to avoid an aimless navigation.
- There are some "closed" spaces in which the child must write the right answers in order to go on with the pathway. The child verifies his spelling mistakes comparing his writing with the suggestions provided by the

Figure 1. Written text and sign language on the same screen.

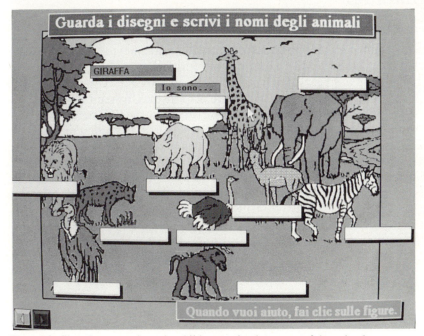

Figure 2. Closed spaces where the child can write the names of the animals.

computer, clicking on the animal in question.
- The child can choose which animal he wants to know more about and which source of information he wants to see.
- There is also a free space, the notebook, which the child can fill in as he pleases.

Film

In selecting the images we again kept in mind the type of children we would be addressing and, within the limits imposed by the availability of the material, we tried to give priority to clarity of image, intelligibility (interpretation as unequivocal as possible, even in the absence of any comment) and duration of the contents (acceptable length and development adequate from the point of view of content). Lastly, our images had to be suitable for management by accessible texts and had to be linkable to contexts which the children were familiar with.

Written Text

The selected content texts referred to and commented the film sequences (just as the choice of filmed material was influenced by the texts). The first draft version was revised and corrected by two speech-therapists, as well as by a group of deaf adults who were responsible for the LIS texts.

As far as the linguistic decisions were concerned, the vocabulary was kept as simple as was compatible with the topics treated. In particular, care was taken to adopt a syntactic organization characterized by short sentences, relations of coordination, subject repetition, the use of the present indicative and, in general, the criterion of being as explicit as possible. Furthermore, "hotwords" were created by using explanatory links in which written explanations in the form of single words or phrases are associated with non-written explanations in the form of fixed images (graphics or photographs) or short film sequences.

Italian Sign Language Comments

Just as a hearing child can normally listen to the commentary of a film in the form of a sound track in the spoken language, so a deaf child in our application can see the commentary in sign language or written Italian. At the end of each film the child can access an explanatory source in sign language by selecting the LIS option from the main menu, which includes also written and graphic explanations.

The child selecting the LIS option will see a short film sequence of a deaf person explaining and commenting the images just seen in sign language. In this way, further information and details may be obtained on the various topics: the characteristics of the Savannah, the animals that live in it, and their food and living habits.

The language used in these films is Italian Sign Language, in the version current in Rome. Nevertheless, every effort was made to ensure that the signs are generally comprehensible and to avoid any strongly dialectal forms.

The LIS explanations are pitched at an intermediate level of difficulty, neither too "low" nor too "high", considered appropriate to the "scholastic" content used in the application. The lip-reading movements accompanying the signs are linked to the contents that the deaf teacher intends to transmit to the children.

The LIS explanation can be called by the children also while reading the written text, in order to see the two languages together on the same screen. Comparison between the written Italian and LIS versions of the same piece of information is used to confirm and highlight an extremely important fact, i.e. the structural difference between the way information is organized in sign language, which uses a visual-gestural channel, and that of vocal languages, in which the acoustic-auditive channel is used.

Sign language is an essentially visual language. It has a spatial grammar and its syntactic structure takes into account the order in which the events appear visually. Written Italian is different in that it is the transposition of a spoken language. It only apparently has a visual form but, instead, retains a method of organizing information which is unrelated to immediate perception, and which tends rather to be governed by the syntactic structure and the shared parameters of the written code (Laudanna & Volterra, 1991).

When the child chooses which option to open (written text or Sign Language, separately or on the same screen), we keep note of his choices and comments (signed and/or spoken). Also, there are in both texts some small details which differentiate the Sign Language text from the written Italian one. For example, when presenting the characteristics of the hyena, in the signed version the expression "*seek food*" (looking for food) is used, where in the Italian text the expression "hunting" is used instead. Another example: at the beginning of the application, when the Savannah is presented, the written Italian text says that "it is very hot", while the LIS text adds an information that isn't found in the Italian text: *"Temperatura 50"* (the temperature is 50° C). But the Italian text has other information that the LIS doesn't mention: "It is never winter".

Thanks to these slight differences, it will be possible to verify whether children refer to both information sources in order to get new information, and which of the two sources (Italian text or LIS description) could be the most exploited. This check can be made with a careful analysis of their spontaneous writings kept in the notebook and of their answers to a set of specific questions.

Graphic Explanations

Throughout the application, other explanations are available to the child in the form of drawings and figures.

We consider the use of graphics as a level of symbolization intermediate between that of the film/documentary and that of the language (LIS, written Italian). This access may be implemented directly through the menu or from within the text (hotwords). Menu-driven access is basically of two types:

- geographic location of the savannah environment and of the animals living in it;
- explanations about the feeding habits and some classification of the animals.

For instance, geographic location is handled by an image showing the various continents and countries, which are suitably highlighted to show where the savannah is located, and then where each animal lives.

More in general, we wanted to give the application an uniformity of semantic value in its global visual layout (buttons, drawings, written text, colours, etc.). In doing that, we followed the criterion of correspondence between the form and its function.

Notebook

Let us now briefly examine the spaces set aside for the children to write in. They are of two types: a closed space, in which the child must write answers, the form of which is fixed inside the pathway; and a free space, the "Notebook", which the child can call up and fill in as he pleases. In the first case we have implemented a corrector which recognizes and corrects only a few of the words specifically introduced along the pathway whose acquisition is to be checked. The Notebook is instead a free space, where mistakes can be learned from and are actually welcomed.

In the notebook the child can write everything he wants: information he has learned about the animals' life or information he already knows and his feelings or preferences. The notebook is saved under the name of each child and, any time the child works again with the application, he can call back his own personal notebook (Conte, Pagliari Rampelli & Volterra, 1991). Furthermore, the possibility to print their own writing (and bring it home) stimulates them to write for their own pleasure, and not because it is a duty imposed by the teachers.

Conclusions

The work done so far represents only the first stage of the full project. In October 1991, a start will be made on testing the prototype at the State Institute for Deaf Mutes in Rome with 25 deaf children, ranging in age between 6 and 15 years. On the basis of these tests, we shall revise and complete the application, adding the parts that are still missing. If it works, we intend to use the same paradigm as a basis for new projects. One of the aims of this application is in fact to investigate and develop an effective didactic model for the transmission of knowledge to both deaf and hearing children. In the course of the work, we have identified several aspects that can be generalized and extended to any type of multi-media application aimed at the visual organization of information. Constructive exchanges with deaf persons working on this project and the systematic comparison with a different way of structuring information, i.e. sign language, have highlighted a number of important aspects concerning the timing and techniques of presenting visual information correctly. For instance, special emphasis has been given to the shape, position and colour of the single elements appearing on the screen. This was done out of necessity, not for aesthetic appeal, as we were fully aware that any carelessness in this domain would have been detrimental to communication with our users.

In our view, the new technologies certainly represent a fundamental breakthrough in the field of educating the handicapped. However, it is also true that the handicapped can make an important contribution to a correct development of technology in the educational field, as they can help those developing and using it better than any other user.

Acknowledgments

We would like to thank S.I.L.I.S. Group (Group for Study and Information on LIS) and PANEIKON (Television Production Company) for their collaboration and support in the production of the application.

References

Battacchi, M.W. & Montanini, M. (1991). *Pensiero e comunicazione nel bambino sordo*. Bologna: Clueb.
Caselli, M.C., Franchi, M.L., Rampelli, L., Volterra, V. & Zingarini, A. (1989). Il bambino sordo al computer. *Golem, 1*, 11-14.
Conrad, R. (1979). *The Deaf School Child*. London: Harper & Row.
Conte, M.P. & De Mola (1989). L'uso di tecnologie informatiche per favorire lo sviluppo cognitivo in bambini sordi. *Logopedia Contemporanea*.
Conte, M.P. & Chiappini, G. (1990). Ambiente di rete telematica per lo sviluppo cognitivo in bambini audiolesi inseriti nella scuola dell'obbligo. *Golem, 3*, 9-11.
Conte, M.P., Pagliari Rampelli, L. & Volterra, V. (1991). La costruzione del testo scritto nei bambini sordi: storia di un caso. In: M. Orsolini e C. Pontecorvo (eds), *La costruzione del testo scritto nei bambini*. Firenze: La Nuova Italia, 391-418.
Devescovi, A., Caselli, M.C., Volterra, V. & Rampelli, L. (in press) Italian Linguistic Competence by Deaf Children. In: *Proceedings of the Second Meeting of the European Group for Child Language Disorders*. Dragvoll, Norway: University of Trondheim.
Donin, J., Doehring, D.G., Browns, F. (1991). Text Comprehension and Reading Achievement in Orally Educated Hearing-Impaired Children. *Discourse Pro-cesses, 14*, 307-337.
Hanson, V. & Padden, C. (1989). The use of interactive videodisk for bilingual education of deaf children. *Golem, 1, 12*, 5-6.
Hanson, V.L. & Padden, C.A. (1990). Bilingual ASL/English instruction of deaf children. In: D. Nix & R. Spiro (eds), *Cognition, education and multimedia: Exploring ideas in high-technology*. Hillsdale, NJ: Erlbaum.
Klima, E.S. & Bellugi, U. (1979). *The Signs of Language*. Cambridge, MA: Harvard University Press.
Kyle, J. (Ed.) (1987). *Sign and school: Using Signs in Deaf Children's Development* Clevedon: Multilingual Matters.

Laudanna, A. & Volterra, V. (1991). Order of words, signs and gestures: A first comparison. *Applied Psycholinguistics, 12, 2*, 135-150.

Maragna, S. (1990). Un'esperienza al computer con una bambina sorda. *Italiano e Oltre.*

Mottez, B. (1979). Ostinarsi contro i deficit significa spesso aggravare il handicap: l'esempio dei sordi. In: M. Montanini Manfredi, L. Fruggeri & M. Facchini (eds), *Dal Gesto al gesto: il bambino sordo fra gesto e parola.* Bologna: Cappelli.

Rampelli, S. (1990). Appunti sulla televisione per chi non sente. *Golem, II, 6*, 7-8.

Stokoe, W. & Volterra, V. (eds) (1985). *Sign Language Research '83.* Roma: Linstok Press and Istituto di Psicologia - C.N.R.

Susini, C. (ed.) (1988). *Informatica, Didattica e Disabilitá.* I.R.O.E. - C.N.R, Firenze, 42-50.

Taeschner, T., Devescovi, A. & Volterra, V. (1988). Affixes and function words in the written language of deaf children. *Applied Psycholinguistics, 9*, 385-401.

Volterra, V. (Ed.) (1987). *La lingua italiana dei segni.* Bologna: Il Mulino.

Volterra, V. (1990). Sign Language Acquisition and Bilingualism. In: S. Prillwitz & T. Vollhaber (eds), *Sign Language Research and Application.* Hamburg: Signum Press.

Volterra, V. & Caselli, M.C. (1990). Acquisizione del linguaggio ed educazione del bambino sordo. In: V. Gallai & G. Mazzotta (eds), *Neuroni, Mente e Corpo - Atti del XIV Congresso Nazionale della SINPI, Vol. 1*, 168-176.

Volterra, V. (1991). Gesti e Segni come strumento d'indagine dei processi linguistici. *Sistemi Intelligenti, III, 3*, 405-427.

A Multimodality and Multimedia Approach to Language, Discourse, and Literacy Development

Philip M. Prinz[1], Keith E. Nelson[2], Filip Loncke[3], Griet Geysels[3], and Conny Willems[3]
[1]Department of Special Education, San Francisco State University, San Francisco, U.S.A.
[2]Department of Psychology, Penn State University, University Park, PA., U.S.A.
[3]Department of Deaf Education Research, Sint-Gregoriusinstituut, Gent, Belgium

Abstract. Recent advances in multimedia technology, especially interactive video-disc, have opened up new avenues for developing interactive contexts for discourse and literacy development in children acquiring spoken, written, and/or sign language. Preliminary reports have emphasized the rich language learning environments simulated through the use of multimedia technology. The present research is an extension of prior work with the ALPHA Interactive Language Program which capitalizes on student initiations and control by providing immediate perceptually salient feedback that incorporates multiple input and output sources and modalities. The program is interactive in that not only does the student interact with the microcomputer and optional videodisc, but, also, with an adult who assumes a major mediational role in ensuring that the language input provided is meaningful to the student. Two preliminary studies are reported: The first involves reading gains using computer plus animated graphics with a group of 10 deaf Flemish children and the second documents 3 case studies involving computer plus interactive videodisc language/literacy-assisted training with limited English proficient (LEP) mentally retarded, autistic and specific language disordered American children. Theoretical and applied issues related to language, discourse and literacy development utilizing multimedia technology are discussed.

Keywords. Multimodality, multimedia, language, literacy, discourse.

Introduction

Advances in interactive multimedia learning environments are revolutionalizing the fields of developmental psycholinguistics, special education, deaf education, communicative disorders, second language learning and bilingualism. The term "multimedia" is defined as the "convergence of video, audio, data and print technologies..." (Elmore, 1991). More specifically, multimedia learning contexts incorporate one or more of the following: animation, graphics, interactive video-discs, audio compact discs (CDs), interactive television, multimedia educational and entertainment installations, numerical data, sound, text and/or video sequences (Laurel, 1990). Multimedia technological applications involving microcomputers, graphic animations and interactive videodiscs have begun to be used in ways that promote interaction beneficial for integrated language, cognitive and social development in various groups of children and adults including deaf, language/learning disabled, second language and bilingual learners.

A fundamental tenet underlying the language and literacy process is the importance of "interaction" and the active participation of the student in the learning process. By integrating conversational discourse within multimedia (e.g., microcomputer and microcomputer plus videodisc) assisted language intervention sessions, new linguistic structures and pragmatic functions are acquired and the student begins to effectively connect pictures and text to language learning (Nelson, Prinz, & Dalke, 1989; Nelson, Prinz, Prinz & Dalke, 1991). The microcomputer and interactive videodisc technology in turn allow the student to gain gratification and motivation from the successful triggering of animations, video images, speech output from synthesizers and text that aid in the acquisition of language.

The multimedia paradigms have frequently incorporated the use of "multimodality" approaches involving text, spoken and/or sign language. One basic assumption underlying this paradigm is the existence of an "internal mental lexicon" with entries from spoken, written and/or sign language whereby the form in one modality (e.g., speech) activates a form in another modality (i.e., writing or signing), (cf. Loncke, 1990). Another basic assumption is that multimedia technology may help a child rapidly assemble in working memory some closely parallel representations between known images (e.g., graphic animation or sign sequences) and representations that have not yet been fully learned such as text sentences (cf. Nelson, 1987; 1988; 1991). Multimedia/multimodality approaches have been effectively combined and adapted to enhance language learning and literacy development in deaf children and adults as well as other groups. The purpose of the current research was to field test a multimedia/multimodality language/literacy program incorporating computer- and computer plus interactive videodisc technology designed to improve the spoken, written and sign language skills of students presenting language differences (i.e., deaf and hearing second language learning or bilingual students) and students exhibiting severe communication handicaps (i.e., autistic, mentally retarded and language/learning disordered). In contrast to more traditional language remediation programs, this interactive language/literacy program capitalizes on student initiations and control by providing immediate perceptually salient feedback that incorporates multiple input and output sources (i.e., video monitor, printer, computer keyboard, special student keyboard, videodisc player - see Figure 1) and several communicative modalities (sign, speech, text). These features are of great relevance to individuals who are primarily visually-gesturally oriented or who exhibit a severe language disability (e.g., autistic children, whose language has been noted for lack of sponteneity, initiation, flexibility and generalization, as well as for limited functional use). The program is *interactive,* in that not only does the student interact with the teaching tool, but also with the teacher, who communicates in the student's best mode of communication (speech, sign language or speech plus sign language) and provides appropriate and stimulating language input. The software program incorporates both sign language from the computer and synthesized speech output to meet the needs of children who rely on speech and/or sign language.

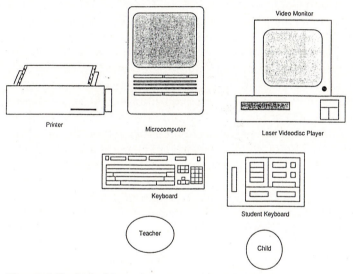

Figure 1. Technical layout.

Multimedia Technological Applications for Language and Literacy Development

Technological advances are increasingly impacting the lives of individuals with handicaps as they provide for often remarkable degrees of adaptation to, or even compensation for basic sensory, motor, linguistic and even cognitive deficits (for overviews, cf. e.g., Hofmeister & Friedman, 1986 or

Esposito & Campbell, 1987). Even the most severely handicapped students have come to benefit from the silicon microchip and multimedia "revolution" (cf. Boraiko, 1982 or Davis, 1983), as relatively low cost microcomputers and related adaptive devices, such as electronic interfaces, augmentative communication devices, microswitches and interactive video (videotape and videodisc) are now within the reach of teachers, administrators and school budgets. Interactive video, a type of "optical media", is now more accessible to educators. It has been defined as: "a system of communication in which recorded video information is presented under computer control to active users, who not only see and hear the pictures, words, and sounds, but also make choices affecting the pace and sequence of the presentation" (Hoekema, 1985). Laser vision videodiscs as well as audio compact discs (CDs) are examples of optical media. Interactive video can be run by personal computers connected to a videodisc player with a monitor. Videodisc technology is used for ease and speed of image access compared to videotape players.

These multimedia technological advances have major implications for the teaching of language and literacy skills, since they could enhance and provide alternative avenues for communication, by allowing individuals who otherwise could not do so, to competently participate in written as well as oral and signed forms of communication. For an overview of specific multimedia applications in first language acquisition see Ahmad, Corbett, Rogers & Sussex (1985) or Meyers (1984). Multimedia approaches used in teaching the limited English proficient or bilingual student are described in De Villar (1990), Edfelt (1989), Johnson (1987) and Wyatt (1984). An innovative approach termed the "Handson" program incorporating multimedia technology for bilingual American Sign Language (ASL) and English instruction for deaf children has been developed by Hanson and Padden (1990). The use of multimedia and interactive technology promises to further enhance alternative and augmentative communication practices, which already have demonstrated their effectiveness with the severely communicatively handicapped (for an overview, see e.g. Blackstone & Bruskin, 1986; Locke & Mirenda, 1988; Reichle & Karlan, 1985; or Wacker, Wiggins, Muldoon & Cavanaugh, 1988).

Instructional Outcomes with Deaf and Communicatively Handicapped Students

The present report draws upon findings of previous studies with a system described as the ALPHA Interactive Language Program (Prinz & Nelson, 1985a; 1985b). The ALPHA program consists of four levels: Preprimer,

Primer, Level I and Level II. The first three levels introduce basic vocabulary through individual noun and noun-verb-noun sequences. Level II incorporates longer and more grammatically complex sentences. Students using this system interact both with the teacher and an interactive video system through a special interface keyboard which activates the computer and an optional videodisc through the use of pictures, words and/or signs (see Figure 1). The program has been shown to be an effective tool in increasing language and basic literacy skills in several sets of deaf and multiply handicapped students with a basic understanding of the core features of language including symbolic representation and grammatical organization (Prinz, Pemberton & Nelson, 1985; Nelson et al., 1989; and Nelson et al., 1991). Additionally, a more advanced program, "The Storyteller", was developed to provide a way to explore written text in a storybook format for students whose reading skills are beyond Alpha Levels I and II.

Prior field testing of the ALPHA program with a group of 63 severe to profoundly deaf children between 3 years, 4 months, and 11 years, 8 months of age demonstrated significant improvement in reading and writing on the microcomputer (Nelson et al., 1989). Assessment involved tests on individual words and on sentences. In both tests animated pictures or animated signs (no text) were displayed on the TV screen and the child was required to "write" answers using a touch sensitive word keyboard. The results showed a significant correlation between language scores, amount of instruction, and reading performance. Children who received more intensive computer instruction performed at a significantly higher level on the Computer Word and Sentence Tests. Additionally, the children were administered a Composite Reading Test. This measure consisted of a series of individual words and short sentences printed on flash cards which the child was asked to read and a standardized reading comprehension test. The level of performance rose from 35.6% at pretest to 50.4% at posttest. The most significant findings were the high performance of the children on the Computer Sentence Tests. Children wrote sentences to describe the meaningful animations they has just seen on the video monitor (e.g., "The dog chases the ball") and the responses were given by pressing word keys on the student keyboards. All of the children learned to use these keyboards competently. Their low levels of confusion and high levels of success in reading and writing is shown by their high range of Computer Sentence scores from a low of 87% to a high of 100% correct.

Additionally, all computer records from a sub-sample of 16 children were intensively analysed to determine if microcomputer tests in realistic (e.g., "The boy lifts the chair") and fanciful sentences (e.g., "The apple chases the house") yielded similar results. The children performed nearly identically on realistic and fanciful-improbable sentences. A detailed report on these outcomes appears in Nelson et al. (1991).

In a variation of the study reported above, a second smaller sample of 16 deaf students between the ages of 5 years, 11 months, and 20 years, 3 months, was selected to participate in a preliminary investigation of gains in text and vocabulary when the ALPHA material from the Apple IIe microcomputer was supplemented with videodisc still and action sequences (Nelson et al., 1989). In addition to material from the Preprimer, Primer, and Level I of the ALPHA program, older subjects were introduced to Level II. Children had average or better intelligence and exhibited a severe to profound hearing impairment. A comparison of performance pre- and posttest scores on the computer-generated sentence test for Level I and Level II material indicated a mean percentage gain of 11% and 12% respectively. Similarly, on a reading flash card test, subjects demonstrated a mean percentage gain of 19%.

Another preliminary study examined reading and language gains by a group of 12 severely multiply and communicatively handicapped children between the ages of 5 years, 7 months and 10 years, 10 months. All subjects exhibited significant motoric impairments. The subjects were randomly assigned to two intervention groups:

- ALPHA only group receiving computer-videodisc-assisted literacy/language intervention and
- a recasting group receiving the interactive videodisc-assisted instruction plus systematic recasting of the children's utterances.

Results of the pilot study indicated gains in reading and language skills in both groups (Prinz, Nelson, Arford & Mugg, 1988). In summary, children seen in earlier phases of our multimedia projects have shown strong gains in reading and writing individual new words. In addition, many have learned to read and write new sentences and to relate these sentences to pictorial animation, and video images. These gains in text skills have been accompanied as well by improvement in general communication skills (see Prinz & Nelson, 1985 a and b; Nelson et al., 1991) -an effect expected because the student-adult interaction is designed to encourage and facilitate the student's overall communication development.

An essential part of the research involves the incorporation of dialogue between the adult and student. Drill and practice is by-passed in favour of interactive activities in which messages are exchanged in the student's best communicative mode (i.e., speech, and/or sign and text). Utilizing a "recasting" approach (Baker & Nelson, 1984), the adult comments on, clarifies, and expands the communicative messages produced by the student so that they are meaningfully connected to knowledge and experience that the child has already accumulated. Previous studies have demonstrated that "recasts" not only occur in parental speech across cultures but also have a record of triggering children's language progress in controlled experiments (Baker & Nelson, 1984; Nelson, 1987; 1988; Nelson, Heimann,

Abuelhaija & Wroblewski, 1989; Prinz & Masin, 1985).

Preliminary language and literacy gains in text and first language skills are reported below for deaf Flemish children in Belgium and hearing American second language learning students with autism, mental retardation and specific language disorders. The first study focussed on computer only intervention while the second study incorporated computer plus interactive videodisc technology. In both studies "recasting" and conversational discourse were built into the instructional design and intervention guidelines to promote language and literacy development.

Study 1: Computer-Assisted Language and Literacy Development in Flemish Deaf Children

A pilot study was conducted on a group of 10 (5 males and 5 females) severe to profoundly deaf Flemish children ranging in age from 7 years, 11 months to 12 years, 2 months using a multimedia approach to language and literacy development. All of the subjects with the exception of one have hearing parents and the communication skills of the children ranged from primarily oral to fluency in Belgian Sign Language (the natural sign language used by deaf Flemish individuals). All of the subjects attend a school for the deaf in Gent, Belgium. The basic communication philosophy of the school is Total Communication and the simultaneous production of spoken Dutch and Signed Dutch (a pedagogical form of sign language adhering to Dutch grammar) is used in the classroom. The school encourages deaf children to explore the possibilities of the visual-gestural modality through sign language. Nine of the children exhibited average or better cognitive skills as assessed on a standardized individual intelligence test. One child was mildly mentally retarded. Two children are reported to exhibit more specific learning disabilities. Most children were beyond the beginning stages of reading and used a variety of psycholinguistic reading strategies including silent reading with accompanying sign language, silent reading without signing, vocalizing aloud with or without sign language, and reading aloud with verbalization and signing. A multimodality approach to language is emphasized in the classroom where students are encouraged and taught to switch from one modality to another (Loncke, 1990).

Equipment and Computer Software

Each subject worked with an Apple IIe microcomputer system (+64 Bytes) a computer monitor, and a printer (see Figure 1). Computer sessions averaged 15-20 minutes each biweekly over a period of 6-8 weeks. During the course of intervention the ALPHA Storyteller Program (Nelson & Prinz, 1989) was utilized. The ALPHA Storyteller Program provides a means of exploring written text within a storybook format for students whose reading skills extend beyond Levels I and II of the ALPHA Interactive Language Program. The Flemish Dutch version of the Storyteller consists of three stories ("Stijn gaat naar het Circus" = "Shawn Goes to the Circus"; - "De Verdwenen Beer" = "The Missing Bear" and "Op Zoek naar een Walvis" = "Let's Find a Whale").

Courseware and Instructional Guidelines

Each Storyteller Program consists of six disks used in sequence from A to F adhering to a basic Pretest-Exploration-Posttest cycle (see Appendix 1). Initially, the teacher pretested the student using Disk A to determine whether the student's reading level was appropriate for the program. The assessment involved a reading comprehension task. Following each graphic presented on the TV monitor, the student was expected to choose the sentence which best described what had transpired in the preceding illustration. The test results (overall percent correct and individual sentence analysis in terms of type of grammatical construction and selection time in milliseconds) were printed out by the printer. If the student's score exceeded 80 percent, the subsequent levels of the Storyteller were pretested until a challenging story was found.

The exploration phase of the Storyteller program covers Disks B through F and involves "reading" the story presented sentence by sentence and through animated pictorial graphics. The students enjoyed the animations and controlled the story, turning the new "pages" by pressing the spacebar. To learn new text skills, the student needed to focus on the text sentences and not just the graphics. On Disks C through E target sentences representing various grammatical constructions (e.g., conditional tense, relative clauses, see Appendix 2) were tested following the corresponding animated illustration.

The sentence tests were designed with four sentence selections appearing at the top of the screen - the target sentence and three incorrect "foils". The foil types include

- a "New Order" foil containing all the words which occur in the target sentence but in a new but grammatically correct order;
- a "Scrambled" foil again containing all the target sentence words, but with their order scrambled; and
- a "New Words" foil containing new words which are visually (i.e., orthographically) similar to the target sentence words in appearance but presenting different meanings.

Disks C through E are designated "Sentence Matching" where the student matches the correct choice to the target sentence listed below the foils. After completing disks B through F, a posttest (Disk A) was administered. If the student performed at or above 80 percent a new and more challenging story was started.

As in prior research with ALPHA, the Belgian teachers working with these stories incorporating text and animated graphics played an active role in communication with the students. For these deaf students the student-teacher communications were in total communication and included "recasts" and other structuring replies by the teacher. At the end of each computer session the teacher completed a Guideline form and attached a printed record from the printer of the student's performance.

Results

A preliminary analysis of gains in reading for 10 Flemish deaf children after 10 weeks of computer instruction revealed the following. A comparison of performance pre and post on the Sentence Matching task on Assessment Disk A indicated an overall mean percentage gain of more than 50%. The students also showed improved reading fluency for posttests versus pretests through more rapid correct selections at posttests. These results are encouraging given the brief duration of instruction. Continued data collection and analysis are anticipated.

Study 2: Three Case Studies

Most of the research to date has involved the use of the original ALPHA Interactive Program (Pre-Primer-Level II - each level consisting of 8 "Packages" with 8 lessons per package) with deaf and multiply handicapped students. In a variation of earlier research, three communicatively handicapped American children from second language learning backgrounds received ALPHA computer/videodisc-assisted language instruction. The three children included: an 8-year old autistic Asian American male, a 6-year, 5 month old severely language disordered Hispanic male, and a 6-year, 1 month old mentally retarded Hispanic female.

Recently, we have begun to pilot the ALPHA program with an eight-year old autistic Asian American male[1]. He participated in two 45-minute

---

[1] The term "autism" is used here to refer to individuals who:
- demonstrate delays in social and language development, which are out of line with their overall level of development,
- exhibit so-called "insistence on sameness" and whose problems started when they were younger than 30 months (Rutter, 1979).

computer-videodisc sessions each week with his teacher. Preliminary reports after 10 weeks of instruction indicate that the child enthusiastically interacts with the computer and teacher and he has begun to make gains in the acquisition of new vocabulary. Preliminary pilot data analysis suggests that the program may be highly effective for students with autism who often appear naturally drawn towards computers and video monitors, and who often demonstrate a fascination with written words and graphics. These informal observations are congruent with the literature that pertains to the linguistic and cognitive characteristics of students with autism. It has been reported that these students do better when stimulus input is spatially organized (e.g. when text, pictures, and keyboards are involved). The results of this initial attempt to use interactive videodisc technology with an autistic child is further corroborated by successful reports of the use of the ALPHA program with a group of Swedish school-aged autistic children (Heimann, Nelson, Gillberg & Karnevik, 1991).

Two additional children from homes where parents speak Spanish and English (a 6-year, 1-month old Down Syndrome, Hispanic female and a 6-year, 5-month old severely language disordered Hispanic male) were seen for 14 weeks of pilot ALPHA instruction. The Hispanic male was exposed primarily to English in the classroom and Spanish at home. He had a diagnosis of specific language disorder and received ALPHA instruction in Spanish and English. By the end of the 14-week intervention period, he had successfully completed Lesson 8 of the Primer Package of the ALPHA program with 86 percent accuracy on the Sentence Test. He consistently demonstrated the ability to read words on the student keyboard with 100 percent accuracy and was beginning to self-correct errors.

The 6-year, 5-month old Hispanic female with Down Syndrome received English instruction at school and was exposed to English and Spanish in the home. She was, also, seen for 14 weeks of ALPHA language/reading instruction (English only program). At the beginning of ALPHA intervention, she was at a pre-reading stage where she could recognize only numbers from 1 to 10 and her own name. By the end of the pilot period, she had completed all of the lessons in the Pre-Primer package and was reading three-word phrases (e.g., "Pig chases girl.").

Discussion

In summary, the children in the studies reported above have demonstrated strong initial gains in reading and writing new words. They have learned to read and/or write new sentences and to relate these sentences both to pictorial animation and optionally to speech. Additionally, there is preliminary evidence that these gains in text skills have been accompanied as well by improvement in general language skills (especially conversational discourse) - an effect expected because the child-adult interaction is designed to encourage and facilitate the student's conversational discourse skills in text, speech and/or sign language.

Results of the present research suggest that multimedia approaches provide an exciting new avenue of language learning by providing a meaningful link between words (whether they be spoken or written), sign language, pictures and context, providing the basis for literacy. Multimedia technology appears to be highly stimulating and motivating since many children are naturally drawn to computers, keyboards, screens, videodiscs, despite communication handicaps as severe as those encountered in childhood autism (Fay, Schuler, & Schiefelbusch, 1980). Through use of a specially adapted keyboard, the student has access to multiple modes, involving speech output, animated pictures, text, sign language and video images. From the outset of instruction the student experiences a sense of competence in using printed words, animated graphics on the computer, and optionally through still and motion picture sequences on videodisc. Moreover, this technology allows teachers to regulate the rate and frequency with which stimulus input is presented and sustained. Thereby, the attention may be gained of even those students who fail to attend otherwise.

Not only does this technology provide the teacher with a fine control over language input, it frees the teacher to act as a mediator of learning. Unencumbered by the need to produce most of the language input the teacher may now act to ensure proper attention, perceptual salience and semantic contingency. In addition, the system proposed may also serve to provide a context for interaction and turn-taking, and not merely function as an end in itself. Afterall, opportunities for joint attention and action are presented when teacher and student are joint observers of the language input presented, and participants as well. Finally, a printer connected to the system allows for documentation of all messages entered by the student or the teacher.

Besides the opportunities for initiations and contingent responses and social interaction at large, a multimedia system may serve to engage users in a variety of "speech acts" (i.e., acts that are performed with words, e.g., "requesting", "promising", "lying", "protesting", see Austin, 1962; Searle, 1969) which is the cornerstone of pragmatics and discourse. While multimedia technology has begun to be adopted to meet the immediate communicative needs of students with mild to moderate communication disorders, broader language learning needs for severely communicatively handicapped students have remained largely unaddressed (Mirenda & Schuler, 1988). Often efforts to teach language do not move beyond basic, but rudimentary requests for tangibles. Meaningful contexts which invite use of language to share, to comment, to problem solve, and to learn, need to be provided.

Another feature of a multimedia-assisted language/literacy training program capitalizes on the visual-spatial processing of information. The acquisition of spoken language requires integrity of temporal processing abilities both in terms of the content of the communication involved and the symbolic code in which that content is expressed. However, both nonverbal as well as verbal communication involve transient signals that fade over time. Consequently, excellent memory for temporal sequences is required. When language is used in reference to human transactions, moods, states of mind, etc., the ability to perceive and give meaning to fleeting information is further taxed - posing special problems for severely communicatively handicapped individuals.

Multimedia approaches - especially interactive videodisc technology - may serve to bypass problems with the temporal processing of transient stimulus input, because of the implicit reliance on more visual and spatial modes of information processing. In addition, it allows for repeated and sustained presentation of information as a result of the processing and storage capabilities of the technology involved. By providing an alternative mode of language learning those individuals who have failed to learn in more conventional ways may now gain access to learning.

Future Technological and Educational Advances

It has taken a number of years to develop the procedures, manuals, software, videodisc, and keyboard arrangements that constitute the current ALPHA Interactive Language System. Clearly this system is a fundamental base for future research. The standard ALPHA software was written to run on Apple II computers with #6502 microprocessor chips because such computers were most widely available in schools when the original ALPHA development began. The Apple II is still widely available, but many clinics and schools that provide communicative training and special education services have purchased or are planning to purchase Macintosh computers. Current work is in progress to develop a new prototype incorporating the use of a Macintosh computer and increased multimedia capacity through the use of hypercard.

In the multimedia teaching reported here the teachers supplemented the technology in important ways - encouraging and motivating the child, providing indirect challenges to the child's current best language, and indirectly helping the child to retrieve relevant representations of prior events. New ventures in multimedia language teaching should also seek ways of doubly enhancing children's processing and learning, combining the strategies of skilled teachers with the powerful and precise presentations of multiple information channels through technology (see Lepper, Woolverton, Muume & Gurtner (in press).

Additionally, future research will concentrate on the development of versions of the program designed to address cultural and linguistic variation within and across individuals. Collaborative work with multiple spoken, written and sign languages (e.g., Dutch, Swedish, Spanish, French, English) and with reading and writing acquisition by individuals whose first language may include sign language variations or may be a dominant or minority spoken language will allow more rigorous testing of psycholinguistic hypotheses and an understanding of how text, sign and speech codes are acquired and used in interrelated ways. Recent advances in multimedia technology for systematically using microcomputers for displaying and assessing use of varied combinations of sign, text, and speech provides a promising new direction for future research on interactive language learning, discourse and literacy development.

Acknowledgments

Many thanks to Cathy Agnostinelli for her graphic work and many other other contributions to the projects reported here. The authors thank the students, parents, and staff at the Sint-Gregoriusinstituut in Ghent, Belgium and the Communicative Disorders Clinic at San Francisco State University, San Francisco, California, for their cooperation in implementing the studies. This research was supported by a gift from the Hasbro Children's Foundation and by National Science Foundation Grant No. INT8722794.

References

Ahmad, K., Corbett, G., Rogers, M. & Sussex; R. (1985). *Computers, language learning and language teaching.* Cambridge: Cambridge University Press.
Austin, J. (1962). *How to do things with words.* London: Oxford University Press.
Baker, N.D., & Nelson, K.E., (1984). Recasting and related conversational techniques for triggering syntactic advantages by young children. *First Language, 5,* 3-22.

Blackstone, S.W., & Bruskin, D.M. (1986). In: S.W. Blackstone & D.M. Bruskin (eds), *Augmentative communication: an introduction.* Rockville, Maryland: American Speech-Language-Hearing Association.

Boraiko, A.A. (1982, October). The chip. *National Geographic,* 421-476.

Davis, M. (1983, July). The chip at 35. *Personal Computing,* 127-131.

DeVillar, R.R. (1990). Computers, software and cooperative learning: Working together to the benefit of the language minority student. In: J.H. Collins, N. Estes & W.D. Walker (eds), *Proceedings of The Sixth International Conference on Technology and Education, Vol. I,* 367-370, Edinburgh: CEP Consultants.

Edfelt, N. (1989). *Computer-assisted second language acquisition: The oral discourse of children at the computer in a cooperative learning context.* Unpublished doctoral dissertation, Stanford University.

Elmore, G.C. (1991). Planning and developing a multimedia learning environment. *The Technological Horizons in Education Journal, Vol, 18 (7),* 83-88.

Esposito, L., & Campbell, P.H. (1987). Computers and severely and physically handicapped individuals. In: J.D. Lindsey (ed.), *Computers and Exceptional Individuals.* Columbus, OH: Charles E. Merrill, 105-124.

Fay, W.H., Schuler, A.L. & Scheifelbusch, R.L. (eds) (1980). *Emerging language in autistic children: Language intervention series.* Baltimore: University Park Press.

Hanson, V. & Paddon, C. (1990). Computer and videodisc technology for bilinguql ASL/English instruction of deaf children. In: D. Nix and R. Spiro. *Cognition, Education, and multi-media: Exploring ideas in high technology.* Hillsdale, NJ: Lawrence Erlbaum and Associates.

Heimann, M., Nelson, K.E., Gillberg, C. & Karnevik, M. (1991). *Increasing language skills in autistic children through microcomputer instruction: A pilot study.* Paper presented to the Society for Research in Child Development, April, Seattle, WA.

Hoekema, B., (1985). Interactive video in special and general education: A development manual. In: G. Nave and P. Zembrosky-Barkin (eds), *Monograph of the International Council for Computers in Education.* Eugene, Oregon: University of Oregon.

Hofmeister, A. & Friedman, S. (1986). The application of technology to the education of persons with severe handicaps. In: R. Horner, L. Meyer, & B. Fredricks (eds), *Education of learners with severe handicaps: Exemplary service strategies.* Baltimore: Paul H. Brookes, 351-368.

Johnson, N. (1987). Current uses of computers in ESOL instruction in the U.S. *CALICO Journal, 5(2),* 71-77.

Laurel, B. (1990). New directions: Introduction. In: B. Laurel, *The art of human computer interface.* Reading, MA: Addison-Wesley.

Lepper, M.R., Woolverton, M., Mumme, D., & Gurtner, J. (in press). Motivational techniques of expert human tutors: Lessons for the design of computer-based tutors. In: S.P. Lajoie and S. J. Derry (eds), *Computer as cognitive tools*. Hillsdale, NJ: Lawrence Erlbaum and Associates.

Locke, P., & Mirenda, P. (1988). A computer-supported communication approach for a child with severe communication, visual, and cognitive impairments: A case study. *Augmentative and Alternative Communication, 4*, 15-22.

Loncke, F. (1990). Sign language and reading in young deaf children. In: M. Spoelders, (ed.), *Literacy Acquisition*. Lier: Van In, 147-159.

Meyers, L.F. (1984). Unique contributions of micro-computers to language intervention with handicapped children. *Seminars in Speech and Language, 5*, 1.

Mirenda, P., & Schuler, A.L., (1988). Augmenting communication for persons with autism: Issues and strategies. *Topics in Language Disorders, 9 (1)*: 24-43.

Nelson, K.E. (1991). On differentiated language learning models and differentiated interventions. In: N. Krasnegor, D. Bumbaugh & R. Schiefelbusch (eds), Hillsdale, NJ: Lawrence Erlbaum and Associates.

Nelson, K. (1987). Some observatons from the perspective of the rare event cognitive comparison theory of language acquisition. In: K.E. Nelson and A. van Kleeck (eds), *Children's Language, Vol. 6*. Hillsdale, NJ: Lawrence Erlbaum and Associates.

Nelson, K. (1988). Strategies for first language teaching. In: M. Rice and R.L. Schiefelbusch (eds), *The teachability of language*. Baltimore, MD: Brookes.

Nelson, K., Heimann, H. Abuelhaija, L., and Wroblewski, R. (1989). Implications for language acquisition models of children's and parents' variations in imitation. In: G.E. Speidel and K.E. Nelson, (eds), *The many faces of imitation in language learning*. NY: Springer-Verlag.

Nelson, K.E. & Prinz, P.M. (1989). *ALPHA Storyteller*. Unpublished computer software program.

Nelson, K.E., Prinz, P.M. & Dalke, D. (1989). Transitions from sign language to text via an interactive microcomputer system. In: B. Woll (ed.), *Papers from the Seminar on Language Development and Sign Language, Monograph 1*. International Sign Linguistics Association. Bristol, England: University of Bristol, Centre for Deaf Studies.

Nelson, K.E., Prinz, P.M., Prinz, E.A. & Dalke, D. (1991). Processes for text and language acquisition in the context of microcomputer-videodisc instruction for deaf and multi-handicapped deaf children. In: D. S. Martin (ed.), *Cognition, education and deafness: Trends in research and instruction, 2.*, Washington, DC: Gallaudet University Press.

Prinz, P.M. & Masin, L. (1985). Lending a helping hand: Linguistic input and sign language acquisition in deaf children. *Applied Psycholinguistics, 6*, 357-370.

Prinz, P.M., Nelson, K.E., Arford, L. M. & Mugg, S.E. (1988). *"Recasting" during microcomputer-aided language intervention with multihandicapped children.* Paper presented at the American Speech-Language Hearing Association Convention. Boston, MA.

Prinz, P.M. & Nelson, K.E. (1985a). "Aligator Eats Cookie": Acquisition of writing and reading skills by deaf children using a microcomputer. *Applied Psycholinguistics, 6*, 357-370.

Prinz, P.M. & Nelson, K.E. (1985b). A child-computer-teacher interactive method for teaching reading to young deaf children. In: D. Martin (ed.), *Cognition, education and deafness: Trends in research and instruction, 1*. Washington D.C.: Gallaudet College Press.

Prinz, P.M., Pemberton, E. & Nelson, K.E. (1985). ALPHA interactive microcomputer system for teaching reading, writing, and communication skills to hearing-impaired children. *American Annals of the Deaf, 130 (5)*, 444-467.

Reichle, J. & Karlan, G. (1985). The selection of an augmentative system in communication intervention: A critique of decision rules. *Journal of the Association for Persons with Severe Handicaps, 10*, 146-157.

Rutter, M. (1979). Definitions of autism. In: M. Rutter & E. Schopler (eds), Autism. New York: Plenum Press.

Searle, J., (1969). *Speech acts.* London: Cambridge University Press.

Wacker, D., Wiggins, B., Muldoon, M. & Cavanaugh, J. (1988). Training students with profound or multiple handicaps to make requests via microswitches. *Journal of Applied Behavior Analysis, 18*, 331-343.

Wyatt, D.H. (1984). The logo syndrome. *CALICO Journal, 5(4)*, 76-82.

Linguistic and Educational Principles of the Computer Aided Language Learning Software A.D.A.M. & E.V.E.
(Automated Document Analysis and Manipulation & Extensible Variety of Exercises)

Leopold Karel Engels
Professor Emeritus, Katholieke Universiteit Leuven, Tiensevest 61, 3010 Leuven, Belgium

Abstract. A language can be compared with the cells of a living organism; every day new elements appear while others vanish. In a language there are finite sets of words which do not increase or decrease: prepositions and particles, deictic words, connectives, collocations, all forms of irregular verbs. They are primarily suited to computational manipulation. A finite series of notional words (nouns, adjectives, adverbs, verbs) can only be obtained by using a tool to measure language: the principle of vocabulary control by means of a frequency count (objective frequency combined with subjective frequency). By applying frequency to a large language-corpus we obtain an almost unchangeable *core* of word-forms. Once we possess that tool, any language document entered into the PC (open system) can be automatically analyzed, controlled as to its degree of lexical difficulty, and the teacher is enabled to "manufacture", also automatically, an extensible variety of exercises on any entered text and to provide his students with a set of exercises which they can do by means of a diskette or on paper.

From the educational point of view the created sets of exercises are intended for mastery learning by the students, i.e. up to the ability of using newly learned words and expressions, or reinforcing formerly encountered elements. There are also exercises for learning grammar (e.g. use of tenses and modalities), studying and applying coherence of texts (connectives, particles, conjunctions), word- and sentence-order. These mastery-learning exercises should be done by the students in between the study & explanation of the text (in the classroom) and the discussion on the contents afterwards.

Keywords. finite sets of words - infinite potentiality of notional words - measuring the occurence of words by the principle of their objective or subjective frequency - clusters of word-forms for each headword - language corpora - automatic analysis of the lexis - open system - measuring lexical difficulty - exercises generated by computer for mastery learning of new words and collocations, connectives, coherence of text - grammar of tenses and modalities - scoring - users' dictionaries - concordances.

Language and Computer in General

If we define a language as a finite set of rules generating an infinite realization of words and sentences (Chomsky, 1965) and we only take into account its infinity, we cannot manipulate it efficiently by means of a computer. A computer is only efficient with strings of any length or depth, but finite, i.e. measurable.

There are a number of finite sets of words in a language; prepositions and particles are of the species. The human being does not invent new elements of that kind within centuries. The same can be said of deictic words, of irregular or anomalous verb-forms (some strong verbs become weak and so-called regular with every human generation, but rarely will a weak verb change into a strong one). Most connective elements in the language are of the same kind. By means of these finite series of words any language teacher might construct computerized exercises for his students by simply matching these words to any text entered into a PC, and gap-filling exercises would be the result.

This is not the case, however, for the notional words of a language; they steadily increase as a follow-up of the ever altering and developing human activities. If we want to detect the almost finite core of the vocabulary of a language we should apply the principle of frequency (objective and subjective) to a large corpus of texts, containing written, written-to-be-spoken and, if possible, spoken language.

A.D.A.M. (Analysis and Manipulation)

Manipulation 1: Frequency

This frequency calculus can be done if there is a language corpus available. By way of example we shall explain what was done for the English language in our centre. At the basis of the objective frequency count were three corpora of about 1,000,000 running words each: the Brown University Corpus (Kucera & Francis, 1967), the Lancaster-Oslo-Bergen Corpus (L.O.B., Johanson, 1980), and the Leuven Drama Corpus (Geens, Engels & Martin, 1975). Brown contained written American and L.O.B. written British English, both were constructed in a parallel way: texts written in 1961; 15 genres, 500 texts and 2000 words per text. The Leuven Drama Corpus contained written-to-be-spoken British English: 61 plays by different authors, written between 1965 and 1971.

In an objective count it is the computer which calculates the frequency of word-forms, putting them in a descending ranklist of frequency without distinguishing their semantic contents. To this objective count we amalgamated a list of 4,495 words denoting concrete objects (Richards, 1971). The frequency obtained here was subjective, because we relied on a familiarity judgement by 1000 native speakers of Laval University in Canada and not on a computer. These words were ordered in a descending ranklist of familiarity. The 1500 most familiar words were matched to the amalgamation of BROWN, LOB and Leuven Drama. Only 642 in 1500 happened to overlap in the objective count. In this way we effected a worthwhile correction to the objective count by adding the remaining 858 not-overlapping words to our list in a descending order of familiarity. These familiar notions of concrete things do not often appear in the written language (e.g. soap, lavatory, towel, etc.), still they should be taught in a foreign-language course.

For the objective count we restricted our ranklist to 2000 headwords in descending order of frequency; for the subjective count we restricted the list to 1500. The CORE of the English language, accordingly, was restricted to 2000 + 858 not-overlapping headwords; it is an almost finite core suited for further computerization (Engels, Van Beckhoven, Leenders & Brasseur, 1981, L.E.T.-list).

In the Section of Applied Linguistics at the K.U. Leuven, we have been doing research on word-frequency for English and Dutch since 1962. The 1981 results in the L.E.T.-list were first intended for the automatic analysis of a set of English texts to be studied by our students in their first propaedeutic year, in order to enrich their vocabulary. About 1985, when we started working on A.D.A.M. & E.V.E., the L.E.T.-list happened to provide an excellent automatic analyser for the lexis of any text introduced into a PC.

The research on frequency as such has not stopped in the Section of Applied Linguistics. Another team has started new experiments (Engels, Goethals, Vanermen, Van Beckhoven & Leenders, 1990).

Manipulation 2: Clustering

As headwords the computer chose the most frequent word-forms of a lemma. Accordingly, the headword of the verb *to be* is its form *is*. Round these headwords we gathered all the other forms of the headword and its derivatives of the same semantic field, e.g. round *is* we gathered in one cluster: *is, 'm, 're, 's, ain't, am, are, aren't, be, been, being, beings, isn't, was, wasn't, were, weren't*. For Dutch we made clusters like: *vinden, vind, vindt, vond, vonden, gevonden, vondst*; and for French: *connaitre, connais, connait, connaissons, connaissez, connaissent, connaissais, connaissait, connaissions, connaissiez, connus, connue, connues, connaissance, etc.*

We rely here on the educational principles of vocabulary learning by Van Parreren (Van Parreren & Schouten - Van Parreren, 1979), who pretend that you learn a word with its morphological forms and derivatives.

The computer's work consisted in calculating the relative frequencies of each item in the cluster, so that we could make a sum of all the relative frequencies in the cluster to finally obtain the rank-position for the whole cluster in a descending order of frequency.

In the list of 2000 descending clusters + the added familiarity clusters, we obtained about 12,000 word-forms in the English frequency list, about 20,000 word-forms for the Dutch language and 30,000 word-forms in the French list. The distinction is due to the different morphological components of these languages.

Manipulation 3: Automated Analysis of Texts

The automatic lexical analyser of texts is now operational. It is a completely *open* system, because it can analyse *any* text, whatever its degree of difficulty. But as we intended to let the program work for beginners as well as for intermediate and advanced students, we have introduced different levels of analysis corresponding to the students' mastery of the language, which a teacher is normally aware of, and to the difficulty of the text he decides to choose for them as an object of study. Therefore the descending frequency list of words present in the computer has been ordered into 4 blocks of 500 words each in descending order of frequency.

For beginners the teacher chooses fairly easy texts which can be analysed and put to the test by the computer by means of only block 1 with the 500 most frequent words, or block 1 + block 2 with the 1000 most frequent words of the language. The teacher can then try out which analysis gives the best results. All the word-forms of the text which happen to have a rank-number beyond these chosen barriers will appear in a block, which is reserved for the "outsiders", viz. the words that will have to be taught and learned. For advanced students the teacher will choose more difficult or specialized texts to be analysed by the whole set of the 2000 clusters contained in blocks 1 to 4. In case they denote concrete objects and do not appear among the 2000 clusters, they still can be "saved" by the added list of words from the familiarity-count.

The teacher need not accept indiscriminately the list of outsiders provided by the computational analysis. He should consult the list of outsiders in order to decide which words he judges suitable for explanation or translation, or for entering the exercises on outsiders. The teacher can store the words to be defined, translated or illustrated by example sentences into a user's dictionary, provided by the program.

Linguistic Manipulation 4: Polysemy

The higher the frequency of a word in a language, the more expanded its polysemy. A data-base was entered into the PC to illustrate the polysemy of the 2000 headwords of the clusters. Round each word there are about 3 to 6 sentences illustrating its polysemy. The computer will generate exercises on the polysemy of any notional word of the studied text which happens to be present in the list of 2000 clusters. In this way we provide continuous revision of formerly learned words, and at the same time we impose the different meanings of the same word so that we enrich the mastery of its semantic contents.

Linguistic Manipulation 5: Verbal Forms Transformed to their Infinitive Form

The computer will perform a syntactic analysis of the verbal forms; it can recognize all the irregular verbal forms, all anomalous finites and the verbal forms that accompany them, all forms of to be and the verbal forms that accompany them (-ing forms and passive voice), all forms of have and the verbal forms that accompany them (perfect tenses). All these forms will be reduced to their infinitive forms and exercises on the use of the tenses and modalities can be generated. The student will learn how to restore the required tense or modality, helped by the context.

Linguistic Manipulation 6: Implementation of a Spoken Dictionary

This manipulation with digitalized sounds has been realized in a proto-type version residing with the publisher. It is operational but not commercially efficient because of its financial implications for the schools (more memory needed on hard discs, etc.).

Until now the work has only been done for the English language. About 6,000 word-forms have been chosen from the frequency-list of clusters, i.e. the headwords and the variations of pronunciation within the same cluster: e.g. advertise, advertisement as to stress variations; go, went, gone as to vowel change. The program enables the student to call up the pronunciation of words in the text being studied; to have his own pronunciation recorded and listened to, comparing it to the native speaker's voice.

The teacher (or a native speaker) can also enter a whole spoken version of the text or part of it, taking into account the intonation catenation and reductions. The student can listen to it or imitate it while recording it. An automated dictation exercise is also made possible.

As soon as this program will be distributed, a new kind of language laboratory will be the result, in which many interactive skills can flourish: reading, writing, pronunciation and intonation training, vocabulary and grammar learning, conversation.

Linguistic Manipulation 7: Implementation of Whole Dictionaries

This is what all language teachers are craving for. As soon as publishers will allow commercialization of dictionaries in a machine-legible form, a new era of how to use computers in *computer-aided language learning* will start; disambiguation of homonyms, definitions to be matched to example sentences, exploration of grammatical categories and semantic depth.

Linguistic Manipulation 8: a Concordance of One or More Texts

It is extremely useful and inspiring, if it is executed when a fair number of texts has already been studied (Engels, 1986).

E.V.E. (Extensible Variety of Exercises)

The numerous linguistic manipulations can realize a number of exercises (extensible, because the list is never exhaustive; the imagination of the teachers using the program provides new kinds of exercises with every new release of A.D.A.M. & E.V.E.).

Manipulations 1, 2 and 3 enable the generation of exercises on outsiders, with different formats such as matching numbers, writing the words in the gaps in full, recalling by means of acronyms; exercises on the cohesion in a language, i.e. prepositions and particles, deixis, connectives: conjunctions and adverbials.

Manipulation 4 will generate exercises on the polysemy of all the notional word-forms present in the 2000 clusters of the frequency-list. There are two kinds of exercises: alternative context (one sentence is chosen at random by the computer displaying a context different from the one in the reading text studied) and pregnant contexts in which the same word is being left out from all the sentences available for the word, so that the student will guess the word by comparing the sentences.

Manipulation 5 will generate exercises on the use of the tenses and modalities in the text studied.

Manipulation 6 will allow pronunciation of single words, of parts of a text, with intonation, and automated dictation exercises.

Manipulation 7: The use of a dictionary will create a large extension of possible exercises, too many to enumerate them in this paper.

Manipulation 8: The study of concordances teaches the behaviour of words in *context*: words that belong together will be detected, idiomatic expressions and collocations.

The C-cloze will exercise *spelling* and *grammar* (morphology and syntax). But it does not require any linguistic manipulation beforehand (Raatz & Klein-Braley, 1981; Van Beckhoven, 1983).

Educational Values of A.D.A.M. & E.V.E.

A.D.A.M. & E.V.E. is a language mastery learning program. In the diagram on the next page we illustrate its place in the study of language materials.

A.D.A.M. & E.V.E. is a cognitive approach in language learning. All the generated exercises possess problem solving qualities; all the gap-filling exercises require memory, but also inductive and deductive operations. All grammar has to be applied in context (use of tenses, order of words in sentence, order of sentences in paragraph). If there are 2 students in front of the screen, the solution to exercises is being done by interaction.

The vocabulary training is extensive: extension of a ready vocabulary to be used in discussions about texts studied; continuous recapitulation of formerly learned words so as to reinforce their mastery; the detection of and exercises on new and useful clusters and collocations.

There is a continuous individual evaluation of the learning process. The exercises are no tests, but they are ways of learning to perfection: the scores must be between 95 and 100%.

One remarkable experiment with A.D.A.M. & E.V.E. is worth mentioning. At the Instituut for the Deaf at Sint-Michielsgestel, the Dutch version of this program is used to train Dutch grammar and vocabulary to boys and girls of 9 or 10 years of age. The reason why this program was chosen is certainly its capacity to analyse simple classroom conversations by means of an automated analyser which adapts itself to even such simple texts. The main reason, however, is that it can be used as an expert accountant while applying the Reflecterende Moedertaal Methode (Maternal Reflective Method), invented by Van Uden (Van Uden, 1977). The children's talks and conversations are made up, perfected and finished with the help of the teacher; the vocabulary which had to be added is filled in. The program will generate the exercises wanted by the teacher. The exercises can be done individually by the children; they get their scores; personal user's dictionaries can be stored in the PC's to take into account each child's proficiency.

Adam & Eve

Students' tasks	Teacher's tasks
	• free choice of text by teacher
	• teacher enters text by means of built-in word processor

	• the level of difficulty is checked against:
	    frequency
	    familiarity
	    covering

• text-study in classroom or at home

Mastery Learning:

• exercise discs are produced and distributed to students	• exercises are automatically generated
• students complete exercises	
• student performance is computed and fed back to teacher and to student	

• discussions, debates, reports, précis-writing, essays

Acknowledgments

A software program such as A.D.A.M. & E.V.E. is not one person's realization. At the K.U.Leuven and in other language institutes we organized teamwork. We are indebted to T. Leenders for 11 years of programming; to M. Goethals for his cooperation from the very beginning when working at the mainframe computer, for his presenting the program at the AILA conference in Sydney in 1987 (Goethals, 1990), for his introducing the program in the teacher's training centre at the university and in postgraduate sessions; to B. van Beckhoven and U. Vanermen for their contributions to further frequency research, tests and text study (Vanermen, 1985; Engels, et al., 1990).

For the Dutch program there is a team of co-operators: L. Baten (K.U.Leuven), L. Dieltjens (ICHEC), M.-T. Claes (U.C.L.), J. Van Parijs (Namur). For their frequency research they relied on a.o. CELEX (Kerkman, 1987; Baeten, Claes, Dieltjens & Vanparijs, 1989). For French, German and Spanish new teamwork is being organized.

References

Baten, L., Claes, M.-T., Dieltjens, L. & Vanparijs, J. (1989). A.D.A.M. & E.V.E. (Nederlands). Tekstanalyse en het genereren van oefeningen met de PC. *Levende Talen, 442*, 419-424.

Chomsky, N. (1965). *Aspects of the Theory of Syntax*. Massachusetts: M.I.T. Press.

Engels, L.K. (1986). Linguistic Exploration of Concordances Produced on Personal Computers. *Interface, Journal of Applied Linguistics (1)*, 29-42.

Engels, L.K. (1987). The Computer as the Language Teacher's Ingenious Companion. In: Atkinson, E. & Janssens, R. (eds), *A Collection of Papers from the 21st IATEFL Conference*. Frankfurt am Main: Westende.

Engels, L.K. & Leenders, T. (1984). Meetinstrumenten en Automering. In: De Coo (ed.), *Computers and Language Instruction, Applications of Interactive Technology. ABLA-papers nr.8*, 29-64.

Engels, L.K., Van Beckhoven, B., Leenders, T. & Brasseur, I. (1981). *L.E.T. Vocabulary-List. Leuven English Teaching Vocabulary-list based on objective frequency combined with subjective word-selection*. Leuven: ACCO.

Engels, L.K., Goethals, M., Vanermen, U., Van Beckhoven, B. & Leenders, T. (1990). Didactic frequency research for English as a foreign language at the K.U. Leuven. In: S. Granger (ed.), *Perspectives on the English Lexicon. A tribute to Jacques Van Roey*. Louvain-la-Neuve, p.269-280.

Geens, D., Engels, L.K. & Martin, W. (1975) *Leuven Drama Corpus and Frequency List*. Interim Report. Leuven, Institute of Applied Linguistics.

Goethals, M., Engels, L.K. & Leenders, T. (1990). Automated Analysis of the Vocabulary of English Texts and Generation of Practice Materials: From Main Frame to P.C., the Way to the Teacher's Electronic Desk. In: N.A.K. Halliday, J. Gibbons & H. Nicholas (eds), *Learning, Keeping and Using Language: Selected Papers from the Eighth World Congress of Applied Linguistics. Sydney, 16-21 August 1987*, 231-268.

Johansson, S. (1980). The LOB Corpus of British English Texts: Presentation and Comments. *ALLC Journal I (1)*, 25-36.

Kerkman, H. (1987). CELEX. Een Centrum voor Lexicale Informatie. *Toegepaste Taalwetenschap in Artikelen.*

Kucera, H. & Francis, W.N. (1967). *Computational Analysis of Present-Day American English.* Providence, Rhode Island: Brown University Press.

Raatz, U. & Klein-Braley, C. (1981). The C-test, a modification of the CLOZE Procedure. In: P. Culhane, C. Klein-Braley & D. Stevenson (eds), *Practice and Problems in Language Testing. Occasional Papers nr.26.* Colchester, Essex University, 113-138.

Richards, J.C. (1971). *Word Familiarity as an Index of Vocabulary Selection with Indices for 4495 words.* Ph. D. Diss, Laval University, Canada. Unpublished ms.

Van Beckhoven, B. (1983). De C-test, een nieuwkomer onder de testen. *Werkmap voor Taalonderwijs, 29,* 1-14.

Vanermen, U. (1985). Collocmatics. An Interim Report. *I.A.T.E.F.L. Newsletter,* 10-11.

Van Parreren, C. & Schouten - Van Parreren, C. (1979) Erwerb eines fremdsprachlichen Wortschatzes. In: K. Detering & R. Högel (eds) *Englisch auf der Sekundarstufe.* 22-36. Hannover.

Van Uden, A.M. (1977). *A world of language for deaf children. Part I: Basic principles, a maternal reflective method.* Lisse: Swets & Zeitlinger (third revision).

Grammar in a Visual Mode: an Alternative for Hearing-Impaired Children?

H. Veenker
State University of Groningen, Grote Kruisstraat 2-1, 9712 TS Groningen,
the Netherlands

Abstract. Deaf children learning a spoken language find it extremely difficult to acquire structural (=linguistic) information like syntax and morphology. Recent research has demonstrated that suprasegmental information contributes significantly to the language acquisition of hearing children (Morgan, Meier & Newport, 1987; Issidorides, 1988; Mehler, Jusczyk, Lambertz, Halsted, Bertoncini & Amiel-Tison, 1988). In the present research project it is assumed that the absence of suprasegmental information like intonation, rhythm and stress may be due to this problem. Due to it's acoustical character deaf children have no access to suprasegmental information. Since suprasegmental information is not represented in writing, another "visualisation" of relevant segmenting cues might be useful.

In a previous psycholinguistic research project it was - in addition to research of others (cf Quiqley & King, 1986)- shown, that deaf children have a major syntactical problem (Veenker & Van Geert, 1990). It was also found, that deaf children lack segmentation skills on word-level (Wilbur, 1982; Veenker, Wever & Van Lenthe, 1991). On the basis of this research two visual grammars were developed: one is concerned with the structure of words and the other with sentences. The aim of these grammars is to segment language forms in a way that looks like suprasegmental information. Of course, only those features that are relevant for the segmentation are selected in the grammars.

First, in this paper attention will be paid to this research that proceeded to the development of the grammars. Some principles behind the grammars will be explained. Second, the two visual grammars and the additional software will be characterized; finally some remarks will be made about a planned evaluation project.

Keywords. (second) language acquisition, grammar, reading, dyslexia, visual mode, computer graphics.

Introduction

Deaf children find it very hard to learn a spoken language. The problems appear not only in the spoken but also in the written modality. Since almost any hearing child can learn a spoken language, irrespective of intelligence, it is suggested that the spoken modality itself contains information about the language that contributes to the learnability of that language (Morgan, Meier & Newport, 1988). This suggestion increases in impact of course due to sign language research that demonstrated that sign languages can formally be compared with spoken languages (Klima & Bellugi, 1979); this also implies, that sign languages contain suprasegmental information as well as spoken languages do, albeit in a different mode. In ASL e.g. one can rhyme (Poizner, Klima & Bellugi, 1987).

It must be emphasized that it is not the semantic aspect of spoken languages that causes the high threshold but rather the grammatical (cf. Quiqley & King, 1980). In our research project the influence of grammatical and semantic cues of deaf children's reading strategies is examined. Some examples will be given later in this paper.

This article deals with the question whether visual grammars can be useful for this rather complex language-acquisition problem of deaf children. Referring to the titel of this article, one might wonder what is meant by "visual grammars"; moreover some attention will be paid to the use of the term "alternative".

Linguistic Reading Strategies

To begin with the latter: in our research we discovered that - in spite of what many researchers claim - deaf children do use rather intelligent linguistic strategies in reading. Some examples might clarify this statement.

In this research project we examined wordorder, wordclasses and concordance or congruentual morpholoy. The children varied in age from 7 to 15 years. In the test for wordorder (Kunst, van der Vlugt, Veenker, Verhagen & Hoijtink, 1988) children had to distinguish Yes-No-questions from declarative sentences by putting a question mark or a full stop behind them. In Dutch inversion may occur both in questions and in declarative sentences. A sentence like: "Toen heb je dat gedaan" ("Then you did it") illustrates inversion in a declaritive sentence. For some deaf children this is a tricky form, because it looks like an interrogative form (Kunst et al., 1988). Nevertheless, word order is still a very important cue in determining whether a sentence is in interrogative or in declaritive form (Figure 1). In Figure 1 verbal elements are placed in the expanded boxes. Each box represents a constituent. The two verbal positions are marked with oversized boxes (Geerts, Haeseryn, de Rooy & van den Toorn, 1984).

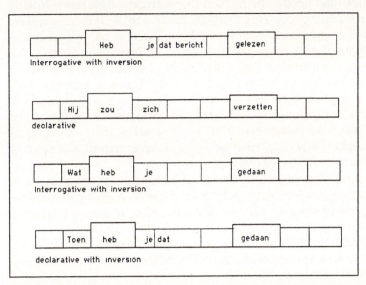

Figure 1. An illustration of word-order patterns in Dutch declarative and interrogative sentences. (Translation: Heb jij dat bericht gelezen?: Did you read that message? Hij zou zich verzetten.: He would show resistance. Wat heb je gedaan?: What have you done? Toen heb je dat gedaan.: You did it then.)

The results of this test show that Dutch deaf subjects tended to use the inverted order "finite verb - grammatical subject" as a framework for interpreting sentences as a question. They misinterpreted many declarative sentences which had this inverted order. We also found a strong correlation between age and this strategy: elder children made more use of this strategy than younger children. The hearing subjects seemed to be more sensitive to semantic or pragmatic features.

It is clear that the strategy used by deaf children - we mentioned it the inversion strategy - is a linguistic strategy. However, it is not an intuitive strategy but rather a cognitive strategy, which means, that the children tend to analyse the test-items with a formal, grammatical vocabulary.

Similar results were found in the other tests: in the tests for congruential morphology we found that deaf children make strong overgeneralizations in the use of word-endings. We also found significant correlations between age and the occurance of overgeneralizations, in the same way as we did before in the test for word-order.

These examples show, that deaf children are able to use linguistic information; the problem, however, is the strong cognitive character of the reading strategies. This can be explained by the nature of the grammar deaf children learn: not seldom they learn a grammar by means of rules, and the rules are applied to sentences. Since the entire framework of the grammar consists of rules that need to be learned (by heart, mostly), much time is required for sentence processing, both productive as well as perceptive. Our alternative is concerned with a non-cognitive, but rather perceptive grammar: a visual one. As is the case with suprasegmental information, the segmentation is self-learning: the pupil does not have to learn how to use the visual grammar, but the other way around: the grammar tells the pupil how the words of the sentence need to be grouped. In order to create such a visual illusion computer graphics are a helpful instrument. At the end of the research phase we had gathered information about the processing of words and simple sentences so that we had a sharp description of the sort of information we had to visualize.

In summary: reading, in spite of the use of linguistic strategies seems to be a game of reasoning, like playing chess for instance. We believe that deaf children can benefit from a grammar, that can easily be perceived during sentence processing. For that purpose we have been developing a grammar in a visual modality in order to approach a natural and therefore perceivable framework for language acquisition. Our point of departure is that learnability and perceivability are narrowly related.

Visual (=graphical) Grammars

We would like to define a visual grammar as a set of graphical structures, that is appropriate for language acquisition purposes.

- A visual grammar serves as an instrument for the representation of formal properties of a language.
- A visual grammar must be easy to learn and to remember so that it can be used easily in language processes, especially at the mental level.
- The most important quality of a visual grammar - especially a grammar for sentence representation - is, that it must be able to represent the development of sentences in time. Not primarily for the sake of rhythm, but rather because the processing of language develops in time. Therefore this time-aspect is more important for the representation of sentences than for words. (This does not mean that rhythm is not important of course; this remark is only meant to be a description of a quality of visual grammars.)
- A visual grammar primarily operates on the descriptive level. It needs to be flexible so that the grammar can describe the structure of any language form. "Exceptions" upon rules should also fit in the system. The grammar must be able to account properly for both simple and complex sentences.

Ortho and Matrix

In our research project we have been developing two visual grammars: Ortho and Matrix. The grammar of Ortho makes it possible to describe the structure of words, the grammar of Matrix visualises the structure of sentences.

Ortho

The basis of Ortho is a template for syllables. Each template consists of 3 positions for consonants, the vowel and consonants resp. (Figure 2). A word that consists of three syllables requires three templates. Besides this general template Ortho furthermore makes use of some additional techniques that can be used for more detailed information about the word.

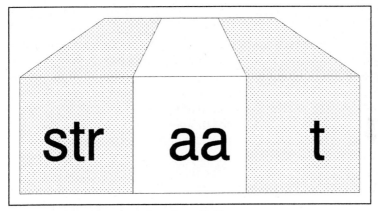

Figure 2. The Ortho-template for syllables.

To begin with, we use colour for the squares inside the template: green for the consonant positions and red for the vowel position. Furthermore, brightness of colour is used to distinguish stressed from unstressed syllables. This is not only useful for pronunciation purposes but also for orthographic rules. In the computerprogram other colours can be chosen as well, e.g. for children who are colourblind.

The second technique is concerned with the use of fonts. This technique enables the user to mark morphological and a few phonological aspects. A special option makes it possible e.g. to create a computer-animation of a "growing" letter (the letter increases from a small point to a big letter on the screen): this option can be used for the distinction between long and short vowels. This distinction is relevant for some phonological and orthographical rules.

The Architecture of the Computerprogram Ortho. Ortho consists of 6 options.

- Looking at words (Woorden bekijken) (1)
- Editing of words (Woorden invoeren) (2)
- Printing of words (Printen van woorden) (3)
- Interactive exercise: "Flash words" (Flitswoorden) (4)
- Standards (Standaard instellingen) (5)
- Font editor (Lettervormen invoeren) (6).

Options 1, 3 and 4 are developed for the children, the others are for the teachers.

The most important module is number 4: the interactive exercise. The child can work individually with this interactive module. When the child has typed in its name the computer asks the child to point to the requested reading speed. Words can be presented fast as well as slow; the speed can be defined in tenths of a second. After the setting of the speed a word appears on the screen during the defined time. The child has to remember the word and then has to type it in. The type screen contains two edit lines and a couple of boxes that refer to special options. First the child has to try to type in the word. If the child cannot remember the word, the box for "I don't know" (a red box with question marks) can be chosen. This choice gives the answer to the problem: the complete word, including fonts and segmention appears on the screen. The next item appears afterwards. If the child on the other hand does remember the word, it can be typed in. After entering the "return" key the word appears in the template. The computer distinguishes vowels from consonants. With this information syllables are automatically placed in the template. If the child thinks that the structuring is o.k. the child can enter the "ready" box with the mouse; if the child wants to modify the word e.g. the segmentation, the stress pattern or the font-choice this can be done first. In this situation the pupil switches from the keyboard to the mouse. The pointer is already set at the correct position, so that quick typing is stimulated. After the typing phase the child may be asked to provide rather complex information. It turned out to be the most efficient, to have this performed with a "click-what you want" -system. Now the answer of the child can be corrected by the computer. If the child enters the "ready" box with the mouse, the computer compares the word of the child with the master-file of the teacher. On the basis of this comparison the computer responds to the answer of the child.

The master-file is a file produced by the teacher. It contains all the required information that the computer needs for corrections. A masterfile can be compiled from the dictionary, but can also be typed in.

In addition to these options there is a small computational program, Ortdata, that can process the results. This module gives statistical information about the responses of the children. With this module one can analyse the behaviour of the children since it can be programmed to give specific information, e.g. about spelling, morphology, segmentation etc.

Matrix

Matrix is a visual grammar for sentences. The basic structure of Matrix is for declarative sentences. A similar structure is built for sentences with the verb in the first position (Figure 3).

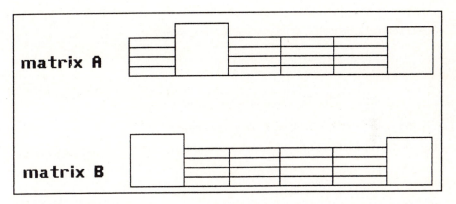

Figure 3. The basic structures of the Matrix-grammar with resp. a verb on the second or the first and the last positions. The large boxes refer to the verb-positions.

The large boxes refer to verb-positions. Each structure contains six positions or boxes. Inside each position-box four segments can be optionally drawn. The basic idea is that each segment can contain a word, and each position-box one constituent.
If a constituent contains more words than four, the computer automatically draws a box without segments. Figure 4 demonstrates the use of the basic structures for main clauses with respect to word order and inversion. Apart from these two basic structures there are two structures for sub-clauses that can be attached to a basic structure. The Matrix-grammar consists of combinations of these graphical structures.

The time-aspect in computer animations: the presentation of sentences word by word Graphics like Figure 4 can easily be presented on a computer-screen. It is also possible to simulate the time-aspect of sentence production on a computer screen. This can be done by presenting sentences word by word just above the Matrix (Figure 5). This technique forces the child to pay attention to the wordorder. At the same time one can present segmentational support at the computer-screen by presenting the appropriate Matrix. The corresponding segment of the matrix lights up, so that the child can perceive the place of the word in the structure.

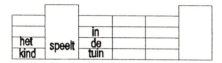

Het kind speelt in de tuin. *(The child is playing in the garden)*

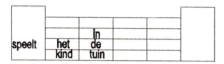

Speelt het kind in de tuin? *(Is the child playing in the garden?)*

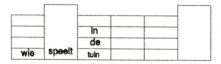

Wie speelt in de tuin? *(Who is playing in the garden?)*

Figure 4. Applications of the Matrix-grammar for 3 different sentences.

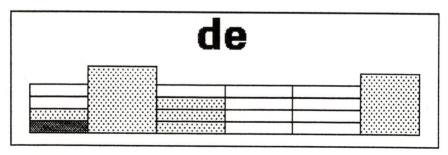

Figure 5. An example of the matrix in the word-by-word mode. The grey segments predict the filling of the forthcoming positions that the sentence will use.

The Surplus Value of the Use of the Computer

One of the main characteristics of both computerprograms is that they are based upon a theory of language acquisition (Morgan, Meier & Newport, 1987; Issidorides, 1988; Veenker & Van Geert, 1990). For that purpose two grammars have been developed. The computer enables us to optimalize the use of the grammars. However, it is not necessary to use the computer permanently. Actually, the running start with Ortho e.g. does not begin with the computer but with boxes like big dice.

With respect to Ortho and Matrix the computer has many advantages that I will sum up:

- First one can mention the large impact of computer graphics and animation: this might enable us to manipulate reading strategies and linguistic processes that are related to those strategies.
- The graphical displays make it possible to pay attention to rather difficult and abstract problems.
- The computer enables the teacher to differentiate in the classroom. This is of particular importance in the education of deaf children since the levels of children even in small groups can vary enormously.
- Thanks to the interactivity of the computer the child (or e.g. two children) can receive feedback; the pupil can learn individually.
- The interactivity of course saves the teacher time.
- Motivation and attractiveness. Grammar lessons are often of the boring kind; thanks to the computer-programs children can have more pleasure; the programs support the motivation of the children better.

Technical Qualities of the Programs

At this moment the development of Ortho for MS-DOS has almost come to an end; Matrix on the other hand is not finished yet. A forthcoming step will be the development of MS-Windows applications of Ortho and Matrix. Matrix may benefit from what we have learnt from Ortho. We paid attention to the following points while Ortho was being developed:

- The operation of the programs should be easy: we wanted to avoid typing in commands: therefore we made use of mouse-directed menus.
- The programs should be attractive to children: grammar has the reputation of being boring. We tried to avoid this effect by means of the graphical quality, and through the choice of the exercises. Ortho e.g. can be manipulated by increasing the reading time of words. The feedback is

also very important because it suggests a game.
- The teacher needs to know what the children have done during the exercises in terms of the learning process. So quantitative information only is not sufficient. The teacher needs to know about qualitative aspects of the learning process as well. This demand is probably fulfilled sufficiently by "Ortdata", the program that gives information about the results of each child. The program gives information about the type of difficulty: can the child remember the orthographic elements of the word, how well are the segmentation skills etc.

A final word must be said: the computer may seem to be the only instrument that enables the teacher to make use of the grammars. As stated before, happily this is not the case. One can draw for instance a large Matrix figure on the playground. Such a simple tool can be used for playing a hopping game on rhymes or plain sentences. Actually, Ortho and Matrix can be processed in or combined with many materials. Another remark that must be made is, that the children learn to develop segmentation skills. The computer serves as a didactic instrument to achieve this purpose. Hopefully the computer makes itself superfluous - just like many other instruments.

Evaluation of the Programs

Both programs are in some stage of development. Therefore we only have very little information about results. In the autumn of 1991 however, we have planned an evaluation-research. In this project the programs will be evaluated by several groups of children: the programs will be evaluated at institutes for deaf, hearing, dyslectic and foreign children learning Dutch.

In the forthcoming research project we will carry out n=1 and n=2 studies. First of all we will try to compute two baselines: an internal and an external one. The internal baseline is concerned with the success of the programs: do the children like the program, do the children understand the templates and graphical structures? etc. The external baseline is concerned with the linguistic progress of the children in general: does their comprehension on wordorder increase? etc. The external baseline measures the existing level of knowledge and it also tries to make an estimation of the linguistic growth: this measure attempts to predict the language development of a pupil; the measure will be obtained from several repeated measures. Having obtained a baseline for each pupil we will introduce the visual grammar and again several repeated measures will be accomplished. For each child we will compute the forthgoing development. The results that we will obtain from the external measures will be compared with control-subjects in n=2 studies according to a matching procedure.

In the forthcoming project we wil also develop for each target-group a reading method. The point of departure will be the present methods of the participating institutes. We will attempt to develop several methods that can be applied in many different educational settings.

References

Geerts, G., Haeseryn, W., Rooy J. de, & Toorn, M.C. van den (eds) (1984). *Algemene Nederlandse Spraakkunst.* Groningen/Leuven: Wolters-Noordhoff/Wolters Leuven.
Issidorides, D.C. (1988). The discovery of a miniature linguistic system: function words and comprehension of an unfamiliar language. *Journal of psycholinguistic Research, 17, 4.*
Klima, E. & Bellugi, U. (1979). *The signs of language.* Harvard University Press.
Kunst, H., Vlugt, C. van der, Veenker, H., Verhagen, A. & Hoijtink, H. (1988). Vraagteken of punt? De rol van woordvolgorde bij het lezen door dove kinderen. *Tijdschrift voor Taal-en Tekstwetenschap, 8, 2,* 89-110.
Mehler, J., Jusczyk, P., Lambertz, G., Halsted, N., Bertoncini, J. & Amiel-Tison, C. (1988). A precursor of language acquisition in young infants. *Cognition, 29,* 143-178.
Morgan, J.L., Meier, R.P. & Newport, E.L. (1987). Structural packaging in the input to language learning: Contributions of prosodic and morphological marking of phrases to the acquisition of language. *Cognitive Psychology. 19,* 498-550.
Poizner, H., Klima, E.S. & Bellugi, U. (1987). *What the hands reveal about the brain.* Cambridge: MIT-press.
Quigley, C.M. & King S.P. (1980). An invited article. Syntactic performance of hearing impaired and normal hearing individuals, *Applied Psycholinguistics, I,* 329-356.
Veenker, H. & Geert, P.L.C. van (1990). *Taalverwerving en leesstrategieën bij dove kinderen.* Eindrapport van het project. Rijksuniversiteit Groningen, HB 89-987-IN.
Veenker, H., Wever, D. & Lenthe, J. van (1991). De herkenning van de structuur van Nederlandse woorden bij dove kinderen. *Interdisciplinair Tijdschrift voor Taal- en Tekstwetenschap (TTT), 10, 2,* 93-109.
Wilbur R. (1982). The development of morpheme structure constraints in deaf children. *The Volta Review,* 7-17.

Oral Communication

Computer Interactive Techniques in Training and Evaluation of Communication Skills

Harry Levitt[1], Karen Youdelman[1], and James J. Dempsey[2]

[1]Center for Research in Speech and Hearing Sciences, Graduate School and University Center, City University of New York, New York 10036 and The Lexington Center, Jackson Heights, New York 11370

[2]Department of Communication Disorders, Southern Connecticut State University, New Haven, Connecticut 06515 and Lexington Hearing and Speech Center, Jackson Heights, New York 11370

Abstract. There are many ways in which computer interactive techniques can be of value in addressing the problems of hearing impairment. This paper describes two computer interactive techniques for training and evaluation of communication skills:

- training and evaluation of speech production skills using computer-based visual displays, and
- training and evaluation of receptive communication skills using a computer simulated version of the method of continuous discourse tracking.

Computer Interactive Speech Training Systems

Visual feedback has been found to be extremely useful in teaching speech to deaf students. A wide range of electronic visual displays has been developed over the years (Strong, 1975; Levitt, Picket & Houde, 1980; Lippman, 1982). Of the many speech-feature displays that have been tried, visual and/or tactile displays of voice fundamental frequency have been found to be particularly useful (Fourcin and Abberton, 1971; McGarr, Head, Friedman, Behrman & Youdelman, 1986). Other speech-feature displays which have shown successful results in experimental evaluations include displays of frication, nasalization, and vowel type (Guttman, Levitt & Bellefleur, 1970; Stevens, Kalikow & Willemain, 1975; Povel & Wansink, 1986).

Despite the positive results obtained in experimental evaluations of visual speech training aids, these devices are not widely used in schools and clinics. Several reasons can be posited for the relatively low usage of modern technology in speech training. Technological aids which work well in the laboratory may not be convenient for use in a classroom setting. Devices that need to be calibrated or adjusted at regular intervals place an additional load on a teacher's already busy schedule. Even if a new speech training aid works well and is easy to use, it needs to capture the interest of both the student and the teacher in order for it to be used effectively. The student needs to be motivated to use the speech training aid and the speech teacher needs to feel confident about using the device and how it can be integrated advantageously into the student's speech-training curriculum. In short, for a new speech training aid to be successful it needs to be "user friendly", motivating for the student, and capable of improving speech skills within a practical speech-training curriculum.

Computer-interactive speech training systems can address these problems in innovative ways and, in so doing, open up new possibilities with respect to the practical use of advanced technology in the classroom. An important advantage of computer-based systems is that software can be written to make even the most sophisticated technology easy to use. Witness the development of the mouse and other user-friendly methods of bridging the interface between people and computers. The experience gained in bringing computers into the classroom can also be used effectively in broadening the use of advanced technology in speech training.

A review of the history of speech analyzing aids shows that the most successful devices are those in which the relevant speech features are determined reliably and displayed in a simple, easy to comprehend form (Levitt, 1986). Voice fundamental frequency (F_0) and frication, for example, can be estimated reasonably reliably from the acoustic speech waveform or alternatively, in the case of F_0, by means of a sensor placed conveniently on the throat. In contrast, articulatory manoeuvers involving tongue placement are not easy to monitor. Estimates of vocal tract shape and, concomitantly, of tongue placement cannot always be estimated reliably from an analysis of the acoustic speech signal. These estimates are invariably based on an imperfect model of the speech production mechanism and are prone to error.

It is possible to measure tongue placement directly by means of sensors placed in the mouth (Itoh & Hiki, 1977; Fletcher & Hasegawa, 1983). A device of this type, the palatograph, uses an artificial palate (similar to an orthodontic retainer) that is placed in the mouth. The artificial palate is very thin and rests against the hard palate. Tiny sensors are mounted in the artificial palate; these sensors monitor any contact between the tongue and the palate.

The palatograph is an extremely useful measurement tool which can be used for both research and the clinical diagnosis of articulatory disorders. It can also be used effectively as a speech training tool. The inconvenience of having to place an artificial palate in the mouth for speech training is not negligible, but this disadvantage is outweighed by the extraordinarily useful information that is obtained from the device and which cannot be obtained reliably by other means.

A pilot study has been performed on the use of the palatograph in a computer-interactive speech training system. The Matsushita speech training system was used. The system contains a range of different sensors for monitoring speech production. These include a laryngeal transducer, a nasal transducer, an air-flow monitor, a voice-activated microphone and an artificial palate. The system is computerized and any of the speech parameters being monitored can be displayed conveniently on a video screen, or stored in computer memory (including the speech waveform) for purposes of record keeping and future analysis. A very useful aspect of the memory feature is that good productions of an utterance by the student can be stored conveniently and then used as a practical target for the student in subsequent training.

Five profoundly deaf students, 15 to 17 years of age, were trained on the system over a six-week period. Each student received individualized speech training with the system for one 30-minute session per week for a total of six such sessions. Measurements of speech production skills were obtained prior to training and at the end of the six-week training program. The Fundamental Speech Skills Test (Levitt, Youdelman & Head, 1990) was used for this purpose in addition to test material specific to the training program.

The focus of the training program was on the remediation of common articulatory errors. The training began with the correction of the most common errors, initially in the context of syllables and syllable pairs, but moving rapidly towards correct productions in words and phrases. Emphasis was placed on the use of speech in a meaningful context.

The palatograph was used to provide the students with visual displays of their tongue placement. This was done both in real time during speech production and later in slow motion in order to show the deaf student when and where errors in tongue placement occurred. Visual feedback in slow motion was found to be very useful in providing the student with clear and precise information on how they had placed their tongue in the preceding articulation. Information of this type is not available using conventional methods of speech training.

Auditory feedback was also provided using the student's personal hearing aid. The students were taught to monitor their own speech production using whatever residual hearing was available. This proved very useful once the visual display was removed.

The results of the pilot study are summarized in Table 1. The table shows the percentage of correct productions for each student before and after training. A set of utterances designed to cover common articulatory errors in the speech of the deaf students was used. Recordings of the test material were obtained without the use of the visual display. The recordings were randomized and played to a skilled rater who identified the errors in each production.

As shown in the table, all of the students showed improved test scores after training. For two of the five students, the improvement in test score was statistically significant. This result is particularly encouraging considering the short duration of the training program and that the articulatory errors exhibited by the students prior to the experiment were problems of long standing.

Table 1. Percentage of correct productions pre- and post-training for 5 subjects with the Matsushita Speech Training System.

Subject	Pre-Training	Post-Training	Significance Level
1	56	61	---
2	38	64	$p < .05$
3	37	43	---
4	28	47	$p < .05$
5	24	35	---

In the pilot study reported above, the interactive speechtraining system was used with older students in order to remediate speech problems that had been acquired over many years and which were deeply ingrained despite previous attempts at remediation using conventional methods of speech training. Since the students were older, it was not difficult for them to grasp the association between the visual displays and the placement of their articulators. It is more difficult teaching young children to interpret these visual displays, yet at the same time it is very important to teach young deaf children to develop their speech production skills correctly so as to avoid the need for remediation at a later date.

Work is proceeding on the use of the computer-interactive speech training system with very young children. Simple visual displays have already been used with children as young as four years of age. The use of the palatograph with very young children, however, raises additional problems because of the small size of the mouth and related developmental considerations.

The use of small, flexible artificial palates of various sizes provides a means for addressing these issues. An important need, however, is that of developing appropriate training strategies that take into account developmental aspects of speech production and which can be used effectively with advanced computer interactive speech-training systems of this type.

Training and Evaluation of Receptive Communication Skills

A very powerful technique for training and evaluation of receptive communication skills is that of continuous discourse tracking (DeFilippo & Scott, 1978). According to this technique, a speaker reads a passage from a text, usually a simple story. The listener repeats verbatim each utterance produced by the speaker. If the listener makes a mistake, then the speaker tries again either by repeating what was said or, alternatively, by rephrasing the target utterance. The procedure continues until the listener repeats the target utterance correctly. The rate at which the listener is able to correctly track what was said (in words per minute) is used as a measure of communication ability.

The method of continuous discourse tracking can be used for both training and evaluation of communication skills. It is widely employed for both of these applications with persons fitted with cochlear implants. The technique is simple to implement, has good face validity and covers a wide range of communication skills.

Alternative methods of evaluating communication skills, such as the use of phonetically balanced word or sentence lists, have a narrow range of performance and are not representative of how people communicate in everyday life. The method of continuous discourse tracking, in contrast, is an interactive procedure that involves communicative exchanges between the speaker and the listener. As such, the technique addresses an important aspect of communication, that of speaker-listener interactions, that is neglected in conventional methods of assessing communication skills. For similar reasons, the technique is also very effective in teaching communication skills.

A serious practical problem with continuous discourse tracking as an evaluative tool is that there are very large individual differences between speakers. There are also substantial differences in the rapport between speakers and listeners. That is, certain speaker/listener pairs communicate very effectively while other speaker/listener pairs communicate poorly (Schoepflin & Levitt, 1991). These differences detract from the reliability of the technique in evaluating the communication skills of an individual listener. This problem is not very different from that which occurred during the early development of speech testing procedures when live-voice testing was used (Fletcher, 1929). In order to reduce inter-speaker differences, standardized recordings of test materials were developed. The use of standardized recordings is now common practice in the evaluation of speech reception skills.

Pre-recorded test materials can be used in continuous discourse tracking provided the interactive nature of the tracking procedure is maintained.

This has been done using a video disc player under computer control. Each video disc has recorded on it several versions of each phrase or sentence used in the test. For example, a paragraph length short story might consist of ten sentences. Each of the ten sentences is recorded in several different ways. The first recorded version of a sentence is produced as it might occur in a typical conversation. The second version would be a repeat of the sentence assuming the listener did not hear any part of the sentence correctly. The third version might be a repeat of part of the sentence with emphasis placed on those words which were not heard correctly on the previous occasion, and so on.

The choice of which version to play at any given time depends on how well the subject repeated the target utterance. In our computer simulation of continuous discourse tracking a human observer is used to make the decision as to whether the listener repeated the target utterance correctly or not. In order to minimize judgmental variability, the observer is restricted to two simple binary decisions, whether or not the listener repeated the first half of the sentence correctly and whether or not the listener repeated the second half of the sentence correctly. These two decisions are fed into the computer which then applies a simple rule for selecting the next recorded utterance.

The following is an illustrative example of how the system works. Consider the target utterance "Susan worked late at the bookstore that night." A video recording of this utterance, as it might occur in everyday conversation is played initially. A typical response by the listener might be "Susan worked late on her book at night." The observer would then indicate, by processing a specified key on the computer, that the first half of the sentence was repeated correctly and, by pressing a second key, that the second half of the sentence was repeated in error. The computer would then select for playback a video recording in which only the second portion of the utterance is repeated, e.g., "at the bookstore, that night." The listener then attempts to repeat the second version of the utterance. This second attempt is evaluated by the observer who, as before, is required to judge whether each half of the utterance was repeated correctly.

The procedure is continued iteratively until the subject has correctly repeated the entire target sentence. The computer then selects for playback the initial version of the next sentence in the paragraph. Alternatively, if the subject is unable to repeat the target sentence correctly then, after a predetermined number of unsuccessful attempts, the target sentence is typed out on the video screen and the system moves on to the next sentence in the paragraph.

The constraint that the observer's judgments be limited to binary form reduces judgmental variability significantly, but it also represents a change from the conventional use of continuous discourse tracking. For this reason, the computerized implementation of continuous discourse tracking developed here is referred to as Computer-Assisted Tracking Simulation, or CATS (Dempsey, Levitt, Josephson & Porrazzo, 1992).

It is conceivable that a fully automated version of CATS could be developed in which the human observer is replaced by an automatic speech recognition system. This has been attempted, but two difficulties were encountered that precluded its implementation in practice, at least for the time being. The first and most serious problem was that although the automatic speech recognition system was trained on the set of target sentences, the system still made occasional errors in recognizing the listener's spoken output. These errors resulted in erroneous repetitions of utterances that were in fact repeated correctly by the listener, thereby providing a misleading estimate of the listener's tracking ability. In the case of communication training, errors by the speech recognition system provided misleading feedback to the listener. A second, less serious problem was that the recognition system required several seconds of processing time at the end of each sentence. This resulted in an abnormal deviation from the interactive pattern of communication typical of continuous discourse tracking. Methods of circumventing these problems are currently being considered.

An experiment was performed in which the version of CATS using a human observer was compared to continuous discourse tracking using a live speaker. The same speaker was used for both the live and computer-interactive versions of the procedure with 18 versions of each sentence in each story being recorded. Ten paragraph length short stories were prepared. Six normal hearing listeners served as subjects. They were required to lip read the target sentences as part of the tracking task. Additive white noise was used to mask the acoustic speech signal. A balanced combination of five live-voice and five computer-interactive sessions was used. The assignment of stories to experimental conditions was randomized subject to the constraint that each listener tracked each story once only.

Table 2. Average Tracking Rates: Live vs Computer Assisted Tracking Simulation (CATS). All entries are in words per minute.

		Subjects						
		1	2	3	4	5	6	Mean
Average Tracking Rate	Live	18.1	18.0	15.9	19.4	25.9	29.4	21.2
	CATS	10.3	10.7	13.6	12.0	16.8	13.6	12.8
Std error	Live	4.9	8.4	6.9	8.1	11.5	13.2	8.8
	CATS	4.1	3.9	6.7	3.3	2.0	4.1	4.0

The results of the study are summarized in Table 2. Mean tracking rates averaged over the ten short stories are shown for each mode of tracking and for each subject. Also shown is the test/retest standard error. Between story differences were found to be relatively small and have been combined in estimating test/retest variability.

The results show that test/retest variability was much smaller for CATS as compared to live-voice tracking. In addition, between-speaker differences have been brought under control by the use of pre-recorded test materials. In this study, the same speaker was used for both the live-voice and the computer-interactive mode of tracking. In practice, it is difficult to ensure that the same speaker is used for all experimental conditions and, as a consequence, live-voice tracking is subject to additional sources of variability if different speakers are used for different experimental conditions. The problem of inter-speaker differences is particularly severe when data from different laboratories or clinics are compared since speakers at different locations often use slightly different rules in implementing the method of continuous discourse tracking. Neither of these sources of variability occur with the computer-assisted version of the technique.

An additional advantage of CATS is that all aspects of the test are monitored and recorded automatically. Consequently, in addition to measuring tracking rate the computer-interactive technique can also provide a statistical analysis of the types and frequencies of errors made by each listener.

The average tracking rate for CATS was found to be lower than that for live tracking. This was largely because in live tracking, the speaker is more efficient in selecting the appropriate repetition after an error than the automated method. The differences in tracking rate are not a major concern since the lower tracking rate was observed consistently for all subjects.

A limitation of CATS, as it is currently implemented, is that the observer is limited to a pair of binary decisions after each repetition by the listener. Although this constraint is effective in reducing judgmental variability on the part of the observer, it also modifies the nature of the speaker-listener interaction, as is evident from the slower tracking rates observed for CATS.

In summary, the method of continuous discourse tracking is a powerful technique that can be used for both the evaluation and training of receptive communication skills. A major problem with continuous discourse tracking is that of uncontrolled speaker differences. This problem can be eliminated by using pre-recorded test and training materials. An additional advantage of using standardized pre-recorded materials is that normative data can be obtained on each set of recordings and different sets of materials (e.g., different stories) can be matched for equality of difficulty. The computer-interactive system is easy to implement and requires no more than a small personal computer and a conventional video disc player with a serial input port for computer control.

Acknowledgements

The research reported in this paper has been supported by Grant #H133E80019 from the National Institute of Disabilities and Rehabilitation Research, a grant from Matsushita Electric Industrial Co., Ltd. and Grant 5R01DC00507 from the National Institute of Deafness and Other Communication Disorders.

References

DeFilippo, C. & Scott, B. (1978). A method for training and evaluating the reception of ongoing speech. *J. Acoust. Soc. Am., 63,* 1186-1192.

Dempsey, J.J., Levitt, H., Josephson, J. & Porrazzo, J. (1992). Computer-assisted tracking simulation (CATS). *J. Acoust. Soc. Am., 92(2),* 701-710.

Fletcher, H. (1929). *Speech and Hearing* (1st ed.). New York: Van Nostrand.

Fletcher, S. & Hasegawa, A. (1983). Speech modification by a deaf child through dynamic orometric modeling and feedback. *J. Speech Hear. Disord., 48,* 178-185.

Fourcin, A.J. & Abberton, E. (1971). First applications of a new laryngograph. *Medical and Biological Illustration, 21,* 172- 182.

Guttman, N., Levitt, H., & Bellefleur, P. A. (1970). Articulation training of the deaf using low-frequency surrogate fricatives. *J. Speech Hear. Res., 13,* 19-29.

Itoh, H. & Hiki, S. (1977). Observation of personal characteristics of lingual articulation by use of electro-palatography. *J. Acoust. Soc. Am., 61,* S31.

Levitt, H., Pickett, J. M., & Houde, R. A. (1980). *Sensory Aids for the Hearing Impaired.* New York: IEEE Press, Institute of Electrical and Electronic Engineers.

Levitt, H., (1986). Hearing impairment and sensory aids: A tutorial review. *J. Rehab. Res. and Dev., 23(1),* xiii-xviii.

Levitt, H., Youdelman, K. & Head, J. (1990). *Fundamental Speech Skills Test, (FSST).* Englewood, Colorado: Resource Point, Inc.

Lippman, R.P. (1982). A review of research on speech training aids for the deaf. In: N.J. Lass (ed.), *Speech and Language: Advances in basic research and practice, Vol. 7.* New York: Academic Press, 105-133.

McGarr, N., Head, J., Friedman, M., Behrman, A.M. & Youdelman, K. (1986). The use of visual and tactile sensory aids in speech production training: a preliminary report. *J. Rehab. Res. and Dev., 23(1)*, 101-109.

Povel, D.J. & Wansink, M. (1986). A computer-controlled vowel corrector for the hearing impaired. *J. Speech Hear. Res., 29(1)*, 99-105.

Schoepflin, J.R. & Levitt, H. (1991). Continuous discourse tracking: An analysis of the procedure. *J. Commun. Disord., 24*, 237-249.

Stevens, K.N., Kalikow, D.N. & Willemain, T.R. (1975). A miniature accelero-meter for detecting glottal waveforms and nasalization. *J. Speech Hear. Res., 18*, 594-599.

Strong, W.J. (1975). Speech aids for the profoundly/severely hearing impaired: Requirements, overview and projections. *Volta Review, 77*, 536-556.

Design and Evaluation of Interactive Trainingprograms for Speech Reading and Hearing Skills (ISEG) for Children and Adolescents with a Profound Hearing Impairment

Frans J. IJsseldijk and Ben A.G. Elsendoorn
Institute for the Deaf/IvD, Sint-Michielsgestel, The Netherlands

Abstract. Two interactive videodiscs have been developed; one for training speechreading and hearing, and another for diagnostic purposes. First the design and the basic characteristics underlying the ISEG training and reference program on one videodisc is described. The evaluation of the ISEG training program was carried out with the ISEG testprogram on the second videodisc. This computerized audiovisual system simulates face-to-face intervention and is specifically designed for profoundly hearing-impaired children and adolescents. In the ISEG training program there is a free choice in various exercises on auditory and speechreading tasks. Exercises range from recognising speech samples in a multiple choice format to exact identification of stimuli on phoneme, word, phrase or sentence level.

The second part of this paper describes the results of an evaluation test carried out to assess the effectiveness of the ISEG training program. A group of 20 profoundly hearing-impaired children and adolescents completed a pre- and post- testprotocol. The posttraining protocol was administered to the students two weeks after the training program. Oneway analyses of variance did not reveal significant differences between pre- and post-test results. More positive effects were found when the training group was divided into two groups consisting of students with a total speechreading score either below or above the median.

Introduction

In the field of education and rehabilitation of profoundly hearing-impaired students there is a lack of adequate instruments that can be used for training communication skills (Montgomery & Demorest, 1988). Speechreading and hearing are two of those skills. Within this context the term 'speechreading' means processing visual information with the support of a sensory aid (hearing aid or cochlear implant). New developments in computer-controlled displays and interactive videodisc technology make it possible to apply new and supportive methods of training and testing communication skills.

In comparison with traditional training methods computerized laser videodisc programs offer the following unique features:

- The profoundly hearing-impaired student no longer depends on the communication skills and patience of the speech therapist.
- The learning environment is more relaxed. The student is allowed to make mistakes without having the feeling that he[1] dissatisfies the speech therapist.
- The profoundly hearing-impaired student can decide for himself when an item will be presented, and how many times.
- The stimulus on the videodisc can be presented in ways that would be impossible to provide in ordinary oral communication settings. The stimulus can be presented with only the lips of the speaker visible, without sound or in slowed-down speech.
- The computer and the videodisc offer possibilities to present drawings and pictures that can be integrated into the program.
- Results are immediately stored.

Experiences with these new possibilities for training are still rather limited. The following computer-based interactive speechreading and communication training programs have been reported on in the literature: In the United States the programs DAVID (Sims, Von Feldt, Dowaliby, Hutchinson & Myers, 1979) ALVIS (Kopra, Kopra, Abrahamson & Dunlop, 1986), CASPER (Boothroyd, 1987) and a program developed at the University of Iowa by Tye-Murray, Tyler, Bong and Nares (1988) are known. Pichora-Fuller and Bequerel (1991) developed the CAST program at the University of Toronto in Canada and in France, ALLAO- an interactive videodisc for teaching speechreading was developed by Guilliams (1991; *this volume*).

DAVID, ALVIS and CAST are programs mainly developed for hearing-impaired people with normal language proficiency skills. The first interactive system, dubbed DAVID (Dynamic Audio Video Interactive Device) was based on videotaped instructional materials for post-secondary students with severe to profound hearing loss. The speechreading exercises required students to view simple sentences on videotape and then type into the compute what was said (verbatim). 'Help' and 'Repeat' keys were available. Training results demonstrated that gains from pretest to posttest were at least comparable to results from speechreading instruction with conventional videotape equipment (Sims et al., 1979).

---

[1] Wherever he/his is written in this article, the female she/her is implicitly implied.

ALVIS was the first program that used a laser videodisc. The videodisc presented in order of increasing difficulty 300 sentences. Kopra e.a. (1986, cited by Sims, 1988) indicated that gains were comparable to results from face-to-face speechreading exercises.

The CASPER (Computer Assisted Speech Perception Evaluation and Training) program was designed by Boothroyd and his colleaques at City University New York. Six laserdisc are available with CASPER. Training activities incorporated into CASPER include detection/identification of speech contrast in nonsense syllables, words and phrases; recognition of phonemes in CVC words, recognition of words in carrier phrases and sentences, and recognition of words in paragraph-length continuous discourse using a semi-automated Continuous Discourse Tracking (CDT) procedure. For a detailed description of the CDT procedure the reader is referred to De Filippo (1988). CASPER was used to compare the effectiveness of analytic and synthetic speech perception training programs. Five adults, recipients of a multichannel cochlear implant participated in an evaluation of this training program. The results suggested that the synthetic speech perception program was more effective than the analytic training program (Boothroyd, 1987).

Tye-Murray et al. (1988) developed an interactive system to assess and train visual speech perception skills and assertive communicative behaviour among hearing-impaired children and adults. The programmed activities ranged from analytical visual consonant discrimination/recognition tasks to identification/comprehension tasks using topic-specific continuous discourse material. Also some training activities were specifically designed to train communication repair strategies. The effectiveness of this training program has not been reported yet.

Pichora-Fuller (1991) and her colleague developed a Computer Aided Speechreading Training (CAST) program. CAST was designed as a visual speech perception training program for preretirement adults with a mild to moderate hearing loss. The interactive automated course consists of eight training lessons each focussing on a particular viseme. Three basic speechreading skills are emphasized: visual speech perception, use of linguistic redundancy and use of feedback between message sender and receiver. Gagné, Dinon and Parsons (1991) assessed the effectiveness of CAST on two groups of 8 normal hearing adults. The evaluation was considered to be a laboratory prototype experiment. It was hoped that this experiment would provide insight into possible clinical applications of CAST with hearing-impaired individuals. One group completed the CAST program. A posttraining testprotocol was administered to the subjects during the two weeks following the maximum time period to complete the training program (10 weeks). The results indicate that CAST was most effective in developing aspects of synthetic visual speech perception skills. No significant differences were measured between viseme recognition scores and sentence understanding. Significant differences between the groups (2*8 persons) were found for total word recognition scores on sentences tests. This is somewhat surprising because the design of CAST was influenced by an analytic approach. The lessons are sequenced according to viseme categories. The potential benefits of CAST for hearing-impaired individuals remain to be determined.

In this volume Guilliams describes the design and the evaluation of the ALLAO system. Results are reported on experiments with 14 hearing-impaired adolescents.

The Institute for the Deaf/IvD in Sint-Michielsgestel have developed two interactive videodisc programs: one for training hearing and speechreading skills (ISEG) and another for diagnostic purposes. These programs were made especially for children and adolescents who have language skills that are generally below what is normal for that age.

To test its effectiveness an experiment was set up in which the training program was evaluated.

Design of ISEG Training Program

The ISEG training and reference program is a flexible training aid, both for students and teachers. Basically it contains four units:

- One for student training, i.e. the actual exercises of the training program
- A second unit for teacher support and instruction in the reference program
- A third unit for leisure purposes, with games and picture books, but still with education in mind
- A fourth unit for research purposes. All training results are stored on disk and can be analysed afterwards.

The Target Group

This interactive program was developed for orally-educated Dutch profoundly hearing-impaired children and adolescents.

Technical Details: Hardware

The program runs on an Amiga 2300 computer with a hard-disk, an integrated Genlock, and a colour monitor. They control a Philips VP 406 videodisc player. A switchboard handles a direct sound connection between the disc player and the student's hearing aid. Results of the training sessions are stored on a separate floppy disk for each student. If needed the results can be printed. All exercises are mouse-controlled.

Stimulus Material

On the videodisc for the training program 50 minutes of continuous audio-visual speech material and 50 minutes of audio fragments have been stored. Speech material consists of words, phrases and sentences spoken by three different speakers. At the recording sessions the speakers have been filmed 'en face' and 'en profil' simultaneously. This makes it possible to do the same exercises both in the 'en face' and in the 'en profil' mode.

Basic Characteristics Underlying the Speechreading Training Program

Speechreading as a Linguistic Process. The training program is based on the concept that speechreading is basically a linguistic process. Speechreading is more dependent on the various linguistic skills of the profoundly hearing-impaired student than on various visual speaker-sender variables (IJsseldijk, 1992). Therefore it is important that the student be offered training material which has a link with language topics already discussed in the classroom. The exercises on the training disc come with three booklets and form an integrated element with the language and reading lessons in school. The exercises on the disc are derived from the language used in these booklets. It is expected that language problems in speechreading are thus minimized.

The Language Ability of Profoundly Hearing-impaired Students and the Consequence for the Program. Since the program is intended for prelingually profoundly hearing-impaired students (i.e. students who have been profoundly hearing impaired since birth or became deaf before the age of one-and-a-half) instructions are expressed in simple, understandable language. Icons are used wherever possible. Errors caused by spelling and writing problems on the part of the student are avoided as much as possible by the method of answering in multiple-choice formats. The menu structure of the program is such that the student is able to keep track of the choices he has made. In this way memory problems can also be avoided.

Freedom of Choices I: the Training Section. Initially the user has to decide between training and reference. Figure 1 shows a flow chart of the main features when *training* is chosen.

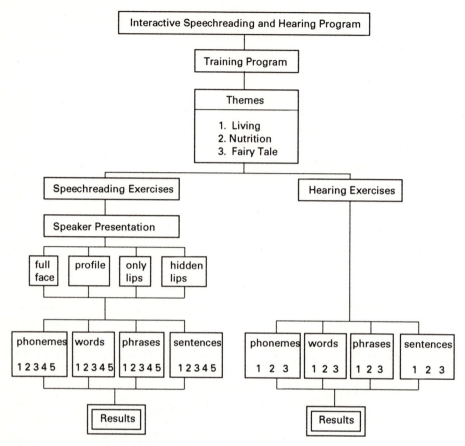

Figure 1. Flowchart of the ISEG training program.

The following choices can be made:

- the theme of the exercise: Living, Nutrition, and a Fairy tale;
- speechreading or auditory training exercises;
- four different language levels, viz. phoneme, word, phrase and sentence level;
- when speechreading is selected, the exercises contain five different levels of difficulty, whereas exercises for auditory training have three;
- speaker presentation: students can select a full face, a profile, a lips only or a mouth covered presentation.

In speechreading both analytic (phoneme and word level) and synthetic skills (sentence level) are needed. There are, however, no empirically verified laws of rankorder regarding acquisition of speechreading (sub)skills which must be met before the student can successfully start with the next. Therefore the program allows the level and type of speaker presentation to be chosen by the student.

The exercises are presented in a matrix. Every cell indicates one exercise containing 10 items, with specified language level, level of difficulty and way of speaker presentation.

Feedback. Feedback is given both immediately during as well as at the end of the exercise. If answers are incorrect, the right answer is presented, sometimes also first repeating the incorrect answer in order to make the student aware of the contrasting difference. This is done when the incorrect answer is also recorded on disc. The correct answer is also simultaneously displayed in print. In some exercises the program may give additional information about the right or wrong parts in the answer. After ten items the general result is given in two ways:

- immediate feedback on how many items out of a series of ten were correct and
- in the presentation of a so-called 'thumb-matrix'; thumbs up indicate a pass for the block of 10 exercises. Thumbs down means that three or more answers were incorrect. (see Figure 2)

Help-functions. During the speechreading exercises the pupil can use some function blocks which are presented at the status line at the bottom of the screen (see Figure 3). These function blocks present options for Stop, Help, Repetition, Slowed-down speech and Correction.

With Help a written hint is given on an essential aspect of the item. Sometimes, at the phoneme and word level, Help is given by spelling the answer.

When Repetition or Slowed-down speech is chosen, the item is repeated.

Freedom of Choices II: the Reference Section. When instead of the *training* section the *reference* section is chosen, the student has the following options which are shown in Figure 4.

In Games the student will find colour, drawing and construction games. Games has been designed to let students (especially the younger ones) grow accustomed to using the mouse. The telephone alfhabet is used as a Help in some speechreading exercises. Words are spelled out by the speaker. In the reference section the teacher or speech therapist can also type words which are then spelled by the speaker. The student must synthesize the right word. In Instruction the speechreading characteristics of the basic vowels (n=15) and consonants (n=17) are visualized and described. For each phoneme drawings and a description are given of the main characteristics of lips, jaws, tongue, voice and breath.

With Extra-Training the teacher may design exercises tailored to fit the specific needs of a particular student. Nearly all visual-auditory (n=291) and auditory words (n=275) are coded according to a number of character-

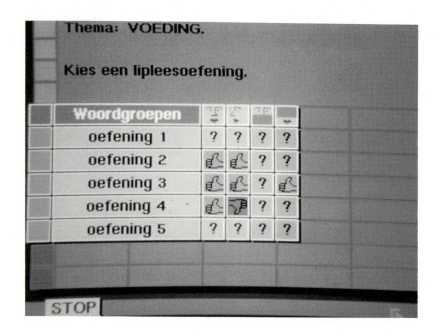

Figure 2. A 'thumb-matrix'.

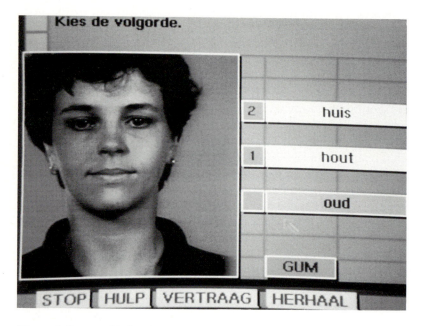

Figure 3. Screen with function blocks on status line.

istics, such as type of vowel, consonant, number of syllables, stress-pattern, etc. By defining certain characteristics the teacher can select particular subgroups of words. Next the type of presentation and the speech rate can be selected. In this way a more theoretical bottom-up training in speechreading and auditory training is possible.

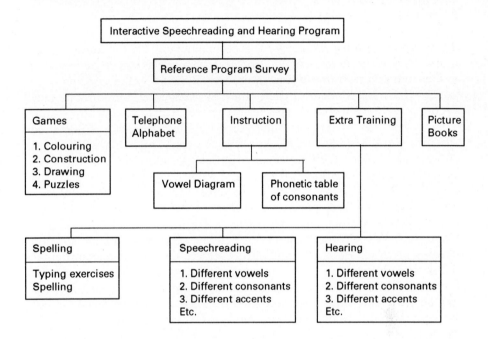

Figure 4. Flowchart of the ISEG Reference program.

Picture books presents different pictures for leisure purposes. The student can choose from a number of different topics. In total 300 pictures are encorporated on the disc. Some of them are also used as stimulus material in the training program.

Evaluation of ISEG Trainingprograms

Method

Subjects. Twenty students of the Institute for the Deaf/IvD took part in the training program. They were students of a special department for profoundly hearing-impaired students with learning problems in the development of language, speech and speechreading. Orthodidactically this department makes extra use of the written word as communication tool.

The students' ages varied between 14 and 20 years. Average hearing loss was 102 dB ISO (Fletcher index, average loss at 500, 1000 and 2000 Hz) with a standard deviation of 11 dB. One student had a hearing loss of less than 90 dB, all others had a greater hearing loss. The students had been examined by the IvD's ophthalmologist and had corrected vision to normal.

Training Procedure. Three systems were available for the training program. They were set up in one room. Each system was directly connected to the student's own amplifying equipment. In this way the students were able to train independent of each other. Watching the thumb menu (see Figure 2) the student could keep track of the exercise selected and the result. Their task was to get as many thumbs up in the exercise matrix. While three students were training one teacher was present. Teachers had been instructed and informed about the aim, the design and the way in which the training program functioned. The experimental design was to let students train themselves as independently as possible. They were free to choose the type of stimulus presentation and the level of difficulty. The teacher only intervened when the student asked for advice in the choices of the exercises. Contrary to this students were not free in the selection of the topic of the training program. Preceding and during the training period one particular theme was discussed in class using one of the booklets that come with the program. Difficult words and notions that returned in the program were explained. One theme appeared to suffice as training material for all students with the exception of one hard-of-hearing student.

Students trained twice a week for 30 to 45 minutes during a six-month period. The total training time ranged between 24 and 36 hours.

Test Procedure. In addition to the training program an interactive test program (IJsseldijk, 1990) was recorded on a second disc. This program contained several speechreading and auditory tests.

The four audiovisual speech perception tests consist of two speechreading tests for sentences, one test for vowel recognition and one for consonant recognition.

- One speechreading test for sentences [Rep-Sent] consisted of ten sentences, each containing eighteen syllables (Van Uden, 1983). The score represented the number of correctly reproduced syllables.
- The other sentence speechreading test [Pict-Sent] consisted of 30 items (IJsseldijk, Wollenberg and Tellegen, to appear). Each item was a phrase or short sentence that students had to associate with one picture out of a possible four that were presented on the screen.
- The items in the vowel and consonant speechreading recognition tests consisted of two stimuli: an orthographic and an audiovisual presentation

of a word. Both are monosyllables. The words are either the same (e.g. orthographic /lake/ - audio-visual [leIk]) [Co-S and Vo-S] or differing in the initial consonant (/lake/-/cake/) [Co-Dif] or in the vowel (/lake/-/look/) [Vo-Dif]. The subject has to decide whether the orthographic and the audiovisual stimulus is the same or different. The score is the number of correct judgements. Scores for same and different items were calculated separately. The consonant recognition test has 84 items (19 same, 65 different items), the vowel recognition test has 110 items (24 same and 86 different items).

In addition to the audiovisual test two hearing tests were used:

- One hearing test was a 25-item auditory word pattern recogniton test [W-Pat], with six or four multiple-choice words. Test and multiple choice words may differ either in the number of syllables or, in the case of words with similar syllable patterns, in stress pattern (e.g. dessert - desert).
- The other hearing test was a 10 x 4 multiple-choice word recognition test [W-Recog]. Test and answer items have the same number of syllables and the same stress pattern.

The test procedure used at the post-training testsession was identical to the one used in the pre-training testsession. The post-training testprotocol was administered to all subjects within four weeks after they had finished the training program. Approximately 1.5 hours were required to complete the testprotocol, which was accomplished in two separate testsessions.

Results

Average scores (expressed in percentages of the total score) and standard deviations for pre- and post-test sessions are shown in Table 1. Using a oneway analysis of variance we compared the results of pre- and post-tests.

The comparison of the results obtained before and after the training period yields one significant difference. After training, initial consonants that are presented pairwise orthograpgically as well as audio-visually in a 'same' pair are recognized significantly better as being the same.

Table 2 presents a correlation matrix for the relations between age, hearing loss (Fletcher index) and the tests used.

The Fletcher index explains about 40% of the variance in W-Pat and W-Recog. Both hearing recognitions tests (W-Pat and W-Recog) significantly correlate with seven out of eight speechreading tests. Coefficients are generally slightly higher for consonant and vowel speechreading tests than for sentence speechreading tests.

In addition three out of four speechreading tests correlate significantly with each other. For this particular group of students the speechreading tests for consonants and vowels do not clearly show any skills that are independent from skills required for speechreading sentences. Speechreading skills are called upon that are common to all four tests.

Table 1. Average percentage correct scores before and after training, with F-values and significance level (oneway ANOVA).

	mean % correct				
	pre	post	df	F	p
Hearing tests					
Word Pattern test	55.6	61.5	38	.60	<.44
(W-Pat) 25 items					
Word Recognition test	65.6	63.2	33	.07	<.78
(W-Recog) 10 items					
Speechreading tests					
Consonant-Same test	76.0	85.6	35	10.4	.0003
(Co-S 19) items					
Consonant-Different test	68.5	66.1	35	.84	<.37
(Co-Dif) 65 items					
Vowel-Same test	89.9	86.2	37	1.69	<.20
(Vo-S) 24 items					
Vowel-Different test	58.2	58.6	37	.02	<.90
(Vo-Dif) 86 items					
Repeat Sentence test	51.8	53.9	38	.33	<.60
(Rep.Sent) 10 items					
Picture Sentence test	31.4	35.9	36	1.16	<.29
(Pict-Sent) 30 items					

It might be that the effect of the speechreading training program is different for good and poor speechreaders. In view of this a total speechreading score was calculated for each student (the average of the summed percentage scores of the four tests in the pre-training test session). Next the students were divided into two groups; one group consisting of students who have an average speechreading score higher than the median, and another group of students with scores that are lower. For each group an analysis of variance was applied to the pre- and post-test training scores for the various tests. Both groups showed a significant improvement in consonant recognition for 'same' judgments. The group with scores lower than the median performed significantly better on the Van Uden test for speechreading sentences, viz. an average of 21% vs. 30% (F=6.96, df=15, p<.02). For the remaining speechreading tests the two groups did not differ significantly.

Table 2. Product-moment correlation between age, Fletcher Index, word-pattern and word-recognition test, sentence-imitation speechreading test, and picture-sentence matching test. Significance levels are indicated by asterisks (* p<.05, ** p<.01, *** p<.001).

	age	Fletcher	W-Pat	W-Recog	Co-Dif	Vo-Dif	Rep-Sent	Pict-Sent
age	1.00							
Fletcher	-.24	1.00						
W-Pat	-.08	-.67**	1.03					
W-Recog	-.04	-.60**	.83***	1.00				
Co-Dif	.10	-.58**	.65**	.44*	1.00			
Vo-Dif	-.22	-.35	.53**	.44*	.44*	1.00		
Rep-Sent	.13	-.28	.41	.54**	.41	.53**	1.00	
Pict-Sent	-.09	-.24	.43**	.45*	.64*	.53**	.85***	1.000

The auditory tests showed the following differences between pre- and post-tests: Differences in scores for word pattern (W-Pat) recognition before and after training just failed to reach significance with the group with lower-than-median scores, viz. averages of 33.7% vs 47.6% (F=3.87, df=15, p<.07).

For the word-recognition (W-Recog) test this was exactly the reverse: The group with the higher-than-median scores performed better after the training period than before (viz. 82% after and 72% before training). However, this difference was not significant (F2.24, df=18, p<.15). These results agree with our expectation that low-scorers will improve on easy tests and high-scorers will do so on tests with a higher degree of difficulty.

Conclusions

The main results can be summarized as follows:
- Using the training program for 24 to 36 hours did not yield significant differences between hearing and speechreading pre- and post-tests for the complete group of profoundly hearing-impaired students.

- Results are slightly more favourable if the group is divided into two groups using the median of the overall result for the four speechreading tests as a criterion. After the training period the group with scores below the median perform significantly better on the Van Uden sentences speechreading test.
- Results obtained for the two auditory word recognition tests correlate significantly with the results for the various speechreading tests.
- Scores for the analytical speechreading tests significantly correlate with those obtained in the sentences speechreading tests (three out of four).

Discussion

Results obtained after the training period only show some sparing effects. However, some observations should be made:
A training period of 24 to 36 hours is still rather limited.
A second evaluation research by De Zeeuw and Van de Ven (1992) showed roughly similar results. They had a group of ten children, who used fingerspelling as their primary communication mode, train with the program during an eight-week period for two hours per week. Before and after this period similar results (i.e. no effects) were reported for the consonants and vowels speechreading tests.

However, the tests used were not specifically designed to measure the effects of the training program. This is notably clear in the sentences speechreading tests; the linguistic material used in the training program is completely different. If the language used is a factor in (not) recognizing the spoken sentences, this would not be changed after the training period. The group of profoundly hearing-impaired students participating in the training program were known to have learning problems in language, speech and speechreading.

On the other hand some positive results can be mentioned. Students remained highly motivated to work with the training program. The self-operative character of the program in a neutral learning environment that allows for mistakes being made appears appealing to the students. The training program itself did not seem to be an insurmountable obstacle either. Numerous exercises were finished successfully, sometimes after many repetitions. The program as a whole positively influences the teacher's as well as the student's attitude, since it points at what a student *can* do, not at what he *cannot* do.

However, viewing the general results induces some caution and the following recommendations:
Chances for improving training results will increase when exercises are

selected more specifically on the basis of the test results. In the present experiment and the one reported on by De Zeeuw & Van de Ven (1992) students were free to choose their exercises.

Students work very result-oriented. They are motivated to finish an exercise with a thumb pointing upwards. They find it less important how to reach this result. Students need to be more actively involved when they make mistakes. Working with the training program they tend to ignore the corrective feedback which is given after an incorrect answer. It also seems desirable to get teachers more involved with the exercises by having them use the 'reference' section.

The speechreading training assumes that the language offered is known with the students. As a consequence teachers should work through and adequately discuss the reading booklet containing the major part of the language offered in the speechreading exercises before training starts.

Also with the profoundly hearing-impaired children and adolescents the use of residual hearing appears to support speechreading. The relation found here is in accordance with the results of a study with students with a profound hearing-impairment reported by IJsseldijk, Van den Wollenberg and Tellegen (submitted), in which 25% of the variance in audiovisual speechreading scores for the Pictures Sentence test was explained by the Fletcher index. Training of residual hearing - in addition to training speechreading - remains an important factor for audiovisual speech understanding by profoundly hearing-impaired people.

The significant correlations between analytic speechreading tests and sentence tests agrees with results found by Gailey (1984), De Filippo (1982) and Huiskamp (1992). This supports our starting point that training of speechreading is useful both at the analytic as well as the synthetic level.

References

Boothroyd, A. (1987). CASPER: A computer-assisted system for speech-perception testing and training. In: *Proceedings of the 10th Annual Conference of the Rehabilitation Society of North America*, 734-736.

De Filippo, C.L. (1982). Memory for articulated sequences lipreading performance of hearing-impaired observers. *Volta Review, 84*, 134-136.

Gagné, J.P., Vinon, D. & Parsons, J. (1991). An evaluation of CA: A computer-aided speechreading training program. *Journal of Speech and Hearing Research, 34*, 213-221.

Gailey, L. (1984). Psychological parameters of lipreading skill. In: B. Dodd & R. Campbell (eds). *Hearing by eye: The psychology of lipreading*. London: Lawrence Earlbaum Association Publishers.

Guilliams, I. (1991). *Acquisition et évaluation de la lecture labiale au moyen d'une videodisque interactif - ALLAO, un systeme, une méthode.* Université Paris 7. Unpublished doctoral thesis.

Huiskamp, H. (1992). *Twee onderzoeken op het terrein van liplezen.* Unpublished master thesis, University of Utrecht.

Kopra, L., Kopra, M., Abrahamson, J. & Dunlop, R. (1986). Development of sentences graded on difficulty for lipreading practice. *Journal of the Academy of Rehabilitative Audiology, 19*, 71-86.

Montgomery, A.A. & Demorest, M.E. (1988). Issues and developments in the evaluation of speechreading. In: C.L. De Filippo & D.G. Sims (eds), New reflections on speechreading (Monograph). *Volta Review, 90*, 193-214.

Pichora-Fuller, M.K. & Benquerel, A.-P. (1991). The design of CAST (Computer-Aided Speechreading Training). *Journal of Speech and Hearing Research, 34*, 202-212.

Sims, D.G., Feldt, J. von, Dowaliby, F., Hutchinson, K. & Myers, T. (1979). A pilot experiment in computer-assisted speechreading instruction utilizing the Data Analysis Video Interactive Device (DAVID). *American Annals of the Deaf, 124*, 618-623.

Tye-Murray, N., Tyler, R.S., Bong, B. & Nares, T. (1988). Computerized laser videodisc programs for training speechreading and assertive communication behaviors. *Journal of the Academy of Rehabilitative Audiology, 21*, 143-152.

IJsseldijk, F.J. (1990). *The ISEG testprogram.* Sint-Michielsgestel: Instituut voor Doven.

IJsseldijk, F.J. (1992). Speechreading performance under different conditions of video image, repetition, and speech rate. *Journal of Speech and Hearing Research, 35*, 466-471.

IJsseldijk, F.J, van den Wollenberg, A. & Tellegen, P.J. (submitted). Construction, standardization, and validation of an audiovisual speechreading test for children and adolescents with profound hearing impairment. *Submitted to Journal of Speech and Hearing Research.*

Uden, A. van. (1983). *Diagnostic testing of deaf children.* Lisse: Swets & Zeitlinger.

Zeeuw, H. de & van de Ven, S. (1992). *Lipleestraining met ISEG het ISEG trainingsprogramma.* Unpublished thesis. Hoensbroek: Hogeschool Heerlen.

ALLAO - an Interactive Videodisc for Teaching Lipreading

Isabelle Guilliams
CRITT Electronique et Communication - 22300 Lannion - France

Abstract. The Allao system attempts to respond to the difficulties inherent in lipreading learning by the use of a specifically adapted technology: the interactive videodisc driven by a computer. The Allao videodisc consists of 800 speech segments uttered by several speakers, used to perform various exercises and tests. A teaching method complementary to classic methods has been developed:

- The hearing impaired exerts a "power" over the speech of the video speaker: he may ask to see the speech segments again, for a slow motion, for an auditory output, for an illustration, for the written text...
- Linguistic categories are used to respectively stimulate the visual decoding (syllables), the lexical access (words) and the global comprehension (sentences).
- A stimulating context is proposed to the learner to observe real speech segments. Thus, he may become aware of his own comprehension mechanisms and be able to build speech decoding rules to be used in a real communication situation.

Speech therapists who regularly use the Allao system observe a noticeable improvement of the deaf person's capability for verbal communication together with a strong motivation. The speech segment replay and the slow motion have been validated as performant teaching functions.

Keywords. Lipreading, education, evaluation, deafness, phonetics, computer, videodisc.

Introduction

Deafness is a sensorial handicap which has the immediate effect of disturbing the oral communication loop. The hearing-impaired person, when lipreading, tries to understand a speaker by observing his lip movements and facial expressions combining this with some auditory information. Lipreading is complex and difficult to master. Spontaneous acquisition of lipreading is seldom encountered, and the apprenticeship is long, often tedious and requires great concentration from the learner. Discouragement and lack of motivation often hinder improvements.

Considering the difficulty to learn lipreading, the study presented here aimed to determine how to facilitate this apprenticeship; it has lead to the realisation of a video-computer training system of lipreading. Physicians, speech therapists and researchers are now aware of the way in which the benefits of the new video and computer technologies can contribute to the assessment and rehabilitation of language disorders, specifically of the most severe, such as deafness (Cronin, 1983, Kopra, 1987) or aphasia (Bruckert, 1989).

The aim of the Allao system (Aide à la Lecture Labiale Assistée par Ordinateur) is to develop the ability of the hearing-impaired person to understand speech when lipreading. The exercises aim to stimulate the various processes involved in speech comprehension, from perception to cognition (Guilliams, 1987). Moreover, the system allows to evaluate the lipreading level by means of various tests. The system is especially dedicated towards postlingually hearing-impaired adults and prelingually hearing-impaired teenagers. A basic level in oral and written French is required to use the system. This limitation is due to the following reasons.

The learner must know the vocabulary and the syntactic structures of the sentences presented by the system. He has to read what is displayed on the TV screen (instructions, words and sentences presented during the exercises). Deaf children under the age of eight are hence not concerned.

For two years, the system has been used on a regular basis in eight experimental centres. Five Institutes for the Deaf assessed the pedagogical contents of the system, whereas three hospitals were using the system to test lipreading skills. After these two years of experimentation, the system has reached a pedagogical and ergonomic maturity. Some two hundred hearing impaired persons took part in the experiment under the guidance of twenty speech therapists (Gosset, 1990; Robic, 1989).

The system and the experiment were realised by Isabelle Guilliams at the Centre National d'Etudes des Télécommunications in Lannion, France (Guilliams, 1991).

Presentation of the ALLAO System

The Allao system comprises the following elements: a standard personal computer PC AT, a Philips videodisc player, a TV monitor, a Videologic IVA 2000 overlay card and the keyboard as the dialogue interface. The software which drives the videodisc player includes some ten classes of exercises and controls a data base describing the segments of speech stored on the videodisc. It analyses the answers of the learner and displays the results.

The videodisc contains some 800 speech segments pronounced by 7 speakers. The speakers are filmed close up so both the head and shoulders can be clearly seen. The segments are syllables, numbers, words and sentences. Owing to the population concerned, easy syntactic structures and familiar words belonging to the common French language have been selected. Frequency lists and a dictionary for children have been used to select the words. More than a third of the corpus should be easy to understand by a 10 year-old deaf child. The contents of the videodisc is as follows:

- syllables (140): they present consonants and vowels in various phonetic contexts. They are nonsense syllables produced in isolation.
  Examples: Initial consonant: pa vi chou ...
  	Final consonant: rap riv rouch ...
  	Median consonant: apa ada afa ...
  	Vowel: pa pi pou ...
- numbers from 1 to 100,
- words (260) gathered around familiar themes (Animals, Christian names, Sports, Parts of the house, ...). They are pronounced with an article.
- sentences (200) either isolated or linked into short stories,
- questions (80) and their associated answers,
- 1200 slides illustrating the words.

Exercises are structured as a linear succession of speech-segments, all segments being either syllables, words or sentences (Figure 1). The system allows the speech therapist to perform a multicriteria selection of the speech segments described by the data base of the system; the selected items are then stored in a working file. Hence it is the speech therapist who determines the linguistic contents of the exercises. The linguistic and phonetic criteria are:

- the initial or final phonemes,
- the vocalic nucleus,
- the number of syllables,
- the familiarity, the difficulty,

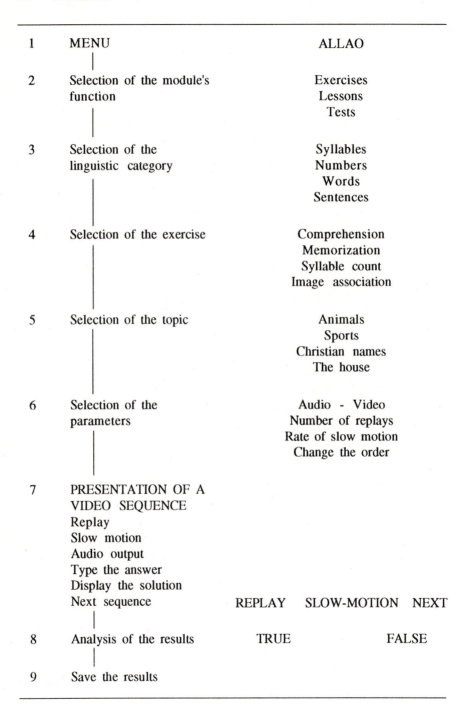

Figure 1. Linear stages of an exercise.

- the theme,
- the speaker,
- the subject of a sentence (I - You - He/She/It).

An exercise results from the association of a working file with a pedagogical module. The pedagogical modules of the Allao system, as opposed to the working files, are permanent programs of the system: they cannot be created or modified by the user. The system comes with a set of three ready-to-use working files for each module.

A module defines the aim of an exercise (e.g., identification of a pronounced number) and its protocol (the learner's task, the assistance he may obtain, the analysis of the answers).

Within a session, the speech therapist and the pupil are seated in front of the TV monitor. They share the keyboard, and so both have access to its functions. On the screen the pupil sees the speaker pronouncing a segment of speech. The pupil observes the face and lip movements and tries to understand the pronounced stimulus. From the keyboard he may obtain assistance:

- ask for an immediate replay of the speech-segment,
- ask for slow motion,
- ask for the auditory output corresponding to the speech segment,
- ask for an illustration of the word, the first letters or to display part of the solution (e.g. the verbal group)
- ask to display the full solution.

Depending on the exercise, the task can be to type what was understood, to find the number of syllables of the stimulus, to memorize a succession of three consecutive stimuli, to choose between two possibilities for a pronounced word, and so on ...

The difficulty of an exercise depends on the task determined by the protocol, the linguistic category of the speech segment (syllables, words or sentences), and on its phonetic, lexical and linguistic characteristics. The therapist hence determines the level of difficulty of an exercise as he creates a working file.

The various ways in which an exercise can be presented stimulate and hold the learner's interest throughout the apprenticeship. They contribute to maintain a high level of motivation. The learner develops personal strategies on the system. During a session, he may:

- choose the exercise and the working file, even create the working file.
- decide on the moment to ask assistance: (repetition, slow motion, auditory output, pictures, display of the solution).

The following table presents the results of a survey describing the actions of the learner with the system. This survey concerns five experimental centres.

Table 1. Actions of the learner with the system during a session.

learner's action	always	often	sometimes	never
types the answers	***	**		
selects the working file	***	*	*	
selects exercise or test	**	*	*	*
asks for Repetition	**	**	*	
asks for Slow motion	*	**	**	
asks for auditory output		****		*
asks for the solution	*	**	**	
creates working files			***	**

* = answer of an experimental centre

The pedagogical justification of the computer driven videodisc for lipreading teaching has been demonstrated during the experiments (Guillem, 1991).

The deaf learner exerts a control on the speech of the speaker. This novel situation of power avoids discouragement and the deaf person is less dependant on the therapist speaker. When he encounters a complex stimulus, the learner chooses from the various possibilities which are most useful to him. He decides how many times he will see the stimulus. During a slow motion repetition, he focusses on the articulatory details. Moreover, he experiments on how the hearing aid contributes to the comprehension.

Fast random access allows the learner to compare two sequences. It is hence possible to point out the similarity between "dauphin" and "cheval" (the small visible difference is the final [1]), the differences between "c'est loin" and "c'est long". The corresponding video segments are successively shown, if necessary in slow motion.

Immediate replay of the video segments and slow motion are precious pedagogical tools enabled by the videodisc technology: during a classical rehabilitation session, the hearing impaired person would not benefit at will from identical repetitions; neither could he obtain a constant slow motion. He probably would not dare to ask nor would obtain the repetitions he may need. Moreover, the hearing-impaired person would not obtain the written text of each word or sentence uttered by the speech therapist. The Allao system displays the solution as soon as the user asks for it.

Such a system is a multimedia tool. It uses data of various natures: video sequence, sound, text and still images. The interactive videodisc is a technology perfectly suitable to the teaching of lipreading.

It must be emphasized that the system aims to assist the therapist in his rehabilitation task; it does not pretend to be a substitute. The Allao system performs what the therapist cannot do easily or willingly (repeat a given sentence the same way, pronounce slowly without modifying the original articulation, give at will the solution in a written manner). The presence of the system modifies the role of the therapist, but his pedagogical function remains.

- He structures the session: choice of the exercises, level of difficulty, duration of each exercise.
- He stimulates the learner: he encourages him to suggest answers, to see a stimulus again, to ask for the solution.
- He corrects and explains the errors.

Once the stimulus has been provided by the system, the therapist is no longer merely the speaker; he may fully exert his pedagogical function. He may observe the reactions of the learner, the manner in which the learner tries to understand the stimulus and above all the nature of his difficulties. From then on, he will be able to determine the exercises or the options best suited for each specific case.

The therapist may also use the system to carry out a conventional rehabilitation. He may for example propose paraphrases, synonyms, or restructure a sentence that has been misunderstood. He may also include the words and expressions of an exercise in others sentences. The system will then participate to perform speech therapy.

The analysis of the questionnaire (Guilliams, 1991) sent to the experimental centres shows that speech therapists think of themselves as very useful, not to say essential, to the accompaniment of the system during the session. None of them felt rejected or replaced by the system. *"The speech therapist is in no case put aside; during the periods when the learner is autonomous, we may carry out a very fine observation of the strategies of the children and adjust the progression of the pedagogical project."* Thus, we may say that the learning situation is up-dated by the mediation of the computer-assisted system.

The Method Associated to the System

Classically, various methods are used to teach lipreading: some deal with the decoding of the movements of the lips (analytical methods); others favours the direct access to the meaning (overall methods), others emphasize the importance of the hearing aid, some encourage to search for a solution while others recommend the observation of the lip movements.

We have considered that none of these methods could alone meet with the requirements of every hearing impaired person, owing to the great number of individual peculiarities and the diversity of the modes of acquisition (Dodd, 1984). This is why the Allao system advocates and implements the use of all these methods within a session (Guilliams, 1989).

The method associated to the Allao system relies on the following principles:

- the learner tries to find the solution by making use of the repetition and if necessary of the slow motion. He learns to make hypotheses, to confront them with the observed speech clues within the phonological and semantics strains.
- the solution may be obtained at any time, in a written, acoustic or illustrative manner. Thus the learner is never in a position to fail.
- once the solution is displayed on the screen, the learner does not need to "guess" the solution any longer, but can focus his attention on a detailed observation of the lips continuum, with the help of the repetition, slow motion and auditory output.
- the exercises respectively link linguistic categories (syllables, words, sentences) to comprehension procedures (visual perception, access to the lexicon, global comprehension) (Figure 2).
- the use of the hearing aid is recommended.

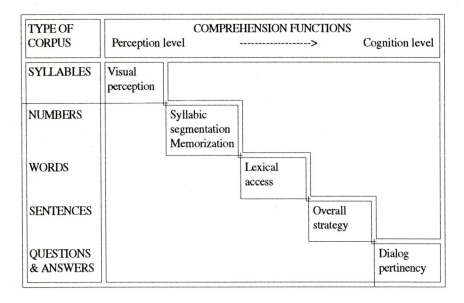

Figure 2. Relation between the corpus linguistic categories and the comprehension functions.

All the exercises on the Allao system are made up of two successive periods. The first one is the discovery period which puts stress on the search of the meaning and stimulates the "problem-solving" process (Gailey, 1984). The system aims to bring the learner to develop personal strategies of comprehension.

The second period or acquisition period aims to draw the attention of the learner to the visual and acoustic characteristics and difficulties of a speech segment. The learner will then be guided by the speech therapist during this analytic task. This second period starts once the solution is displayed on the screen and the learner knows the meaning of the observed speech segment.

Stimulation of the Search of the Solution: the Discovery Period

The quality of the lipreading seems to be closely related to the capability of a person to quickly propose hypotheses once he has seen the lip movements (Dodd, 1987). The discovery period aims to develop the aptitude to find and express these hypotheses. The deaf learner asks for the repetition of the stimulus, if necessary in slow motion or with the auditory output (the stimulus is usually presented the first time without the auditory output). He quickly becomes increasingly aware of the actions useful to help him in his comprehension task and when he must undertake them. It is not necessary to extend this period of seeking for the solution (Le Huche, 1984). Too many repetitions are of little use (an average of two repetitions is appropriate for words, two to eight repetitions for a sentence) (Guilliams, 1991). In case of errors, a limitation of the number of repetitions avoids extending the failure situation and the risk of anchoring in memory an erroneous association between the visual continuum and a wrong answer. The learner asks for the solution when he wishes to check a response and when he is unable to propose a hypothesis.

Once he has formulated an answer, the learner is usually unable to propose another one, even if he is aware that his response is wrong; he is stuck with his first response.

Free access to the solution has appeared essential during the experimentation; it avoids the discouragement of the learner unable to understand a stimulus.

Stimulation of the Observation of the Lip Movements: the Acquisition Period

This exercise is not finished once the solution has been displayed. This display either confirms or invalidates the answer of the learner. The speech therapist then explains the errors; he takes advantage of the repetition, slow motion and auditory output during these explanations. Thus, the repetition is used not only when the deaf person searches for the solution, but above all during the acquisition period that follows. Since the learner does not have to search for an answer, his mind is receptive to observation and acquisition of lipreading characteristics.

The acquisition period is not always motivating. Left alone, the learner asks for the solution and then is tempted to immediately proceed with the next speech-segment.

It is thus useful that the therapist be there to give explanations, to pronounce the stimulus himself and to diversify the modes of presentation of the sequence.

With the task of the speaker being taken care of by the system, the therapist may focus his attention on the difficulties of the learner. Slow motion will help the therapist to designate specific difficulties of lipreading, these characteristics are difficult to show with one's own speech. It also helps to become aware of the mechanisms involved with lipreading difficulties such as coarticulation. Speech is not the most appropriate manner to explain the difficulties of lipreading to a deaf person who must lipread the explanations.

The Use of the Hearing Aid

The hearing aid must be used during the acquisition period. The sound perceived through the hearing aid can be an efficient tool for lipreading acquisition; the learner will quickly find it useful. The speech therapist must take care to alternate periods of lipreading with and without the hearing aid. He will make the learner sensitive to the complementary information delivered by the hearing aid (Summerfield, 1983). The speech therapist will prompt the learner to utter the speech segments after the speaker, or at the same time. Thus, the learner becomes aware of the articulatory dimension of the lip movements he observes. *"The deaf trains himself to repeat the words at the same time as the speaker, ..."*

Relationship between the Linguistic Category and the Comprehension Function

The aim of teaching lipreading is to improve the learner's capacities to understand speech in an ordinary communication situation. The comprehension of spoken language involves several stages, from perceptive level to cognitive level (Campbell, 1989). An apprenticeship in lipreading must concern all these stages; that is why the Allao system uses specific exercises and adequate linguistic categories.

By means of these specific exercises, the Allao system tries to stimulate the perception of the visual speech units, the awareness to the coarticulation difficulties, the sense of rhythm, the segmentation of a sentence into syllables, the memorization of sequences of growing length, the lexical access and the capacity to propose hypotheses, and also to take into account the semantic and syntactic constraints of a sentence (Erber, 1976).

The exercises being dedicated to the improvement of these functions, an appropriate linguistic category corresponds to each of them (Figure 2):

- syllables (improvement of visual decoding of lip movements),
- numbers (segmentation of the visual continuum of speech, memorization of successive lip movements),
- words (lexical access) - sentences (overall comprehension).

Description of Some of the Exercises

Syllabic Pairs. A syllable is pronounced by the speaker. The learner sees two possible answers displayed at the bottom of the screen and he selects one of them. If his answer is wrong, the learner can in turn observe both stimuli to compare them. The instructions being simple and the task far from the tasks of comprehension and communication, this exercise is often used to increase the learner's self-confidence, to show him the possibilities and the limits of lipreading. This exercise contributes to lessen the apprehension of the learner for this apprenticeship, especially when postlingually deaf adults are concerned.

Comprehension of Numbers. The learner sees the stimulus and types at the keyboard the number he has understood. In case of error (e.g., 45 misunderstood 47), both numbers can be observed in turn. This exercise belongs to the pedagogical modules the most asked for by both the learners and the speech therapist. It is considered *"as rewarding because the learner finds it easy"*. *"This vocabulary is very much appreciated by all the children, it allows to work on the basis of lipreading, whatever the age and time during the rehabilitation"*. Hence, this exercise is often used at the beginning of the rehabilitation for its relative ease; it is appropriate to the difficulties and reluctances of the learner while working with the system for the first time.

Comprehension of Words. The learner sees a word, sees it again, with or without the auditory output, and/or in slow motion. Then, he types in his answer which is displayed at the bottom of the screen; a correct spelling is not required. While the learner is searching for an answer, he may benefit from some comprehension aids with the keyboard:

- the solution displayed letter by letter;
- the solution displayed syllable by syllable;
- an illustration of the word (a picture representing the word which is stored on the videodisc).

This exercise is unanimously appreciated by both the learners and the speech therapists. Its level of difficulty is obtained by selecting the theme and the working file; the learners often choose them by themselves.

Syllable Count. A video segment (word or sentence) is displayed. The learner types the number of syllables he has identified. (e.g. LE / KAN/ GOU/ROU = 4) This exercise is entertaining and especially appropriate for group work. Its aim is to develop the learner's awareness to the notion of the syllable and to the segmentation of the visual continuum of speech. This exercise is essentially used together with the hearing aid.

Memorization. The learner observes three words one after the other and must type his answers in three boxes. The task is to recognize a list of stimuli and to memorize it in the correct order. The learner becomes aware of the necessity to remain attentive throughout the whole utterance. The lipreader often uses only the first clues to interpret a stimulus, and therefore often wrongly. In spite of the difficulty of the task, this exercise is incentive especially with a group of learners.

Comprehension of Sentences. It is a necessity within the apprenticeship of lipreading to stress on the importance of overall comprehension. Using sentences allows the learner to come closer to a real communication situation. This exercise deals with isolated sentences, short stories and pairs of questions and answers. The learner does not have to write what he has understood, as in the other exercises. He observes the stimulus and then tries to understand. He can obtain the written solution by displaying successively the syntactical groups of the sentences. For instance, he will ask for the subject in a sentence. Thus he will benefit from lexical and grammatical clues, which will help him to understand the whole sentence.
Ex.   La boulangère   / ...?...   / ..?....   / .....?....
       La boulangère   / vend   / du pain   /de campagne.
The exercises with sentences are usually thought to be difficult and less rewarding than the exercises with words. The possibility of obtaining the solution by the syntactic groups contributes to the motivation of the learners and to their desire to progress. Work on the sentences allows to lead to a more general work on the language.

Results

Replay and Slow Motion

We have determined how the replay and the slow motion influence the comprehension of words; pedagogical principles have then been settled (Guilliams, 1991). The replay has two main functions. It is essentially useful to help the learner to express a hypothesis when the first visualisation has not been effective. The replay also allows the learner to test his first hypothesis. The replay is less effective for correcting a previously wrong answer, and on unfamiliar words.

The slow motion display yields similar, although lower scores than normal speed visualisation. It does not help the learner to understand a word during the discovery period. At the beginning of the rehabilitation, slow motion is often asked for; afterwards it is gradually abandoned. But slow motion is asked for by both the learner and the speech therapist during the pedagogical period: it allows a detailed analysis of the lip movements, it helps to segment the visual continuum of speech and to memorize these movements. Slow motion is therefore used as a pedagogical tool by the speech therapist.

Contribution of the System to Speech Comprehension

According to the speech therapists, the most impressive effect of Allao is the action of remotivating the learners for lipreading, more generally for oral communication. The apprenticeship and practice of lipreading does not appear so complex or out of reach to the deaf learners. A greater motivation, the desire to improve, and the active interest to the learning sessions are described by most of the therapists as the most sensible and immediate consequences of the system application. The motivation of the participants was still high after a full year of regular use (two sessions per week), very few cases of rejection were encountered. The therapists stress the increase of the overall capacity to understand speech: *"The progress can simply be evaluated by an easier comprehension of the speech"*. The learners become aware of the limits of lipreading, they realise that not everything can be visually perceived. In some cases, an improved quality of speech production was observed: the deaf learner speaks more fluently, with a greater ease; the articulation, and the awareness of the rhythm and intonation can improve.

Recent experiments have been performed with fourteen hearing impaired teenagers from an Institute for the Deaf, all of them using a hearing aid. They have trained with the Allao system during a ten-month period (two individual forty-minute sessions per week). The experiments show the progress performed in speech comprehension (Guillem, 1991).

At the beginning of the training period with the system, initial tests have been carried out on syllables, numbers and words. The final test, at the end of the training period with the system, consisted of the stimuli of the initial test which had obtained the lowest comprehension score (more than 9 errors for the 14 subjects). Tests on syllables and on numbers have been performed both with and without auditory output.

Table 2 gives the improvement achieved by the students as a function of the linguistic categories. No reference population (with traditional lipreading training), have performed the tests; therefore it is not possible to ascertain if the improvement is due to the system or to the general training of the Institute.

Table 2. Improvement in the comprehension of syllables, numbers and words after a 10 month training period with the Allao system (14 subjects).

Linguistic category (number of items)	Number of stimuli	Number of correct answers initial test	final test	Improvement
Syllables (14)				
without auditory output	196	0	20	10,2%
with auditory output	196	20	41	10,7%
Numbers (12)				
without auditory output	168	66	98	19%
with auditory output	168	100	135	21%
Words (without auditory output)				
Christian Names (14)	196	40	84	22,5%
Animals (14)	196	26	88	31,9%

A 10% improvement in the comprehension of syllables is classically observed after a training period (Summerfield, 1983). A further analysis of the results concerning the comprehension of numbers shows that it is the profoundly hearing-impaired teenagers which best improve their comprehension score, severely hearing impaired achieving already fairly good scores.

The improvement obtained for words is greater than the one obtained for syllables or numbers. This linguistic category is more significant, thus indicating that the progress deals less with the decoding of the lips movements but involves lexical access.

Conclusion

The interest of the system appears to lie in the possibility for the deaf to freely control a speaker, who will repeat and sub-title his sentences. The observed improvements result from both the pedagogical content and the renewed learning situation. The deaf learner acts on his rehabilitation, he becomes aware of the personal strategies needed to have a better comprehension of speech.

References

Bruckert, R., Henaff Gonan, M.A., Michel, F. & Bez, M. (1989). The use of a computer driven videodisc for the assessment and rehabilitation of aphasia. *Aphasiology, 3, 5,* 473-478.

Campbell, R. (1989). Lipreading. In: A. Young & H. Ellis (eds), *Handbook of research and face processing.* North Holland, Amsterdam, 187-205.

Cronin, B. (1983). The David System: The Development of an Interactive Video System at the National Technical Institute for the Deaf. *American Annals for the Deaf,* 616-623.

Dodd, B. & Campbell, R. (1984). Non-Modality Specific Speech Coding: The Processing of Lip-Read Information. *Australian Journal of Psychology, 36, 2,* 171-179.

Dodd, B. & Campbell, R. (1987). *Hearing by Eye: the psychology of lipreading.* London: L E A Publishers.

Erber, N. & McMahan, A. (1976). Effects of sentence context on recognition of words through lipreading by deaf children. *Journal of Speech and Hearing Research, 19,* 112-119.

Gosset, A. & Marniquet, S. (1990). Etude comparative des stratégies de compréhension en lecture labiale entre une population devenue sourde et une population entendante. *Mémoire d'Orthophonie, Université Paris 6,* U.F.R. Pitié Salpêtrière.

Guillem, A. & Lefaivre, V. (1991). Expérimentation du système Allao (Aide à la Lecture Labiale Assistée par Ordinateur). *Université de Montpellier, Mémoire d'Orthophonie.*

Guilliams, I. (1987). ALLAO - Un système d'apprentissage et d'évaluation de la lecture labiale à partir d'un vidéodisque interactif. *Bulletin d'Audiophonologie, 3, 5,* 589-615.

Guilliams, I., Boulakia, G. & Viallet, J.E. (1989). Acquisition de la lecture labiale: une méthodologie utilisant le vidéodisque. In: C. Dubuisson & F. Demaizière (eds), *L'ordinateur au service des déficients auditifs.* Paris: AEM, Ophrys.

Guilliams, I. (1991). *Acquisition et évaluation de la lecture labiale au moyen d'un vidéodisque interactif - Allao, un système, une méthode.* Université Paris 7, doctorat de linguistique.

Kopra., L., Kopra, M. & Abrahamson, J. (1987). Lipreading Drill and Practice Software for an Auditory-Visual Laser Videodisc Interactive System (ALVIS). *Journal for Computer Users in Speech and Hearing, 3, 1,* 58-68.

Le Huche, F. (1984). A propos de lecture labiale. *Bulletin d'Audiophonologie, 17,* 99-106.

Lutman, M.E. & Haggard, M.P. (1983). *Hearing Science and Hearing Disorders.* London: Academic Press Inc.

Robic, M. & Fuentés, K. (1989). *ALLAO - Expérimentation auprès d'enfants sourds profonds.* Mémoire pour l'attestation d'études complémentaires sur la déficience auditive de l'enfant, Faculté de Médecine et de Pharmacie de Besançon.

Summerfield, Q. (1983). Audiovisual speech perception lipreading and artificial stimulation. In: M.E. Lutman & M.P. Haggard (eds), *Hearing Science and Hearing Disorders.* London: Academic Press, 1311-180.

Voice and Intonation - Analysis, Presentation and Training

Adrian Fourcin, Evelyn Abberton and Virginia Ball
EPI[1] Group, Department of Phonetics and Linguistics University College London,
4 Stephenson Way, London NW1 2HE, UK

Abstract. Voice, intonation, and the lexical tone contrasts in tone languages, provide essential foundations for intelligible and socially acceptable speech. Control of phonation and basic voice pitch/fundamental frequency patterns is acquired very early by the developing child, and is notoriously difficult to acquire - in one's own or a foreign language - after the first few years of life. Despite early provision and use of hearing aids, phonation and intonation are often inadequately controlled by hearing impaired children and adults. This paper gives examples of their improvement as the result of two complementary approaches; speech pattern element interactive training and pattern element hearing aids. The focus here is on voice and intonation -factors which carry a primary functional load in all languages- but the principles are capable of application to other speech receptive and productive skills.

Principles of the Present Approach

Conventional acoustic hearing aids provide users with frequency-weighted, intensity controlled amplification of both speech and environmental sounds. More modern digital, speech-processing aids can counter the interference of ambient noise and reverberation, and take some account of characteristics of the listener's hearing disability by dynamic level adjustment. However, neither of these types of aid reflects the special nature of the acoustic patterns of speech nor their perceptual and linguistic characteristics.

Work by the EPI Group (Faulkner, Ball, Rosen, Moore & Fourcin, 1992;

---

[1] EPI (External Pattern Input) refers to the group of workers at University College London, Guy's Hospital, and Cambridge University concerned with electro-cochlear and speech pattern element hearing aids.

Ball, Rosen, Walliker & Fourcin, 1987) is directed towards the development of hearing aids, and associated interactive visual displays, based on the analysis of speech into physically separate pattern elements which carry quantitative and qualitative information on perceptually relevant linguistic features such as voicing, pitch, loudness, friction, and vowel timbre (Fourcin, 1989). These pattern elements may be presented separately or in combination. They may also be transformed physically so that they are matched to auditory, or visual, ability and yet retain contrastive pattern information. Hearing aids applying these principles are particularly relevant as complements to lip-reading for the very profoundly deaf user who cannot make adequate speech receptive use of conventional aids. They also have an application as training aids for adults with more hearing ability and, in a developmental context, to assist hearing impaired children's speech perception and production in a structured, hierarchical way. We have found the same approach to be of benefit to the totally deaf user through electrical rather than acoustic stimulation (Abberton et al, 1985).

Visual Displays of Speech

Displays of speech that provide visual feedback on performance for the user are available for both prosodic and segmental aspects of speech, and are essentially of two types: those that are based on an analogue "whole speech" approach such as the use of the realtime spectrograph (Houde, 1982), and those that are based on the extraction and display of a particular parameter such as fundamental frequency or amplitude (Destombes, this volume; Povel & Arends, this volume). Within this latter approach there are differences of philosophy concerning the type and amount of processing applied to the signal to make it conform to a particular view of speech perception (see Spaai (this volume) for some discussion of this in relation to the display of speech fundamental frequency for intonation training). At issue here is the question of the use of visual feedback in learning or refreshing not only neuro-muscular patterns but also auditory and linguistic forms and rules for their use (Fourcin & Abberton, 1971; Abberton & Fourcin, 1975). Our experience indicates that it is this combination which determines what to display and how best to help a user acquire control of new material.

The "speech pattern element" displays that we use (Abberton, Fourcin, Rosen, Walliker, Howard, Moore, Douek & Frampton, 1985; Ball, 1991) are designed to make it easy to focus on and clarify particular aspects of difficulty in a hierarchical manner. They are designed to enhance the use of residual or restored partial hearing ability as well as speech production intelligibility when used in an acoustically, phonetically and linguistically motivated programme of speech perceptual and productive rehabilitation (Abberton et al., 1985; Fourcin, 1978). Pattern matching is involved; hence the feedback provided by the learner's displayed responses must be readily interpretable and patterned: it is not helpful simply to receive binary "right/wrong" feedback. On its own, quantification relating only to the global congruence of whole word production using template matching without normalisation is similarly undesirable (Kewley-Port, Watson, Elbert, Maki & Reed, 1991).

Normalisation of auditory and visual pattern presentations is essential both to take into account auditory perceptual equivalence, and to enable speakers with different vocal tract sizes to communicate with each other. High frequency features from fricative consonants can then, for example, appear relatively low down on the frequency scale to give visual integration with fundamental frequency contours. This gives a simple correspondence to the auditory integration of such phonetic features in speech (Bootle, Fourcin & Smith, 1988). Pattern elements can be presented singly or in combination. Thus, for example, fundamental frequency contours can be presented on their own, or with the trace thickened and or brightened to represent greater loudness on particular syllables, and/or combined with voiceless fricative information (Figure 4 gives an example of thickening where there is a linear relation between acoustic amplitude and line width of the fundamental frequency contours).

The selective structured approach which is available with the use of pattern elements can be used at every level. For voice it could be "psycho-phonetic", to focus the learner's attention on poorly appreciated psycho-acoustic dimensions which are of phonetic relevance such as "long-short", "high-low", "rough-smooth", "rising-falling pitch"; linguistically to assist with sentence prosody, and with cognitive/semantic use. For children such work on dimensions can lend itself to a "games approach" while never asking for nor rewarding non-speechlike vocal activity - a problem with displays that depend heavily on computer graphic games (Destombes, this volume). From the very beginning, speechlike patterns are used in both perceptual and productive activities. Such early work must be designed to relate to a later more obviously linguistic approach with phonological, language-specific exercises which are rule-based. This teaching style is essentially cognitive throughout.

Interactive Visual Training - with only intonation patterning

Figure 1 gives a particular example of a typical change in voice productive ability associated with the use of a speech pattern interactive intonation display. The profoundly deaf speaker is a twenty year old man, congenitally hearing impaired, but with an oral educational background. His three frequency average hearing loss (500, 1000, 2000 Hz) is 100 dB HL. The two examples relate to a change in productive ability in a four month period between February and June. The two samples of intonation are derived from the utterance "three hours later the seven scouts came back and said". The top part of the figure relates to the initial condition of productive ability whilst the lower trace shows, for exactly comparable utterances, the situation following training (by VB). The improvements in frequency range, temporal control, and vocal fold vibration regularity (Ball, Fourcin & Faulkner, 1990, all come from the use of this type of interactive display (PCLX - made by Laryngograph Ltd).

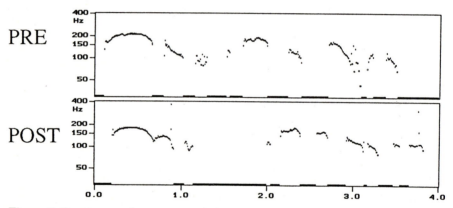

Figure 1. Spontaneous improvement in intonation contour control with Fx display training.

Figure 2 gives more detailed analyses of these utterances - from the same speaker before and after training. Sp refers to the acoustic pressure waveform extracted from the utterance "came back" and Lx relates to vocal fold closure, synchronously recorded using the electro-laryngograph. The European computer compatible SAMPA[2] broad phonetic notation has been used (Wells et al., 1989). The pre-training analysis shows the glottalisation associated with [k] at the end of the sequence and markedly irregular phonation with strong amplitude fluctuation at the beginning of the utterance. The situation following training is quite different, for example

---

[2] SAMPA is a broad phonetic alphabet which has the special advantage that it only uses standard keyboard symbols and has systems devised and already in wide application for many EC languages. The only symbol requiring explanation here is [{], which corresponds to the vowel in *cat*.

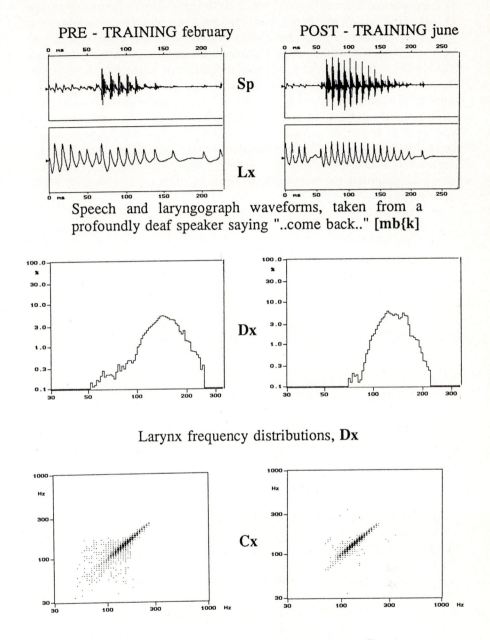

Figure 2. Speech improvement with an Fx display.

[k] is produced normally and there is little variability in period to period closure. The larynx frequency distributions, Dx, come from samples of at least two minutes of read text and are based on simple counts of larynx periods. They show two salient features associated with training; a reduction in overall range and a marked reduction in low frequency larynx vibration. This low frequency voice activity, which is so typical of the speech of the profoundly hearing impaired, is characterised by irregularity, shown clearly in the Cx plots. Cx prior to training shows a much greater scatter than is the case following training. The Cx distribution simply indicates the way in which successive vocal fold vibration periods are organised in time. For good regular speech the concentration of points is along the diagonal, the points depart from the diagonal by a degree which depends on the irregularity.

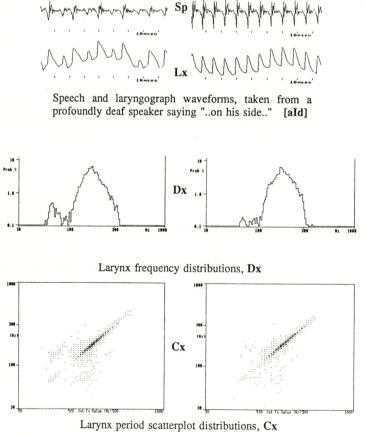

Figure 3. Speech improvement with a SiVo hearing aid.

Auditory Pattern Presentation

Figure 3 shows a set of speech productive analyses corresponding to those of Figure 2 but now based on another profoundly deaf speaker's use of a SiVo (Faulkner et al., 1992; Fourcin, 1990) speech pattern element hearing aid (in this case providing larynx frequency alone). Vocal fold vibration regularity is improved (as above the Sp and Lx examples are specially selected). Here, however, auditory monitoring enables the improvement to be sustained over time. In our experience, visual training is only effective in the long term when it enables the listener to make effective use of residual hearing. In this instance the effect is purely auditory. The speaker only used a SiVo aid to improve, and the change in her speaking ability is an immediate (and reversible) result of change of prosthesis.

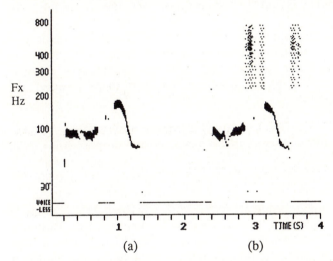

Figure 4. Combined pattern element displays. Two seperate utterances of "I was really surprised"; (a) fundamental frequency and amplitude, (b) fundamental frequency, voiceless friction and amplitude.

Structured Analysis and Training Using Pattern Element Combinations

Figure 4 gives two examples of more complex displays. They have been printed from the real-time interactive system which we use in training the hearing impaired (Bootle et al., 1988); for the sentence 'I was really surprised'. Figure 4 (a), on the left contains information relating to:

• larynx frequency -Fx- indicated by the vertical height of the contour at

any point along the horizontal time axis. Since Fx is derived separately for each larynx period, an irregular contour also indicates voicing irregularity.
- voicing amplitude -Ax- shown by the vertical width of the Fx contours and derived, from a microphone input, on the basis of larynx synchronous processing.

Information is also intrinsically present in regard to the voiced segmental groupings of the utterance. There are four distinct blocks of voicing: the first corresponds to *I was*; the second to *really*; the third, of very brief duration, to the first voiced component of 'surprised' *ur*; the final downward sweep of Fx corresponds to *ised*. This last block of voicing is contained within the tonic syllable, and carries the perceptually prominent nuclear tone. The voiceless segments of the complete utterance can only be inferred from this particular way of displaying the speech pattern information and this deficiency is remedied to an important degree in the adjacent example.

Figure 4 (b) gives a printout for another production by the same man speaker of the same sentence but on this occasion the basic display has been augmented by the further real-time addition of voiceless fricative information. In addition to the timing of these segments there is now also information relating to:

- spectral quality - shown by the vertical distribution of the points printed above the main Fx contours - this is based on the outputs from eight bandpass filters extending to 7kHz (Bootle et al., 1988), but shown using a Mapitch type approach (Fourcin et al., 1984) between 200 and 800 Hz on the vertical axis. (Acoustic energy for fricatives in speech is typically most prominent in the frequency region above 1kHz, here this range is mapped down so that it is visually represented below 1kHz. Auditory normalization allows the same process of mapping also to be used so that both friction and voicing are presented in and matched to the region of usable residual hearing via a SiVo type speech pattern hearing aid.)
- friction amplitude-activity in this part of the display indicates the existence of voiceless friction and the concentration of the points gives a qualitative measure of the overall intensity of the friction within the corresponding part of the spectrum.

Figure 4 (b) now clearly shows three segmental groupings of voiceless friction. The first is for *s* in 'surprised', the second is for *pr* and the third comes from the release of the final consonant *d*. The use of these visually different components in regard to their shape is quite possible with only a monochrome monitor. In our own work, however, a colour distinction is used in addition to shape. The Fx pattern components are green whilst the voiceless vertically speckled components of the complete display are white. These differences enhance the scope of the analytic discussion for almost any presented utterance. For example, the second *s* in the word 'surprised' relates to a voiced segment and this difference between the spoken realisations of the two graphemes is clearly shown. The presence of visually evident silent interval or friction "anchor" points, clearly displayed whilst speaking, is a substantial help to user and therapist in making an immediate conceptual relation between the overall form of the prosody and its segmental constituents.

The prospect of using these displays analytically opens up a large range of practical possibilities in work with the mildly to the profoundly hearing impaired. Interactive teaching with a hearing impaired child who needs guidance in order to make better use of existing auditory ability, or help with, for example, a profoundly deaf adult who is beginning to wear a speech pattern hearing aid, may both benefit from the structured use of separate speech pattern components. The way to the use of the fuller complexity of natural utterances can be directly linked to the sequence of acquisition followed by the normal child in the first case and in the second to the quite different needs of the adult with acquired loss.

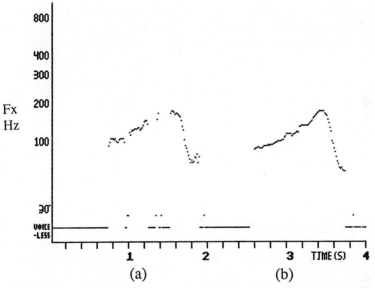

Figure 5. Single pattern element display. Two separate utterances - with and without voiceless segments; (a) "I was really surprised", (b) "Now I'm really annoyed".

Figure 5(a) shows an Fx only, 'stripped down', version of the same sentence "I was really surprised", whilst on the right, the sentence "Now I'm really annoyed" is shown, both produced again by the speaker of Figure 4. This latter utterance is voiced throughout and the basic similarity of prosodic forms in spite of the differences in voiced/voiceless segments is quite obvious. Micro-intonational differences are always present when an accurate method of analysis is used (Fourcin & Abberton, 1971) but in our experience are never a source of difficulty. At the earlier stages of work they are simply ignored by adult or child since it is the large effects which are of consequence and when more detailed segmental exercises are in progress, the interaction between segment and intonation pattern form is of enormous assistance.

It appears to us that it may be a disadvantage to hide the nature of the speech pattern form by, for example, a process of interpolation between voiced stretches. This technique will necessarily introduce features into the final display which are essentially intrusive - not helpful for a child and bewildering even for an adult. The simple contrasts between (a) and (b) in Figure 5 could not even be discussed if such a signal processing strategem were to be applied. However, if this approach were to be allied with speech pattern and phonetic information concerning the nature of the speech string being displayed, then much more powerful and interactively effective displays could result, at the cost of only a delay of one segment. To give just one example, vowel segments could in this way be selectively enhanced in width as a consequence of their phonetic role rather than as a consequence, as in the present approach, of their physical properties.

With only Fx and the appropriate choice of training material, attention can be successively directed to the most basic aspects of intonation control.

- The presence or absence of voicing, as in this example in Figure 5(a)
- The use of a high or of a relatively low voice 'pitch', either sustained or, as here at the end of 'annoyed', in an intonational change.
- The presence of voice irregularity, or 'creak', either sustained or as here, of brief occurrence, at the end of 'surprised'.
- Finally, at this first level of training, work involving only Fx can be organised in regard to the use of falling as opposed to rising intonation, gradual - as at the beginning of 5(b) or sharp, as at the end.

This groundwork has concentrated on the use of pattern forms which are observed in the course of natural development. The skills which it reinforces can now be used to lead to the first stage of phonologically important patterning. We have always deliberately avoided the use of larynx frequency exercises which do not map on to the use of intonation contrasts in language. The 'games' approach, for instance, which requires the child to negotiate an un-speechlike obstacle course with his larynx frequency is - we believe - not helpful in the short term, and in the long term directly analogous to the demoded use of exaggerated articulations in segmental skill training.

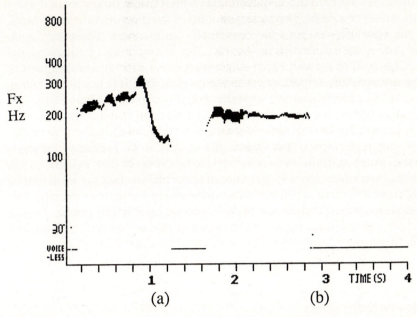

Figure 6. Stress placement and neutralisation. Fx*Ax displays; (a) with appropriate stress placements, (b) with no Fx and misplaced Ax; for the sentence "Now I'm really annoyed".

A further simple range of interactive training becomes feasible when Amplitude of voicing, Ax, is combined with the larynx frequency contour, Fx. Figure 6 shows a pair of utterances produced by a woman speaker for the fully voiced sentence discussed above, "Now I'm really annoyed. Figure 6(a) corresponds essentially exactly to the previous discussion and, as for Figure 4(a), the use of amplitude modulation clarifies structure. Figure 6(b), however, has no substantial change in Fx and the only large variation is in Ax. It is easy to see that the words "now I'm" have been given only 'loudness stress'. Once more the use of Ax in the first utterance has simplified interpretation and the inappropriate use of Ax in the second production of the same sentence is quite evident.

In Conclusion

An essential feature of the use of this type of interactive procedure is that the use of different speakers does not prejudice phonetic and linguistic interpretation. For instance, it is normal, in our use of these facilities, that a woman speaker should give examples which might be responded to by either a man or a child. The patterned form of the displays is what matters, not the absolute values of the coordinates on the axes. These particular examples of the combined, or separate, use of amplitude, frequency, and voiceless pattern elements in a single interactive display are designed to make phonetically important components available. It is not the intention to provide a presentation which is immediately capable of being a phonological interpretation in its own right. Communication depends on the use of contrasts and, in order to encourage their structured use and development, salient aspects of the speech signal have to be presented clearly - whether they are 'right' or 'wrong'. It is to be expected that, in some cases, speech communication will make use of abnormal forms. Our work will be at its most effective when the techniques which it employs provide this freedom to evolve and do not seek to impose prior assumptions coming from phonological normality at the outset of interaction with a deaf adult or child.

Acknowledgments

We are glad to acknowledge all the help and input to this work from our colleagues in the EPI Group, David Miller of Laryngograph Ltd and the earlier associated work on interactive displays of Ann Parker, Angela King and Yvonne Paris, and to thank Colin Bootle of the RNID for his important contribution to the last section of this paper, both in respect of the printout software for combined element presentations and for his design of the display which was used.

References

Abberton, E. & Fourcin, A.J. (1975). Visual feedback and the acquisition of intonation. In E.H. Lenneberg & E. Lenneberg (eds), *Foundations of language development. A multidisciplinary approach.* London: Academic Press. Volume 2, 157-165.

Abberton, E., Fourcin, A.J. & Howard, D. (1989). Laryngographic assessment of normal voice: a tutorial. *Clinical Linguistics & Phonetics, 3,* 281-196.

Abberton, E., Fourcin, A.J., Rosen, S., Walliker, J.R., Howard, D.M., Moore, B.C.J., Douek, E.E.& Frampton, S. (1985). Speech perceptual and productive rehabilitation in electro-cochlear stimulation. In: R.A.

Schindler & M.M. Merzenich (eds), *Cochlear Implants*. New York: Raven Press, 527-538.
Ball, V. (1991). Computer-based tools for assessment and remediation of speech. *British Journal of Disorders of Communication, 26,1,* 95-114.
Ball, V., Faulkner, A. & Fourcin, A.J. (1990). The effects of two different speech coding strategies on voice fundamental frequency control in deafened adults. *British Journal of Audiology, 24,* 393-409.
Ball, V., Rosen, S., Walliker, J. R. & Fourcin, A. (1987). A Speech Pattern approach to electrical hearing. *Proceedings of the International Cochlear Implant Symposium, Duren, FRG,* ed. Banfai. Springer-Verlag, 241-265.
Bootle, C., Fourcin, A. & Smith, J. (1988). Speech pattern element display. In: W.A. Ainsworth & J.N. Holmes (eds), *Proc. SPEECH '88, 7th FASE Symposium (Edinburgh, Institute of Acoustics),* 179-185.
Coninx, F. (ed.) (1990). *Research Symposium, Instituut voor Doven, Sint-Michielsgestel, The Netherlands.* IvD/RES/9103/00.
Destombes, F. The IBM Speechviewer. This volume.
Faulkner, A., Ball, V., Rosen, S., Moore, B.C.J. & Fourcin, A. (1992). Speech pattern hearing aids for the profoundly hearing impaired: Speech perception and auditory abilities, *JASA, 91* in press.
Fourcin, A.J. (1989). Links between voice pattern perception and production. In: B.A.G. Elsendoorn & H. Bouma (eds), *Working Models of Human Perception.* London: Academic Press, 67-92
Fourcin, A.J., Douek, E.E., Moore, B.C.J., Abberton, E.R.M., Rosen, S. & Walliker, J. (1984). Speech Pattern element stimulation in electrical hearing. *Archives of Otolaryngology, 110,* 145-153.
Fourcin, A.J. (1978). Acoustic patterns and speech acquisition. In: N. Waterson & C. Snow (eds), *The Development of Communication,* John Wiley.
Fourcin, A.J. (1990). Prospects for speech pattern element aids. *Acta Otolaryngol. (Stockholm) Suppl. 469,* 257-267.
Fourcin, A.J. & Abberton, E. (1971). First applications of a new laryngograph. *Medical & Biological Illustration, 21,* 172-182.
Hermes, D., 't Hart, H., Spaai, G. & Storm, A. (1990). Automatic stylisation of pitch contours in the teaching of intonation to the deaf. In: F. Coninx, (ed.) 16-22.
Houde, R. (1982). *Development and application of an instantaneous speech spectograph.* Papers from the Research Conference on Speech Processing Aids for the Deaf. J.M. Pickett (ed.), Gallaudet Research Institute, 189-195
Kewley-Port,D., Watson, D.S., Elbert, M., Maki, D. & Reed. D. (1991). The Indiana Speech Training Aid (ISTRA) II: training curriculum and selected case studies. *Clinical Linguistics and Phonetics 5, 1,* 13-38.
Povel, D.-J. & Arends, N. (1992). The visual speech apparatus. This volume.

Spaai, G. (1992). Teaching intonation to the deaf through visual displays. This volume.

Wells, J.C., Barry, W. & Fourcin, A. (1989). In: A. Fourcin, G. Harland, W. Barry & V. Hazan (eds), *Speech input and output assessment*. Ellis Horwood.

Teaching Intonation to Deaf Persons through Visual Displays

Gerard W. G. Spaai
Institute for Perception Research/IPO, P.O.Box 513, 5600 MB Eindhoven, the Netherlands
Institute for the Deaf/IvD, Sint-Michielsgestel, The Netherlands

Abstract. The broken auditory feedback loop of a deaf person inhibits the monitoring of his or her speech. This, in turn, frequently creates deficiencies in the segmental and suprasegmental aspects of speech. The incorrect suprasegmental aspects of speech, for example, often involve the generation of inappropriate intonation contours. The deaf person's intonation can be improved by means of sensory aids that display the pitch of speech. This paper is concerned with the development of a visual intonation-display system for the teaching of intonation to the deaf. In contrast to other visual intonation-display systems, the visual feedback of intonation is given as a continuous representation of the pitch contour. This contour contains the perceptually relevant aspects of the intonation pattern and the display of vowel onsets. The reliability of the visual intonation-display system is tested and discussed and applications of the system for the teaching of intonation to the deaf are described.

Keywords. visual feedback of intonation, aids for the deaf, speech training aids

Introduction

The absence of adequate pitch control is one of the most obvious features of the speech utterances of the deaf (Osberger & McGarr, 1982). For example, the average pitch is often either too high or too low with respect to age and gender (Martony, 1968). A low pitch may be caused by a low tension of the vocal folds, whereas a high pitch may be due to a high tension or an increased subglottal pressure. Willemain and Lee (1971) observed that deaf speakers sometimes tend to begin a breath group with an abnormally high pitch and then tend to lower their level to a more normal pitch level. They hypothesized that the deaf speaker uses extra effort in the larynx to generate high-pitched tones in order to provide proprioceptive cues of voicing. Martony (1968), however, ascribed the increased tension of the vocal folds to the extra effort which is devoted to the articulators. That is, as the tongue muscles are attached to the hyoid bone and the cricoid and thyroid cartilages, extra effort in their use would result in increases in the tension of the vocal cords and therefore in increases in pitch. According to Hudgins (1937), however, the high pitch is caused by the erroneous conception of many deaf speakers that laryngeal rather than respiratory muscles control air flow during speech.

Inappropriate average pitch may detract attention from the speaker's message and give conflicting cues about age and gender. Furthermore, if the average pitch is at the top or at the bottom of the normal dynamic range, there is little room left for providing variations in pitch. This lack of variation may result in pitch contours being perceived as flat, i.e., devoid of melody and reflecting a monotonous voice (Martony, 1968; Nickerson, 1975). In fact, objective measurements have shown that deaf speakers produce insufficient variations in pitch, particularly in their production of interrogative versus declarative utterances (Sorenson, 1974).

Problems with pitch control may differ from speaker to speaker. Whereas some studies report that deaf speakers produce reduced variation in pitch compared to normal hearing speakers, others indicate that deaf speakers produce excessive variations in pitch which can give rise to inappropriate pitch changes (Monsen, 1979). Such variations are not simply normal rises and falls, but rather pitch breaks and erratic changes that do not serve any intonational purpose. It has been suggested that some of these unusual variations in the speech of deaf persons may result from the attempts by the speaker to increase the amount of proprioceptive feedback received from the activity of producing speech.

Incorrect production of pitch contours in the speech of deaf persons may affect voice quality (Monsen, 1979) and seriously hamper speech intelligibility (McGarr & Osberger, 1978). Staccato-like speech productions (i.e., equal production of stress on all syllables) and pitch breaks in particular, are highly negatively correlated with speech intelligibility (McGarr & Osberger, 1978). A correct production of the pitch contours in the speech of the deaf contributes significantly to its intelligibility provided the segmental aspects of speech are produced correctly (Maassen & Povel, 1985; Metz, Schiavetti, Samar & Sitler, 1990). Therefore it is necessary to teach the deaf speaker the regulation of the pitch of his or her speech. This is, however, extremely difficult. First, the major variations in pitch are determined by the action of the cricothyroid muscle (Collier, 1975); this means that it is not possible to give visual cues on the regulation of pitch. Second, the regulation of pitch is mainly controlled by auditory feedback, whereas tactile and proprioceptive feedback play only a minor role (Ladefoged, 1967). However, a deaf person may not have sufficient residual hearing to perceive the auditory cues for control and variation of pitch. In sum, two important conditions for pitch control, i.e., visual and auditory feedback, may not be available to the deaf. This makes it extremely difficult to teach the deaf speaker the regulation of pitch. They even may lack a conceptual appreciation of what pitch is (Martony, 1968). Hearing people describe pitch in terms of a high-low dimension. This description is, however, somewhat arbitrary and may only be meaningful to a hearing person who has had the opportunity to learn to hear the relative reference of 'high' and 'low' in the auditory domain. A lack of intuitive understanding of the concept may help to explain why deaf people attempt to raise their pitch by increasing their vocal intensity (Phillips, Remillord, Boss & Pronovost, 1968).

In general, the speech training of the deaf is often focused on forming speech sounds by learning how to use and position the articulators, i.e., the so-called process-oriented approach (Povel & Arends, 1991). For the teaching of intonation, however, this process-oriented approach can not be applied as no visual cues can be given on how to regulate the pitch of speech. Therefore it seems more suitable to provide information on the pitch of speech, i.e., the so-called product-oriented approach (Povel & Arends, 1991). Pitch information can be given in three different ways to the deaf person. First, information on pitch can be given through the auditory channel. This is the preferred technique in instructing pitch control as the deaf speaker will learn to use his own feedback modalities in order to control pitch. In addition, this method corresponds with the way hearing people learn to control the pitch of their speech. Some deaf speakers, however, do not have sufficient residual hearing for the recognition and control of pitch patterns. For these deaf speakers this auditory method is not appropriate. Second, pitch level can be indicated by means of a visual cue provided by a speech trainer (e.g., raising and lowering the hand). This method has been used fairly frequently in regular speech training lessons. The disadvantage of this method is that the provision of information on pitch is delayed and subjective. Third, information on pitch can be given by means of aids that extract the fundamental frequency from the speech signal and present this parameter as a visual or a tactile display that can provide feedback on pitch contours almost immediately in a consistent and objective way.

The advantage of a tactile display is that it can be made portable, thus feedback can be made available continuously without requiring the active attendance necessary for a visual display. It therefore follows that a tactile aid could possibly support speech reading. However, a major problem arises in the use of a tactile aid due to the "limited frequency-analysing capacity of the skin and the spatial spread of masking" (Abberton & Fourcin, 1975: 158). Much more work has been done, however, in developing visual displays for the teaching of intonation to the deaf (see for an overview Braeges and Houde, 1982), as visual displays are particularly well suited to speech training for two reasons in particular. First, a model or a desired pattern can be presented to a pupil and the model pattern can be stored for comparison with the deaf speakers' own pattern. Second, a stored visual pattern is easy for the speech trainer to point to for the purpose of indicating some part of the desired pattern.

Visual Display of Pitch

The development of visual sensory aids that display the pitch of speech in order to support the teaching of intonation to the deaf has received more attention than any other speech training aid (Abberton & Fourcin, 1975; Houde & Levitt, 1980; Lippmann, 1982). Although some of these speech training aids may be helpful in the teaching of intonation to the deaf, none of them are in general use in schools for the deaf. Several factors contributed to the lack of widespread use of these speech training aids. First, some of these aids are unreliable or very costly, whereas others involve complex processing of speech to extract the fundamental frequency which results in a delay of the visual display (Abberton & Fourcin, 1975). Second, empirical evaluations of these aids are scarce. Third, a curriculum for the use of the aid during speech training is often not available (Houde & Levitt, 1980). Fourth, fundamental frequency is displayed in a complex way. That is, fundamental frequency is measured and directly fed back in an unprocessed form to the deaf person by a visual representation on a display (Lippmann, 1982).

Two difficulties arise when deaf persons are provided with the unprocessed visual feedback of the pitch contour of their speech. Even if the pitch is measured correctly, as is done for instance by a laryngograph (Abberton & Fourcin, 1975), interpretation of the result is hampered by the presence of unvoiced parts and of many perceptually irrelevant details, the so-called micro-intonation: on a screen, the interruptions during unvoiced speech segments are at variance with the continuously perceived pitch contour. Micro-intonation, which can be very conspicuous, especially at transitions between consonants and vowels, can barely be perceived, if at all, by persons with normal hearing, let alone imitated. Only the perceptually relevant aspects should be given as visual feedback of intonation. This is possible by giving a continuous representation of the pitch contour. This approach concurs with the study of intonation based on "close-copy stylisations" (De Pijper, 1983), in which pitch contours are reduced to the smallest number of straight lines possible, without affecting the perceptually relevant properties.

Another difficulty arises from the dependence of the perceptual identity of a pitch movement on its position in the syllable, in particular with respect to the vowel onset. In Dutch intonation, the perceptual identity of a pitch movement depends upon its position in the syllable. It appears that the vowel onset is one of the most relevant moments in this respect ('t Hart & Collier, 1975). One of the prominence-lending rising movements in Dutch starts on average about 70 ms before the vowel onset and ends about 50 ms after the vowel onset. A continuation rise, occurring before a comma in read text, and which does not lend prominence to a syllable, starts much later in the syllable. Hence, a correct interpretation of the pitch contour of a sentence requires that the pitch movements are presented in relation to the vowel onsets of the syllables in which they occur. That is, in order to learn to intonate correctly, positioning the pitch movements with respect to the vowel onsets of the syllables is crucial. The feedback of the pitch contour of a sentence has to indicate the moments of occurrence of the vowel onsets.

In summary, it is argued that for the teaching of intonation to the deaf visual feedback of intonation should be given as a continuous representation of the pitch contour with nothing but the perceptually relevant pitch movements, and also including information on the moments of occurrence of the vowel onsets. At the Institute for Perception Research/IPO in Eindhoven a system has been developed that presents visual feedback on intonation in a way that corresponds with this approach. A further description of this system is given and its reliability is discussed. In addition, applications of the system for the teaching of intonation to the deaf will be described.

The IPO Intonation Meter

Hardware

The core of the IPO intonation meter consists of a Philips NMS9100/ AT286 computer reinforced with a TMS320C25-based Digital Signal Processor DSP) board from ARIEL and a 50 Mb hard disk. Speech input is obtained from a headset MKE 48 (Sennheiser) microphone. The speech signal is led via an audio interface to the anolog input of the ARIEL board. This audio interface is a separate device which basically amplifies the signal level and filters the input microphone signal with a cut-off frequency of 2500 Hz. In this way the output signal to be produced matches the requirements and restrictions of the hardware, that is the ARIEL board, and the software. Two input microphones corresponding to the speech-trainer and the pupil can be linked to the audio interface. In addition to these microphones, connections can be made to an external tape deck or cassette deck, an external amplifier/loudspeaker combination or two headphones.

Software

The software was written in C and implemented on the DSP-reinforced AT286 computer. The time-consuming routines were optimised in assembly language on the DSP board.

Pitch Measurement, Stylisation and Vowel-Onset Detection

Three algorithms have been developed for determining pitch and vowel onsets, and stylizing the intonation contours. The determination of pitch is based on the subharmonic summation technique for pitch determination (Hermes, 1988). The pitch measurements are performed every 16 ms, and after a very short period of postprocessing, displayed on the computer screen. The pitch movements in speech intonation are expressed on a psycho-acoustic scale that takes the frequency selectivity of the auditory system into account. The psycho-acoustic frequency scale is intermediate between a linear and a logarithmic frequency scale. This frequency scale has been used as it is the only one whereby pitch movements with similar excursions and presented in different pitch registers lead to the same degree of prominence (Hermes & Van Gestel, 1991).

Stylisation amounts to an approximation of the course of the fundamental frequency with a minimum number of straight lines while the perceptually irrelevant variations are left out ('t Hart & Collier, 1975). This straight-line approach has the advantage that pitch movements are represented as discrete units with well-defined beginnings and well-defined endings. In the IPO intonation meter stylisation is performed automatically. This is done by first determining the points in a measured pitch curve where the curvature reaches a relative maximum or minimum. These points serve as the turning points of the line segments that constitute the stylisation. Regression lines between these points of extrema are then calculated from the original series of pitch measurements with the restriction that successive line segments must be continuous (Hermes, in preparation).

The detection of vowel onsets is based on the idea that vowel onsets are characterized by the appearance of strong resonance peaks in the amplitude spectrum of the speech signal (Hermes, 1990). This leads to the concept of "vowel strength", i.e., the combined strength of the spectral peaks below 2500 Hz. This is measured every 16 ms. The instants at which the vowel strength rises rapidly are assumed to be the vowel onsets.

An example is shown in Figure 1 for the Dutch sentence "Op een dag kwam een vreemdeling het dorp binnenwand'len" (One day a stranger came walking into the village). The separate points show the unprocessed pitch measurements and the continuous straight lines show the stylised contour. The verical arrows indicate the vowel onsets.

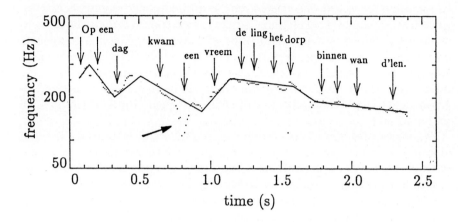

Figure 1. Display of the unprocessed pitch measurements, stylised pitch contour and the vowel onsets (vertical arrows). The thick arrow points at a severe micro-intonational pitch movement.

The Reliability of the IPO Intonation Meter

To verify whether the algorithms for the pitch measurement, stylisation and vowel-onset detection can be applied to the speech utterances of deaf children and their speech trainers, an evaluation was carried out. Audio recordings were made while a prelingually deaf child imitated the speech utterances of the speech trainer in a simulated-speech-training situation. Sixteen deaf children, seven boys and nine girls, aged four to fourteen participated in this evaluation. All children had a hearing loss of more than 90 dB. They had no motor handicaps. Their speech trainers were five males and two females. Speech materials consisted of continuous vowels, isolated words and short sentences. The results showed that, in general, the measurement of pitch worked adequately. Only for the speech utterances of one pupil did the measurement of pitch appear to be problematic due to an extremely strong second harmonic. The stylisation algorithm appeared to perform very well too. On the other hand, the vowel-onset detection algorithm did not operate very satisfactorily: for vowels, isolated words, and sentences too many vowel onsets were detected (the so-called false alarms). Furthermore, the results revealed that the vowel-onset detection algorithm is better suited for sentences than for carefully articulated speech (i.e., vowels, isolated words). This tendency was also found for speech utterances of hearing speakers (Hermes, 1990). In addition, results also showed that the vowel-onset detection algorithm worked slightly better for speech utterances of speech trainers than for the speech utterances of their deaf pupils. This is probably due to the fact that in comparison to the speech utterances of the deaf speakers, the utterances of speech trainers were less strongly pronounced. However, also for speech utterances of speech trainers the application of the vowel-onset detection algorithm resulted in an unacceptably high number of false alarms (Spaai, Storm & Hermes, in preparation).

The major problem of the system is posed by the large number of false alarms. The majority of these false alarms occurred in diphthongs and long vowels. As there is a gradual transition between a diphthong and a double vowel, these speech segments are likely to cause errors. However, it is clear that the vowel-onset detection algorithm does not work properly in this case. Another major category of false alarms consists of the nasals /n/ and /m/ and the liquids /l/ and /r/. Although some modification of the parameter setting appeared to reduce the number of false detections, the number of false alarms produced by the vowel-onset detection algorithm is still too high.

Conclusions and Future Developments

The algorithms for determining pitch and for measuring the stylisation appeared to perform very well. The vowel-onset-detection algorithm, however, did produce too many false detections, whereas the number of missed vowel-onset detections was acceptable. The most important phonetic context in which too many vowel onsets are found consists of diphthongs and long vowels. The solution to this problem might be to determine the spectral envelope just before and just after the vowel onset. A vowel onset is correctly detected whenever the spectral envelope just before and just after the detection differs. It is assumed that the majority of false detections within vowels will be removed by comparing the spectral envelope just before and just after the vowel onset. Another large category of false alarms consists of the nasals and the liquids /l/ and /r/. It is difficult to conceive of a proper solution to the problem of falsely detected vowel onsets before consonants like /m/, /n/ or /r/, as these consonants become vowel-like as soon as they are fairly carefully articulated. In some languages these phonemes can even play the role of vowels, e.g., in African languages in names such as Mbosa and Nkomo. Even in English these phonemes can function as syllabic consonants such as in 'rhythm', 'person' or 'apple'. If words like these are carefully pronounced, the consonants will have so much of a vowel-like character that any vowel-onset detector will detect them as such. Since speech utterances of deaf speakers are frequently characterized by a strong degree of overarticulation (Nickerson, 1975) this might constitute a problem for the use of the vowel-onset detection algorithm in a computer program for the teaching of intonation to the deaf. As there is at present no solution to tackle the problem of false detections found for these consonants, it is suggested that these vowel-like consonants should be avoided when developing a computer program to support the teaching of intonation to the deaf. This means that a program should be developed in which training takes place on a limited speech corpus.

In the computer program currently being developed at IPO the deaf person will gradually be taught to become conscious of pitch and pitch movements and will be taught to produce pitch movements in a correct way. For successful usage of this computer program it is necessary that a curriculum is available, as it is unlikely that a speech trainer himself or herself is going to develop a curriculum for the use of the computer program in teaching. Furthermore, it is important that this computer-based curriculum fits in with the regular speech curriculum in order to increase the possibilitiy of the acceptance of this computer program in schools (Woodward & Jones, 1988). A remaining problem, however, is the lack of a well-defined curriculum for the teaching of intonation to the deaf even though several attempts have been made to develop such a curriculum. For example, Ling (1976) roughly described a curriculum that included both auditory discrimination and the production of discretely and continuously voiced patterns, approximating the high, mid and low points in the vocal ranges of teachers and students. Osberger, Johnstone, Swarts and Levitt (1978) also developed a curriculum that included auditory discrimination, imitation and production on demand of syllables varying in duration, pitch and intensity. More recently, a curriculum was developed by Youdelman, MacEachron and McGarr (1989) to remedy insufficient variation in pitch production. In none of these curricula, however, is the serial order described in which certain pitch movements are to be taught. Moreover, the sequence in which the speech materials (e.g., vowels, syllables, isolated words, sentences) are to be presented in order to teach the production of correct pitch contours efficiently, is unknown. In future work at IPO it is planned to develop a computer-based curriculum that contains a specification of the sequence in which several pitch movements are to be taught and of the speech materials that are to be presented. This curriculum will also contain a specification of four different exercises. In these exercises special emphasis is placed on drill in order to promote automaticity of speech production (Osberger et al., 1978).

In the first exercise, the child will be instructed to discriminate and identify an auditory signal. In this exercise a speech signal containing a rising or a falling pitch, or a combination of both, is presented to the deaf child. The child is asked to indicate whether it has heard a rise, a fall or a combination of both. As intonation involves frequencies below 500 Hz (Lieberman, 1967) and deaf people frequently have residual hearing in this frequency range, it is to be expected that differences in pitch contours can be perceived by these deaf persons (Engen, Engen, Clarkson & Blackwell, 1983). This exercise aims at making the deaf more aware of pitch and pitch movements, which is considered to be an important prerequisite for the development of production skills. It is suggested that as perception skills are sharpened, improvement in production and control of pitch through self-monitoring will follow.

In a second exercise the deaf speaker is instructed to imitate the pitch contour of an utterance produced by the speech trainer and visually displayed on the computer screen. Visual feedback will be presented on the pitch contour of the deaf speaker's utterance almost without a delay in a stylised form to make the interpretation of the contour as easy as possible. Furthermore, the moments of occurrence of vowel onsets are displayed in order to teach the deaf speaker to time the pitch movements correctly. This feature, however, can only be implemented after the vowel-onset detection algorithm is modified for improved performance. Feedback on pitch contours will also be provided in auditory form, as it is suggested that information along this modality plays an important role in learning to regulate the pitch of speech. Auditory feedback will be provided in accordance with the deaf speaker's residual hearing.

In the third exercise the deaf speaker will be required to spontaneously produce various pitch rises and falls. The spontaneous production of these pitch movements will be elicited by visual cues (e.g., sentences, words or pictures).

In the fourth exercise the deaf speaker is prompted to make a judgement regarding the correctness of his or her speech production. Both the accuracy of the judgement and the accuracy of the speech production are finally evaluated. It is suggested that this type of drill is an important step in the carry-over process of speech skills beyond the regular speech training because the deaf speakers have to learn to evaluate and/or modify their own speech productions via the internal feedback modalities. For that purpose it is necessary that the deaf speaker learns to attend to the proprioceptive and acoustic cues associated with intelligible speech.

However, as there is little known about the optimal way these exercises should be implemented in order to achieve the best learning effects, it is necessary to conduct further experimental research. Furthermore, evaluations of these exercises in educational settings are necessary to gain insight into their usefulness with respect to the teaching of intonation to the deaf.

Acknowledgments

This work was supported by a grant from the Institute for the Deaf at Sint-Michielsgestel, The Netherlands. The author would like to express his gratitude to the principals, staff and pupils of the Dr. Van Udenschool. Thanks are also due to Maddy Brouwer, René Collier, Dik Hermes, Teddy McCalley and Arent Storm for their comments on an earlier version of this paper.

References

Abberton, E. & Fourcin, A.J. (1975). Visual feedback and the acquisition of intonation. In: E.H. Lenneberg & E. Lenneberg (eds), *Foundations of language developments. A multidisciplinary approach.* Volume 2, 157-165.
Braeges, J.L. & Houde, R.A. (1982). Use of speech training aids. In: D. Sims, G. Walter, & R. Whithead (eds), *Deafness and Communication: Assessment and Training.* Baltimore: Williams & Wilkins.
Collier, R. (1975). Physiological correlates of intonation patterns. *Journal of the Acoustical Society of America, 58*, 249-255.
De Pijper, J.R. (1983). *Modelling British English intonation.* Dordrecht: Foris Publications.
Engen, T., Engen, E.A., Clarkson, & Blackwell P.M. (1983). Discrimination of intonation by hearing-impaired children. *Applied Psycholinguistics, 4*, 149-160.
Hart, J. 't & Collier, R. (1975). Integrating different levels of intonation analysis. *Journal of Phonetics, 3*, 235-255.
Hermes, D.J. (1988). Measurement of pitch by subharmonic summation. *Journal of the Acoustical Society of America, 83*, 257-264.
Hermes, D.J. (1990). Vowel-onset detection. *Journal of the Acoustical Society of America, 87*, 257-264.
Hermes, D.J. & Van Gestel, J.C. (1991). The frequency scale of speech intonation. *Accepted for publication in Journal of the Acoustical Society of America.*
Hermes, D.J. (in preparation). Automatic stylisation of pitch contours.
Houde, R.A. & Levitt, H. (1980). Speech-training aids. In: H.Levitt, J.M. Pickett & R.M. Houde (eds), *Sensory aids for the hearing impaired.* New York: John Wiley & Sons.
Hudgins, C. (1937). Pitch deviancy and the intelligibility of deaf children's speech. *American Annals of the Deaf, 82*, 338-363.

Ladefoged, P. (1967). *Three areas of experimental phonetics*. London: University Press.
Lieberman, P. (1967). *Intonation, Perception and Language*. Cambridge MA: MIT Press.
Ling, D. (1976). *Speech and the hearing-impaired child: Theory and practice*. Washington: A.G. Bell Association for the Deaf.
Lippmann, R.P. (1982). A review of research on speech training aids for the deaf. In: N. Lass (ed.), *Speech and Language: Advances in basic research and practice*. Volume 7. New York: Academic Press, 105-133.
Maassen, B. & Povel, D.J. (1985). The effect of segmental and suprasegmental correction on intelligibility of deaf speech. *Journal of the Acoustical Society of America, 78*, 877-886.
Martony, J. (1968). On the correction of voice pitch level for severely hard of hearing subjects. *American Annals of the Deaf, 113*, 345-349.
McGarr, N. & Osberger, M. (1978). Pitch deviancy and the intelligibility of deaf children's speech. *Journal of Communication Disorders, 11*, 237-247.
Metz, D.E., Schiavetti, N., Samar, V.J. & Sitler, R.W. (1990). Acoustic dimensions of hearing-impaired speakers' intelligibility: segmental and suprasegmental chracteristics. *Journal of Speech and Hearing Research, 33*, 476-487.
Monsen, R.B. (1979). Acoustic qualities of phonation in young hearing-impaired children. *Journal of Speech and Hearing Research, 22*, 270-288.
Nickerson, R.S. (1975). Characteristics of the speech of deaf persons. *The Volta Review, 77*, 342-363.
Osberger, M.J., Johnstone, A., Swarts, E. & Levitt, H. (1978). The evaluation of a model speech training program for deaf children. *Journal of Communication Disorders, 11*, 293-313.
Osberger, M.J., McGarr, N.S. (1982). Speech production chracteristics of the hearing impaired. In: N. Lass (ed.), *Speech and language: advances in basic research and practice*. Volume 8. New York: Academic Press.
Phillips, N.D., Remillord, W., Boss, S. & Pronovost, W. (1968). Teaching of intonation to the deaf by visual pattern matching. *American Annals of the Deaf, 113*, 239-246.
Povel, D.J. & Arends, N. (1991). The visual speech apparatus: theoretical and practical aspects. *Speech Communication, 10*, 59-80.
Sorenson, J. (1974). *Fundamental frequency contours in the speech of deaf children*. Term paper, MIT.
Spaai, G.W.G., Storm, A. & Hermes, D.J. (in preparation). An intonation meter for the teaching of intonation to the deaf.
Willemain, T.R. & Lee, F.F. (1971). Tactile pitch feedback for deaf speakers. *The Volta Review, 73*, 541-554.

Woodhouse, D. & Jones, A.J. (1988). Integrating CAL with other instructional activities in schools. *Computers in Education, 23,* 85-91.

Youdelman, K., MacEachron, M. & McGarr, N. (1989). Using Visual and tactile sensory aids to remediate monotone voice in hearing-impaired speakers. *The Volta Review, 91,* 197-207.

Conceptual and Technical Considerations in Developing Visual Aids for Speech Training

D.J. Povel[1] and N. Arends[2]
[1]Nijmegen Institute for Cognition and Information Technology (NICI), Psychological Department, University of Nijmegen, The Netherlands
[2]Instituut voor Doven, Sint-Michielsgestel, and Psychological Department, University of Nijmegen, The Netherlands

Abstract. In building a visual aid for speech training one is confronted with many conceptual and technical problems. Conceptual problems relate to speech analysis (how to extract the speech parameters), mapping (how to display the parameters on the available visual dimensions) and teaching (how to use the displays in an effective teaching device), while the technical problems relate to the implementation of these functions into a properly working device. In this paper we shall describe the theoretical framework used in the development of a visual aid and show how in the three versions of the 'Visual Speech Apparatus' problems at the different levels have been solved. We shall also briefly discuss future developments and the type of problems expected to be encountered in developing the next generation of visual aids.

Keywords. Deaf, speech education, visual aid.

Introduction

A visual aid for speech training is basically a system that transforms selected acoustic information about speech into the visual domain in a way that is useful for speech training of children with speech-related problems (e.g. deaf children). Although this may seem a relatively simple task, our experience has been the contrary. During the past 6 years we have found that actually building a viable, reliable and comprehensive visual speech training aid is rather a difficult undertaking. Why is this so? In this paper we shall deal with this question by discussing the conceptual and technical problems that researchers working in this area are confronted with. Subsequently we shall suggest ways in which we think these problems can best be handled. Next, we shall present a brief summary of our own activities and we shall end by examining a few problems involved in the development of the next generation of visual aids for speech training.

The Development of a Visual Aid for Speech Training

We begin by considering the question why the development of a viable visual aid is a difficult task and why it took several decades to develop the first more or less successful devices. The main obstacles on the way towards a visual aid are the following.

First, there is the diversity of problems, both at the theoretical and practical level. Theoretical problems pertain to such different fields as phonetics, automatic speech recognition, speech perception and production, learning theory and didactics, ergonomics, system development and computer programming. Practical problems are related to the management of the project: the coordination and timely performance of the different tasks which include theoretical and technical research, practical testing and formal evaluation.

A second basic problem results from the fact that the final aim of the project cannot be completely formulated at the start. The final aim changes continuously because of the growing insight in the feasibility of the pursued goals. Of course, at the start of the project basic theoretical viewpoints and global goals will be formulated. However, in a project of this kind, it is impossible to foresee the theoretical and technical problems in detail and what type of didactic problems will have to be met in the practical speech training setting. Perhaps, most importantly, one cannot predict future technological developments and resulting changes in technical possibilities. As we shall show later, this latter aspect has greatly influenced the actual course of our project.

It thus follows that the formulation of the ultimate goals, or more specifically, the definition of the device to be developed, is a substantial and continuous activity in a project of this kind. At each moment the current definition will depend on the theoretical and practical insights in the desired characteristics of the device on the one hand, and on the actual possibility of realizing it (that is the availability of the necessary equipment) on the other hand.

In order to successfully accomplish a project of this kind, we believe that an adequate set up of the project is of great importance. In particular the following recommendations are relevant:

- Ensure that the needed expertise in the different fields mentioned above are available. These different kinds of expertise should preferably be present in the group that actually performs the project, so that they can be applied in a coherent way. Otherwise the project group should be able to consult expert advisors who can provide the necessary knowledge.
- The project should be executed in immediate interaction with the people for which it is developed, i.e. the speech therapists and the children who will be using the system.

- The work in the project must be guided by a thorough insight in the essential aspects of its purpose: to help a child acquire basic speech skills. Consequently, the project should be based on appropriate scientific assumptions with respect to what has to be learned, in what order and in what way.
- The daily work in the project must be organized on the basis of a list of requirements that completely describes all aspects of the developing device. This list must be updated regularly.

The Development of the Visual Speech Apparatus

We shall now briefly describe the development of the Visual Speech Apparatus (VSA). The project started in March 1985 and will terminate in December 1992. We shall first look into the recommendations just mentioned and see how we have tried to satisfy these in the project.

- Expertise within the project group was rather broad. Almost during the whole period, the project group consisted of psychologists, technical engineers and speech therapists, while during specific periods the group was enlarged with research assistants from various fields. Besides, we had a quite diverse group of research consultants that proved very helpful in solving specific problems at different stages in the project.
- From the very beginning of the project, speech therapists participated in the project. They helped in defining the basic speech components to be taught with the help of the visual aid and they made suggestions as to the concrete form of the exercises which they tested during speech lessons. They also played an important role in the formal evaluations of the system.
- During the different phases of the project, the work was guided by a theoretical framework that had been formulated early on in the project (Povel, 1987; Povel & Maassen, 1987) and further elaborated in later stages (Povel & Arends, 1991). This framework deals with two basic aspects of the project. One pertains to the question of how to teach basic speech skills to a deaf child with the help of a visual aid. The other relates to a structural description of a visual aid, distinguishing different functional modules. Figure 1 shows the latter aspect. It indicates that a visual aid can be conceived of as a system that performs three functions respectively called *filtering*, *displaying*, and *norm induction*. The filter component extracts the necessary parameters from the speech signal. The display component carries out a number of transformations on the parameters and maps them on selected visual dimensions. The last

component adds a norm (standard, model) in order to make the system a real teaching device. The structure is described in Povel & Arends (1991) in more detail.

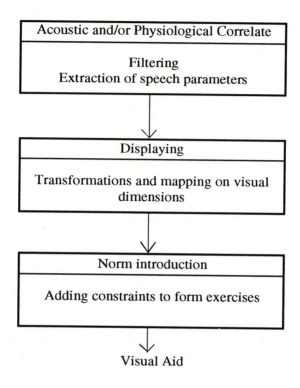

Figure 1. Levels of processing of a visual aid for speech training.

- The major criteria used in the development of the VSA, falling into different categories are:

- General. The system should be complete in the sense that it provides help about all (in as far as possible) relevant aspects of speech. Rational: if there must be a machine for speech training, let it be one machine that incorporates help for all basic speech skills in a coherent way.
- Didactic requirements. The exercises within the VSA should be designed such that learning is optimally supported:
    - by designing displays that are easily understood by its future users
    - by defining basic skill components of speech that can be trained separately
    - by teaching these skills until they are performed automatically
    - by designing the exercises in such a way that maximum adaptability

to the pupil's needs is guaranteed
- by designing the exercises as attractive games that motivate the child and thus increase frequency of training
- by storing learning results which can be shown upon request to the teacher
- by having an option in which the child can practice independently
- by displaying the speech parameters in real time.
• Technical requirements:
  - the device should have sufficient computational power and graphic capabilities to enable real-time speech processing and attractive animations
  - the system must be built, both for its hardware and software, in such a way that future extensions are possible
  - the system must be modularly designed to obtain flexibility needed to handle complex programming tasks and to anticipate future adaptations and expansions
  - irrespective of the complexity of the ultimate system, its operation should be simple and clear so that it will be easy to use.

Preparatory Research

Since a visual aid for speech training fulfils three basic functions: speech analysis, displaying the results of these functions and presenting exercises, we did preparatory research in each of these fields.

With regard to speech analysis, we have performed studies to discover parameters corresponding to the desired speech aspects. In one study we examined several characteristics of the Electro-laryngograph (ELG) signal to find predictors of voice quality (Arends, Povel, van Os & Speth, 1990). In a second study we evaluated various multi-dimensional techniques to derive a vowel space from a spectral description obtained from Fast Fourier Transform (FFT), (Groenen, 1989). The technique we have ultimately implemented in the system is based upon the Physical to Perceptual Space algorithm of Zahorian & Jagharghi (1988). Finally, a real-time version of the pitch algorithm of Reetz (1989) has been developed and implemented for pitch displaying purposes.

With regard to the displaying function of the system, we have studied several methods to show the basic acoustic parameters separately, as well as in a combined fashion, using multi-dimensional visual displays (Veenendaal, 1989).

A relatively great amount of time has, of course, been dedicated to the construction of the system itself. In cooperation with the speech therapists the optimal form of the different exercises was developed by designing prototypes which were tested in the practical situation, leading to further improvements. In addition, an easy-to-operate user-interface was developed as well as a preliminary curriculum incorporating the VSA.

Brief History: VSA Versions 1.0, 2.0, 3.0

In the course of the project three versions of the VSA were developed. Table 1 schematically presents the hardware characteristics of the three versions and describes the major characteristics of each component.

Table 1. Main characteristics of the different versions of the VSA developed during the project.
* ELG=Electro-laryngograph. C.M.=Contact microphone. Both transducers are optional.

Version	Transducer	Signal Interface	DSP	Master system
VSA 1 (1987)	Microphone Laryngograph	External, Manual control	Home-built	Gespac, Atari
VSA 2 (1989)	Idem	Idem	Ariel DSP-16	Amiga-2000 with PC-XT
VSA 3 (1991)	Microphone (ELG, C.M*)	Internal, Automatic	Ariel PC-C25	Amiga-2000 with PC-XT

. As can be seen considerable differences exist between the three versions, due to the developments in hardware and software that took place in the period that we were developing the system. For version 1 we had to build our own signal processor (DSP) which was based on the TMS32010 processor that became available at that time. This resulted in a rather bulky case containing all the circuitry needed for sampling, signal conditioning, memory management etc. Moreover this DSP, being 'home made', was of course quite expensive and difficult to replicate.

In version 2 the 'home made' DSP was replaced by the DSP board developed by Ariel®, the DSP-16. This became feasible as the main system was replaced by an Amiga-2000 computer that came on the market in 1987, and which could be extended with a IBM-PC board accommodating the Ariel® board.

A major improvement in version 3 is the replacement of the laryngograph by a software algorithm that computes the pitch from the speech signal (Reetz, 1989). This makes the system at the same time more reliable and more user-friendly (the children greatly dislike wearing the laryngograph electrodes). Optionally, the ELG can be used for remediating severe speech quality problems. So, if we compare the latest version with the previous ones, we may conclude that it has greatly improved in reliability, flexibility, user-friendliness, compactness, and price-performance ratio.

The hardware of the current version of the Visual Speech Apparatus (VSA v3.0) consists of the following components: 2 microphones (Shure SM10A), a software-controlled Signal Interface System (SIS v3.0), a digital signal-processing board (Ariel, PC-C25) and an Amiga-2000 extended with a PC-XT board, a 40 MByte harddisk, 2Mbyte internal Ram (optional), and an extra 3.5" diskdrive. As both the Signal Interface System and the Digital Signal Processor are housed inside the Amiga, the complete system is quite compact. All components of the system, except the signal-interface, are commercially available.

Since all components, except for the SIS, are general purpose systems, once the hardware system has been assembled, the design activity is mainly concerned with software development. But since the processors used are highly complicated systems (this applies to the DSP as well as to the Amiga with its multi-processor system), this is not really less difficult than developing special purpose hardware, especially since programming has to be done in rather low level languages in order to assure the necessary speed. Indeed, in the project thousands of hours have been spent to develop software programs for controlling the different processors in the system. The main problems that had to be solved were related to the combined requirements of real-time display and attractive animations on the one hand, and the mutual communication between the different processors on the other. Table 2 presents an overview of the main tasks performed by the different processors in the system.

A more detailed functional description of the system, including its operation and the implemented exercises for voice and speech training can be found in Povel & Arends (1991).

Table 2. Main functions performed by the different processors in the VSA v3.0
*SIS=Signal Interface System

Part	DSP	PC-XT	Amiga
Processor	TMS320C25	8088	MC-68000
Language	Assembler	C	C, assembler
Functions	sampling pitch extraction energy comp. FFT Vowel space Vowel quality	control DSP data transfer data transform	exercises user-interfaces SIS* control administration

Discussion

We conclude by stating that thanks to the impressive developments in computer technology we have been able to construct a basic speech training aid that has many of the properties considered prerequisites for a viable visual aid. VSA v3.0 is a low-cost, compact, easy-operable, user-friendly, flexible device that trains basic speech skills in a didactic way using attractive game-like exercises. It is built in a way that allows future extensions in all directions that we can now foresee.

During the school year 1989-1990, the practical efficacy of the device has been evaluated in a study in which the performance of 22 deaf children from the Instituut voor Doven who practised daily for 15 minutes with the VSA, was compared to the performance of children in a control group that had the same amount of daily training, but without the VSA. This evaluation, described in Arends, Povel, van Os, Michielsen, Claassen, & Feiter (1991) clearly indicates that the VSA, apart from increasing the motivation of both pupils and teachers, speeds up the acquisition of the trained basic speech skills significantly.

Some final remarks are in order concerning the direction of future developments of visual aids for speech training. Future projects will not be hampered by the technological hardware limitations as our project was and for that matter all similar projects in the past. Therefore, in future projects attention can be focussed on the central problems related to visually displaying speech for training purposes. Future aids could thus aim at displaying speech in a more complete way. Complete in the sense of providing information about more aspects at the same time (in multidimensional visual displays), as well as in the sense of providing information about longer stretches of (running) speech.

To develop such aids two very different types of problems have to be solved. One is related to the question of how to extract the pertinent information from running speech. The other pertains to the question of how to display this information visually in a way which is understandable to the average user, who has a very limited understanding of the phonetic aspects of speech. With regard to the latter point, answers have to be found to suitable ways of presenting information that varies simultaneously in different dimensions, for presenting visual information that changes very rapidly over time (given the limited temporal resolution of the eye) and for showing and explaining to the pupil what visual information corresponds to which aspect of a speech gesture that is part of a series of speech gestures.

Given the baffling complexity of these problems, we do not expect future developments to proceed much faster than they have in the past.

Acknowledgments

This project was funded by the Instituut voor Doven and co-funded by the Praeventiefonds.

References

Arends, N., Povel, D.J., Os, E. van, & Speth, L. (1990). Predicting voice quality of deaf speakers on the basis of glottal characteristics. *Journal of Speech and Hearing Research, 33,* 116-122.

Arends, N., Povel, D.J., Os, E. van, Michielsen, S., Claassen, J., & Feiter, I. (1991). An Evaluation of the Visual Speech Apparatus. *Speech Communication, 10,* 405-414.

Groenen, P. (1989). *Dimensionele reductie van klinkerspectra.* Internal Report, Department of Psychology, Nijmegen.

Povel, D.J. (1987). Enkele theoretische overwegingen bij de ontwikkeling van visuele hulpmiddelen ten behoeve van het spreekonderricht aan dove kinderen. *Tijdschrift voor Logopedie en Audiologie, 17,* 105-129.

Povel, D.J., & Arends, N. (1991). The Visual Speech Apparatus: Theoretical and practical aspects. *Speech Communication, 10,* 59-80.

Povel, D.J., & Maassen, B. (1987). Visual information and speech acquisition of the deaf. *Proceedings of the 11th International Conference of Phonetic Sciences, Vol. I.,* 373-376.

Reetz, H. (1989). A fast expert program for pitch extraction. *Proceedings European Speech Technology, Paris, Vol. I,* 476-479.

Veenendaal, M. (1989). *Parallel processing capacity for combined visual dimensions in the Visual Speech Apparatus.* Internal Report, Department of Psychology, Nijmegen.

Zahorian, S.A., & Jagharghi, A.J. (1988). *Transformations from 'physical' to 'perceptual' spaces.* Manuscript

Sprach - Farbbild - Transformation (SFT) - the Conversion of Sound to Coloured Light as a Visual Aid in Speech Therapy

Peter Nolte, Renate Printzen, and Günter Esser
Research Laboratory for Medical Acoustics and Audiology at the University Clinic of Düsseldorf, Moorenstraße 5, 40225 Düsseldorf, Germany

Abstract. The Sprach-Farbbild-Transformation (SFT) attempts to provide support via the visual sensory channel for the auditory function of the defective ear of those with hearing defects. SFT synchronously transforms spoken language into coloured curves on a screen to use feedback processing by the visual sensory channel. Various research projects consist of speech therapy and evaluation techniques (i.e. Klangvektor-Analyse).

Keywords. Transformation of speech to colour - Feedback-processes - Speech therapy - Klang-Vektor-Analyse

The Conversion of Sound to Coloured Light

The SFT - Concept

The technical aid SFT (Sprach-Farbbild-Transformation, i.e. speech to coloured light transformation) attempts to provide support via the visual sensory channel for the auditory functions of the defective ear of those with hearing defects. This concept is based on the principle of sensory interchangeability (Sinnesvikariat; Breiner, 1982), which is enabled by the cognitive performances within the neuronal net (intermodale Synthese; Hajos, 1980, - intersensorische Integration; Ayres, 1979). According to this principle, the visual sensory system is used to support the perception and monitoring of spoken language - subject to the application of residual auditory facilities. In order to achieve this, those auditory stimulants which are lacking must be transformed in such a way that they can also be perceived via the non-acoustic, visual sensory channel.

Description and Possible Working Applications of the SFT Aid

The SFT basic model consists of a computer equipped with a disk drive, a screen, a keyboard and two microphones. Spoken sounds, words or sentences are represented on the screen in the form of envelope curves blocked in with colour. In order to make the techniques understood, the listening procedure must be explained: the basilar membrane of the inner ear is a frequency filter with rather flat leading edges. If the human being would "listen" with only one ear he would only be able to distinguish between sounds which are separated by one octave minimum. This corresponds to a frequency difference threshold of 100 percent. Contrary to this, our frequency difference threshold is approx. 3,5 permille. This incredible contrast intensification of 100 percent to 3,5 permille is enabled by the brain, i.e. by the focal area of the central audible path within the brain, to be more precise. The "switching mechanism" which causes this contrast intensification is called the "laterale Hemmung". In adaptation to the listening procedure, SFT operates with a very flat filtering as well. Further processing is left to the brain, in this special case, however, to the focal areas of the central visual path within the brain which is also organized according to the principle of "laterale Hemmung". Since television composes all colours out of the components red, green, and blue, three filters are needed. The passbands are shaped as triangles. This enables a three-dimensional vector containing the components red, green, and blue to be allocated to any acoustic frequency. Thus, a certain colour range is uniquely assigned to each acoustic range.

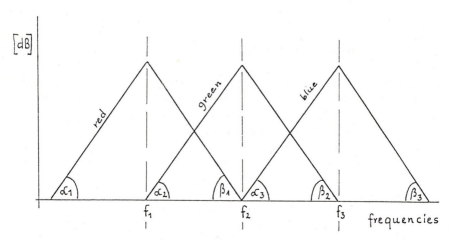

Figure 1.

Figure 1 shows the schematic passband curves of the three filters with allocated colours. The output signals of the low frequency filters (up to 500 Hz) contribute the red components to each SFT image, the output signals of the middle frequency filter (500 Hz - 1000 Hz) the green components, and the output signals of the high frequency filters (above 1000 Hz) the blue components. The three medium frequencies of the passbands which are identified in Figure 1 by f1 - f3, are variable: variable as well is the declivity of the signal edges, which are identified in Figure 1 by the angles a1 - a3 as well as b1 - b3. The parameters have been selected in such a way that the differences in sound which are important when working with hard of hearing or deaf people are clearly recognizable in the SFT image. Graphic representation is achieved by displaying time on the x-axis synchronously with amplitude on the y-axis. The height of the amplitude corresponds to the level of sound intensity. A special problem occurs with the handling of the basic sound. Within the basic sound area, the peak of the deeply frequenced triangle filter is practically truncated. This will cause each basic sound within the range of 100 Hz to 300 Hz to contribute approximately the same share of red to the total colour. Thus, also teachers with deep voices are enabled to train the children in front of the screen. The monitor displays simple and straight forward forms which are easily assimilated and retained by the short-term visual memory (Esser, Nolte & Printzen, 1983).

When switched on, the monitor displays two "tracks": the upper is the "teacher's track", the lower a "learner's track". Both tracks can be independently discussed, fixed, erased, labelled, duplicated, saved on disk, and altered at working speed.

A Visual Aid

The Transformation of Speech

The perception of the segmental properties of speech and their permissible range of variation is a prerequisite for the encoding and decoding of speech. It is, however, not sufficient to identify and reproduce a complex linguistic structure. Speech is perceived as an entity and a transformation of speech must represent the spoken language as a "phonic continuum" (Ternes, 1987). Linguistic comprehension depends to a great extent on an uninterrupted flow of speech. The proximity of phonemes in a phonic string engenders a motorial linkage in the process of which the phonemes involved are subjected to a physiologically conditioned and reciprocal influence. This dynamic process is recorded during transformation in a visually perceptible form in the guise of a changed colour spectrum.

Figure 2 shows some examples of SFT-processed speech.

By way of the suprasegmental (prosodic) components (such as lengthening, rhythmitisation, stress by volume or overlapping intonation patterns) significant contents can be characterised and longer speech acts can be ordered. This property of the acoustic signal as a "multi-dimensional signal" is exploited by SFT's technical capabilities; its adjustable recording speed, for example, makes it possible to fix speech units of different lengths.

The combination of colour, curve and variable recording speeds enables SFT to transfer those properties of a speech continuum which have combined effects to a visually perceptible form of symbolisation.

Information Processing

The principle on which SFT rests requires an examination of information processing:

Feedback - Processes. A listener perceives and processes speech signals primarily via the acoustic channel; in the case of hearing defects, the acoustic channel is impaired. As a result, the person suffering from a hearing defect is impaired in the acoustic perception of signals, in the production of signals and in the monitoring of signals produced by herself/himself. The transformation of the acoustic signals into a visually perceptible signal by means of SFT is intended to close the feedback circuit via the intact visual sensory channel. The listener receives a visually perceptible signal rather than an acoustically perceptible signal. The processing of the optical linguistic signal is entrusted to the brain, in this case, however, to the core areas of the central visual channel where it can be related to linguistic contents.

Neuronal Development of Cognitive Processes. The visual sensory system is stimulated by the provision of transformed, visually perceptible linguistic signs. Visual stimulants are provided in place of the lacking acoustic impressions. Cognitive processing leads via storage processes occuring by means of the generation and decomposition of codes to unique "space-time patterns" (engrammes) in the long-term memory. By way of the brain's capacity for "intermodal synthesis", these engrammes are linked to new patterns via neuronal processes. These can serve as a knowledge base for language acquisition and comprehension. An activation of these patterns implies a recall of the stored information. The presumptions in regard to the influence of the SFT on the information processings are backed-up by the recognitions of the information theory (Erkenntnisse der Informationstheorie /Meyer-Eppler, 1969), the learning and development theory/cognitive psychology (Lern- und Entwicklungs-

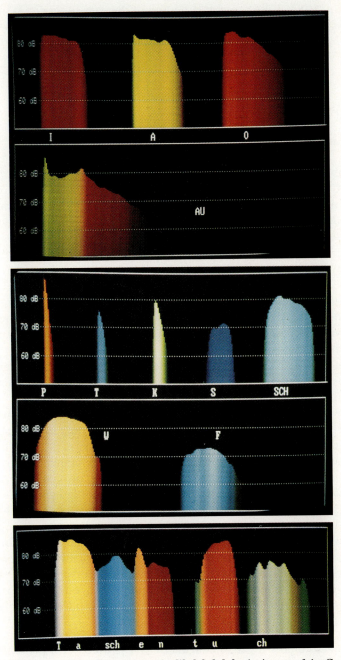

Figure 2. a. The image of the German vowels: [i], [a], [o], **b.** the image of the German diphthong: [au], **c.** the voiceless consonants of the German language, **d.** the voiced consonants of the German language, **e.** the German word "Taschentuch" [taʃntux].

theorie/kogn. Psychologie; Beatty, 1975; Vester, 1975; Piaget, 1982; Szagun, 1983, 1986), and the creation of theories of artificial intelligence (Theorienbildung der Künstlichen Intelligenz; Engelkamp, 1984; Klix, 1986; Anderson, 1988).

In Speech Therapy

Research Projects (1979 - 1991)

The research works on SFT (1979 - 1987) have financially be supported by the Ministry of Science and Research in North Rhine-Westphalia. Since 1989 the research project is financially supported by the Federal Ministry of Labour and Social Affairs. Systematic research results are available for the use of the SFT-system.

The results of several research work on SFT with hard of hearing and prelingual deaf young adults (aged 16-24) and school children (aged 6-16) can be summarised as follows:

- A substantial improvement in articulation is achieved with screen control within a matter of only a few minutes, i.e. switching from the impaired auditory feedback channel to the visual feedback channel is accomplished rapidly.
  However, as soon as the visual control is removed, speech again deteriorates immediately, i.e. the improvement in articulation has not been definitively stored as an engramme.
- The first improvement in spontaneous articulation is perceptible after a period of between 4 to 6 weeks though initially only in the test situation, i.e. if the test words are read out and the test person is aware that her/his speech is being recorded on magnetic tape. Spontaneous articulation in free speech remains poor initially. This finding provides support for the view that although the improved speech patterns have been stored as engrammes, they can only be activated at the cost of great concentration on the part of the test person.
- A clearly appreciable improvement in spontaneous speech in free conversation is noted after a period of approximately one year. This is particularly noticeable in the case of those test persons whose speech had been incomprehensible prior to their embarking on the course of articulatory exercise but which was easily understood after one year even though the speech itself sounded unnatural.

Whether and how the technical aid of SFT is used in the preschool speech training of deaf and hard of hearing children depends on the correspondence of its transformation potential with the perceptual and cognitive abilities of the child concerned. The outcome of these studies with preschool children and an evaluation of the literature speak in favour of the use of SFT as a multi-sensorial feedback technique in the preschool training of children with hearing defects, but also indicate the necessity of developing a methodology which is adapted to age and development stages and to its integration within a holistic, interactive preschool programme of support (Esser, Nolte, Printzen, 1983; Esser, Nolte, Printzen, 1984; Printzen, 1991).

Since 1989, a research project has been dealing with young people suffering from impaired hearing or deafness and who are preparing to enter professional training. An enhancement of articulation and prosody and an extension of job-related vocabulary constitutes the objective to be achieved with the aid of SFT in accordance with a concept developed for adult education (Figure 3). The intention is to facilitate the integration of these young people into professional life and to enable them to pursue employment in a qualified position.

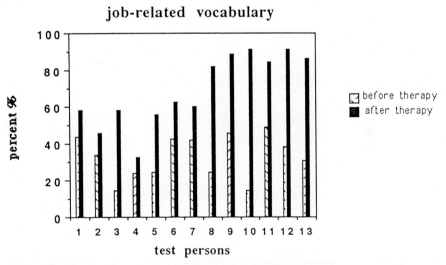

Figure 3. The increase of job-related vocabulary after therapy.

Various evaluation techniques have been developed for the SFT research projects in order to be able to measure articulation and sound formation qualitatively (Dickenbrock, 1984) and quantitatively.

Evaluation Procedure: Speech Intelligibility Test (according to Dickenbrock). The speech intelligibility test is a transformed listening comprehension test in which a test person with normal hearing reproduces that which the test person with impaired hearing has recorded on magnetic tape. The number of words understood completely with an amplification of

45dB - 75dB was evaluated in percentage terms. The values were recorded in a coordinate system. In order to provide orientation, a normal curve (i.e. a test which had been spoken by persons with normal hearing) was inserted into the coordinate system (Figure 4).

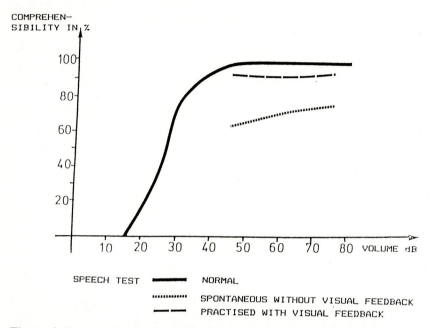

Figure 4. An example for the qualitative evaluation procedure according to Dickenbrock.

In the case of the evaluation of the speech recordings of this test person, an improvement of articulation with visual feedback versus spontaneous articulation without visual feedback is registered with all participants.

Evaluation Procedure: Klang-Vektor-Analyse (according to Esser). An objective evaluation procedure is desirable when appraising the success of speech therapy. In the current research project, an evaluation system is being developed and tested which carries out a sound vector analysis in order to produce an objective evaluation of articulation. An acoustic spectrum is characterised by a three-dimensional vector. The basis is provided by the filtering technique learned in the SFT. By means of this filtering technique, each acoustic frequency is unambiguously associated with a certain colour combination of *red, green*, and *blue* according to the frequencies (as mentioned earlier on). These three components can be arranged in a coordinate system. There results a three-dimensional vector for each sound with the components *red, green, blue*.

As a spectrum of a sound is comprised of individual tones, a sum vector is generated by vectorial addition of individual tones. This represents the sound. It provides a quantitative measure of the sound and is designated as "Klang-Vektor-Analyse".

The SFT computer is capable of measuring the three components of the sum vector directly, for instance the sound [a] in the German word "Maß" (Figure 5).

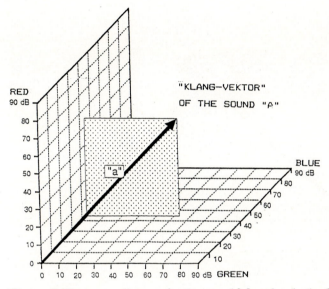

Figure 5. The vector diagram for the vowel [a] spoken in the German word "Maß".

This vector is not representative for every [a], but only for the [a] in this word as spoken by a certain speaker. Intraindividual divergences arise partly as a result of co-articulation or as a result of differing pronounciations of a phoneme even when it is in the same phonemic environment. Intraindividual differences arise from the voice register and from the anatomical relations of the articulatory organs.

The articulation of a sound can be defined by two values in vectorial representation:

- by the length of the vector (the measure of volume) and
- by the direction of the vector (the measure of the spectrum, i.e. of the sound).

In order to determine the success of therapy for articulation, a standard vector is initially required for each sound (this involves 16 vowels and 20 consonants for the German language). Standard vectors can be produced on the basis of the pronounciation of the test words by a normal speaker. The angle between the sound vector of the normal speaker and the sound vector of the test person is a measure for each sound of the acoustic divergence from the articulation of the normal speaker.

The following figure shows the "Klang-Vektor" of the German consonant [k] spoken by a male test person prior to therapy and after therapy. The figure also shows the "Klang-Vektor" of the German consonant [k] spoken by a normal speaker (Figure 6).

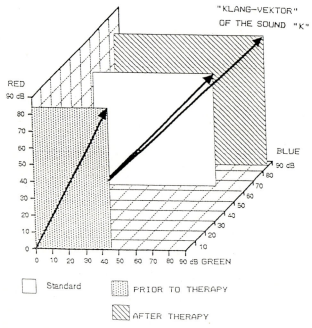

Figure 6. The vector diagram for the consonant [k].

This vector is not representative for every [k], but only for the [k] spoken by this particular speaker. It shows very cleary the change of articulation. Prior to therapy the high frequencies were largely lacking (blue components), the [k] is now somewhat over articulated - the vector is longer as the standard vector - an effect which in the case of the consonants is initially desired and which in the course of time tends to dissipate again. On completion of therapy, the direction of the test person's vector has also drawn closer to that of the standard. Thus, the test person's [k] sounds very similar to the [k] of the normal speaker.

The Central Associations of the German Health Insurance Funds (Krankenkassen) decided on November 5, 1986, to recognise the SFT (version III) subject to certain prerequisites as a therapeutic device within the framework of speech therapy (182 section1 No1 , letter b RVO in conjunction with 10 No3 RehaAng.IG).

Sprach-Farbbild-Transformation (SFT) is used in schools for the deaf and the hard of hearing pupils in speech training.

References

Anderson, J.R. (1988). *Kognitive Psychologie: Eine Einführung*. Spektrum, Heidelberg.
Ayres, A.J. (1979). *Lernstörungen - sensorisch-integrative Dysfunktion*. Springer Verlag, Berlin.
Beatty, J. (1975). *Introduction to physiological psychology*. Brooks/Cole Pub. Co., Monterey, California
Breiner, H. (1982). Erarbeitung der äußeren Seite der Sprache und kommunikative Hilfsmittel. In: H. Jussen, O. Kröhnert (eds), *Handbuch der Sonderpädagogik, Bd. 3 (Pädagogik der Gehörlosen und Schwerhörigen)*. Carl Marhold Verlagsbuchhandlung, Berlin.
Dickenbrock, H. (1984). *Spontane Artikulationsverbesserung unter Sichtkontrolle bei der Sprach-Farbbild-Transformation - Vergleich zweier Meßverfahren*. Dissertation Universität Düsseldorf.
Engelkamp, J. (ed.) (1984). *Psychologische Aspekte des Verstehens*. Springer Verlag, Berlin.
Esser, G., Nolte, P. & Printzen, R. (1983). *Sprach-Farbbild-Transformation (SFT) - Erweiterte Möglichkeiten beim Sprachunterricht Hörgeschädigter*. Tagungsbericht Bund deutscher Taubstummenlehrer, Arbeitstagung für Hörerziehung, Burg Feuerstein.
Esser, G., Nolte, P. & Printzen, R. (1984a). Verbesserung der Sprachentwicklung und der Artikulation durch visuelle Übermittlung von Sprache. *Biesalski - Pädaudiologie aktuell,* Universitätsverlag Dr. H. Krach, Mainz.
Esser, G., Nolte, P. & Printzen, R. (1984b). Sprachtherapie durch Sprach-Farbbild-Transformation (SFT). *Mortier - Moderne Diagnostik und Therapie bei Kindern*, Grosse-Verlag, Berlin.
Esser, G. (1987). Sprach-Farbbild-Transformation (SFT). In: K.R. Fellbaum (ed.) - *Elektronische Kommunikationshilfen*. Weidler Verlag, Berlin.
Hajos, A. (1980). *Einführung in die Wahrnehmungspsychologie*. Darmstadt.
Klix, F. (1986). Über die Nachbildungen von Denkanforderungen, die Wahrnehmungseigenschaften, Gedächtnisstruktur und Entscheidungsoperationen einschließen. In: K. Daumelang & J. Sauer (eds), *Aspekte psychologischer Forschung* - Festschrift zum 60. Geburtstag von Erwin Roth, Verlag für Psychologie Hogrefe, Göttingen, Toronto, Zürich.
Meyer-Eppler, W. (1969). *Grundlagen und Anwendungen der Informationstheorie*. Springer Verlag, Berlin.

Neblung, N. (1984). *Ermittlung spektraler Unterschiede in der Sprache Gehörloser, Schwerhöriger und Normalhörender zur Festlegung optimaler Filterparameter bei der Sprach-Farbbild-Transformation (SFT)*. Dissertation Universität Düsseldorf.

Nolte, P. (1986). SFT - Sprach-Farbbild-Transformation. *Zeitschrift für Sonderschulpädagogik des Verbandes Deutscher Sonderschulen e.V., Heft 1*.

Nolte, P. & Printzen, R. (1983). Sprach-Farbbild-Transformation (SFT) - erweiterte Möglichkeiten beim Sprachunterricht bei Hörgeschädigten. *Hörgeschädigte Kinder, Heft 4*.

Piaget, J. (1982). *Sprechen und Denken des Kindes*. Päd. Verlag Schwann, Düsseldorf.

Printzen, R. (1991). *Die Sprach-Farbbild-Transformation in der kommunikativen Erziehung hörgeschädigter Vorschulkinder*. P. Lang-Verlag, Frankfurt.

Schweter, G. (1990). *Vorläufige Normalwerte für die Komponentenvektoren der Konsonanten der deutschen Sprache bei der SFT*. Dissertation Universität Düsseldorf.

Szagun, G. (1983). *Bedeutungsentwicklung beim Kind*. Urban und Schwarzenberg, München, Wien, Baltimore.

Szagun, G. (1986). *Sprachentwicklung beim Kind*. Urban und Schwarzenberg, München, Wien, Baltimore.

Ternes, E. (1987). *Einführung in die Phonologie*. Wiss. Buchgesellschaft, Darmstadt.

Vester, F. (1975). *Denken, Lernen, Vergessen*. Dt. Vlgs.-Anstalt, Stuttgart.

Wolter, R. (1987). *Auswertung der Sprachverbesserung nach SFT-Intensiv-Therapie bei einem gehörlosen Erwachsenen durch eine dreidimensionale Vektoranalyse*. Dissertation Universität Düsseldorf.

The Development and Application of the IBM SpeechViewer

Francis Destombes
IBM France CESMAP (8/3580)
75592 Paris Cédex 12, France

Abstract. SpeechViewer is an IBM product (both hardware and software) which provides visual and auditory feedback on voice and speech parameters. It is a tool to help speech therapists in the reeducation of speech and/or hearing impaired patients, and provides feedback either as graphs or colorful games. The paper describes briefly the history and evolution of the prototypes which preceded SpeechViewer, provides technical details on its design and implementation, gives examples drawn from its actual use in speech therapy for deaf patients in various countries, and concludes with a short description of its successor, SpeechViewer II.

Keywords. Speech therapy, deafness, voice disorders, communication disorders, speech processing, visual feedback, auditory feedback

Some History

SpeechViewer is a commercially available product derived from a long series of prototypes designed and built at the IBM France Scientific Center in Paris. The "Deaf Children project" at this centre was started in 1978 to explore how speech processing techniques could be used to help the deaf, particularly in the area of speech therapy.

SpeechViewer is one result of this project, and offers a speech therapy tool based essentially on visual and auditory feedback. This, in itself, is of course not original: visual feedback has been used for many years in speech therapy, and has been the basis for many research efforts, such as Risberg (1968), Nickerson & Stevens (1973), Crichton & Fallside (1974), Haton, Haton & Lamotte (1974), Barth (1975), Haton & Haton (1979)...; such citation is necessarily incomplete, because of the many teams which worked on this subject, but one should not forget the visible speech cathode ray tube of Riesz & Schott (1946), nor the work of Mrs. Borel-Maisonny using an oscilloscope... back in the 30's and 40's (no reference available).

Since the beginning, the research project emphasized on building and experimenting prototypes in a real life environment. The first prototype was installed at the National Institute for Young Deaf Children in Paris (INJS: Institut National de Jeunes Sourds) at the end of 1979, and was experimented by a teacher at this institute.

This first prototype was based on a System Design Kit for the Intel (TM) 8086 microprocessor (SDK86), to which home-made interfaces for speech input and graphics output were added. Speech input was on 12-bits at 10 kHz, and the graphics interface allowed displaying a 256x256 black-and-white image on a TV set. The program was kept in a ROM, and the user interface was the 16-key hexadecimal keyboard of the SDK86.

This prototype already exhibited characteristics which were carried through all further follow-up prototypes and into SpeechViewer itself. Apart from the antialiasing filter and analog to digital conversion chip, the system was entirely digital: all necessary processing, such as pitch detection, graph display, game animation, was performed entirely by software. It is probable that this prototype was in fact the first speech therapy tool entirely based on digital processing. By using a software implementation from the very beginning, it was possible, throughout the project, to build successive prototypes mostly by software modifications, based on the remarks of the users (teachers of the deaf, speech therapists).

In addition to graphs of pitch and intensity versus time, the system offered some voice-activated games: a camel was guided by pitch variations through the desert, trying to dodge palm trees and reach water ponds; a duck was guided in the same manner through wolves towards worms. This early emphasis on making the system attractive to the patients by using game representations of speech parameters, in addition to more technical graphical displays, was also carried and increased through future developments, and explains to a large extent why patients find it so pleasant to work with SpeechViewer.

Two copies of this early prototype were built, one for development, one for experimentation at INJS. Based on the remarks of the users, more elaborate prototypes were then designed and built, still using Intel microprocessors as a base.

This initial choice proved to be a lucky one when the IBM Personal Computer was announced in 1981, since it was also based on an Intel 8088 and readily offered a compatible base for a new prototype line. It also allowed expanding the user base considerably: the French project had attracted the attention of other national IBM companies, which wanted to carry similar experimentation within institutes for the deaf in their countries.

In order to make replication of prototypes easier, the project then started designing a speech processing board for the PC, using an Intel 80186; a hundred such boards were built by the IBM France plant in Bordeaux, and shipped to IBM companies throughout the world.

At the end of 1986, the project decided to use a more powerful speech processing board, based on an IBM product developed in Austin, Texas, using a Texas Instruments® TMS32010 digital signal processor. By modifying this board and programming it to extract acoustical speech parameters in real time, a new line of prototypes was initiated, which was installed on PC's in 29 countries.

This considerably increased the number of users for the prototype, particularly in the USA, where test sites provided valuable information which was eventually used as requirements for a product.

Finally, towards the end of 1987, we were contacted by the Special Needs Systems group (SNS) in IBM Boca Raton, Florida, which had started to develop products for handicapped people, or more generally, persons with special needs. This group used the prototype system from the Paris Scientific Center as a base for the development of SpeechViewer, which was announced in the US and Canada in November 1988, and in Europe in March 1989. This was an important step in the life of this project, since SNS not only made SpeechViewer available to many more people than could be done with prototypes, but also added important features such as file management, which was lacking in the earlier systems.

Design and Implementation

The hardware and software of SpeechViewer, and the nature of the computations performed, were selected as a compromise between performance and cost. The goal was *not* to provide a full general purpose speech laboratory, with many advanced analysis functions, a wide frequency range and complex graphical representations. Rather, it was necessary, using the technology available at that time, to define a system providing a useful assistance to speech therapists and patients, with an emphasis on the ease of use for people who had little or no experience in data processing.

Cost was also a design criterion, since potential users, whether institutes for the deaf or private practitioners, were not likely to be able to spend large sums over a complex system of which they might use only a small part. This is why the hardware selected has a frequency range which is convenient for vowels, but not for consonants. A higher frequency range would have meant a higher sampling frequency, a faster DSP chip (Digital Signal Processor), and would have increased the cost beyond what was then considered acceptable by most users.

Experimentation of the early prototypes in real life situations had allowed to gather many observations, criticism and suggestions from users. Those were used to influence the design of application modules, trying to make them as easy to use as possible, with standardized function keys, on-line help screens, etc. System messages are kept in external files rather than embedded in the application code, thus allowing many national versions to be produced easily. At mid-1991 more than 18 different national versions of SpeechViewer existed, including most European languages as well as Hebrew, Arabic and Russian.

Product Description

SpeechViewer consists of two elements:

- SpeechViewer hardware: a microphone, a loudspeaker and a SpeechViewer adapter (a speech processing board, AT-bus format)
- SpeechViewer software: two 3.5 inch diskettes with the software, and a user manual.

This combination of hardware and software is designed to work on an IBM PS/2 (TM) model 30 or 30-286, i.e. a computer with an AT-bus architecture, 640K bytes of main memory, and a MCGA or VGA screen. A graphics printer is optional, and allows printouts of graphs.

General Organization

SpeechViewer is actually a multiprocessor system, since two programs are concurrently active to perform cooperative tasks on two processors: an acoustic coprogram running on the SpeechViewer adapter, and an application module running on the host system.

The main module of SpeechViewer offers a menu to select individual application modules, which in turn communicate with the coprogram to perform the required tasks.

Application modules are presented in three groups:

- awareness modules, which offer a quick and colorful representation of basic speech parameters
- skill building modules, which ask the patient to work towards a goal set by the speech therapist
- patterning modules, offering graphical representation of the patient's and therapist's voices for comparison.

Coprogram

The coprogram uses the TMS32010 DSP of the adapter to perform the following functions:

- speech input, with an antialiasing filter at 3.8 kHz, 12-bit samples including sign, 9.6 kHz sampling rate
- speech output with the same characteristics
- speech processing to perform real time computation of the following parameters 75 times per second, i.e. for fixed-length, non overlapping frames of 128 samples:
    - signal amplitude
    - intensity
    - pitch period
    - zero crossings count for the original and differentiated signal
    - 12 normalized autocorrelation coefficients (obtained after differentiation and Hamming multiplication of the samples in a frame).

Further computations such as LPC analysis (Linear Predictive Coding) are performed by the host program based on the autocorrelation coefficients provided by the coprogram.

Awareness Modules

Those modules are simple and colourful games centered on one or two speech parameters:

- A kaleidoscope moves when sound amplitude is greater than a given level. The level can be adjusted by the therapist to force the patient to speak louder.
- A red balloon inflates according to voice intensity.
- A "thermometer" shows pitch frequency for voiced sounds, and allows finding the maximum and minimum frequency for an utterance.
- A train moves on tracks each time a voiced sound is started; the movement does not continue while the sound is produced, this module is meant to show the voicing onset, rather than the continuation of voicing.
- Finally, a clown's face shows a mouth which grows larger with sound amplitude, while red dots appear on the bow-tie for voiced sounds (of course, in real life, voice loudness has no effect on mouth shape or size; but it was necessary to have a simple graphical relationship between loudness and an object on the screen, and it was more natural to let the mouth grow rather than the nose or eyes, for example. The patients did not complain about this representation -nor about the even more bizarre change of colors on the bow-tie-, but quite a few deaf children pointed out

an oversight in the picture: the symbolized clown face had no ears... an error which was corrected in the follow-on product, SpeechViewer II).

Awareness modules are very simple to operate and provide an easy introduction to SpeechViewer, both for the therapist and the patients. Most can be used with very young patients, such as two-year old deaf children.

Skill Building Modules

Although still based on games, those modules are more demanding than the previous ones, since the patient must reach a goal set by the speech therapist. Two of the modules provide feedback on pitch and voicing, the other two focus on vowel articulation.

- A camel moves through the desert to reach lakes while dodging palm trees; its ordinate on the screen is proportional to pitch frequency, its movement continues as long as voicing is sustained.
- A hot-air balloon flies over mountains as long as voicing is sustained. The profile of the mountains (length, separation) is drawn by the speech therapist.
- A monkey climbs a palm tree to reach a coconut, according to the spectral distance between the sound pronounced and a vowel model.
- A mobile moves in a maze according to the vowel pronounced; four vowel models are attached to each of the four movement directions.

Patterning Modules

Those modules present a graphical representation of speech parameters.

- The pitch and loudness module shows amplitude and voicing versus time (red or green is used to show voiced and unvoiced segments), but also allows showing a pitch graph. The screen is divided in two parts, one normally for the speech therapist to show an example, the other for replication by the patient.
- The waveform module shows and amplitude graph, and allows viewing the waveform of a segment delimited by cursors.
- The spectrum module shows a frequency spectrum obtained by linear predictive coding. Computation is performed by the host system based on the autocorrelation coefficients delivered by the SpeechViewer adapter. It is therefore not truly real-time, but is refreshed often enough to appear as real-time for the users.

Both the pitch/loudness and waveform modules allow the user to save or retrieve sentences from disk. This facility therefore permits saving a given sentence pronounced by a patient at different stages of his reeducation, so that the speech therapist may listen to those sentences later on and judge the progress or lack of progress made by the patient. Statistics on pitch frequency (mean and standard deviation) are provided to help in such comparisons.

Customizing SpeechViewer

SpeechViewer contains many parameters which can be customized by the speech therapist to fit a specific patient. For example, the pitch range can be adjusted for games and graphs as well, game layouts may be altered, etc.

More important, the vowel models used in articulation games can be gathered individually, using a simple model setup module. This module prompts the user to pronounce each of the different vowels in a given language, and asks the therapist to accept or refuse each utterance. The therapist can therefore capture the best productions of a patient, and use them as reference models for practice with the articulation games. Later on, when the patient has improved his articulation thanks to speech therapy, old models can be discarded, and new models gathered, to better reflect the patient's ability.

Using SpeechViewer with Deaf Patients

SpeechViewer has been used by speech therapists with patients suffering from a variety of disorders: deafness, cerebral palsy, dysphonia, dysarthria, stuttering, head trauma, and even with trisomic children and, in one case, with an autistic child.

To concentrate here on the subject of deafness, speech therapists who use SpeechViewer with deaf patients are unanimous in reporting an increase in the motivation and interest of their patients. This is due to the colourful and animated exercises offered by the system, as well as to the variety of displays which help keeping system use from becoming boring. In some cases, for example, deaf teenagers who had completely abandoned speech therapy sessions came back to them because of SpeechViewer. One must also note that SpeechViewer helps to preserve the quality of the voice of very young deaf children, which is often good.

On a different level, many therapists also report that patients prefer discovering their speech errors directly on the screen, by themselves, rather than being told by the therapist without any objective "proof". Contrary to what some people might fear, the system does not impact the relationship by introducing a "third party" in the patient-therapist relationship, it improves this relationship and reinforces the quality of the reeducation work.

SpeechViewer's graphs offer a representation of speech parameters which is easy to understand even for young patients, with help from the therapist. They allow clear distinction of voiced/voiceless segments, show differences for sounds which look alike on the lips, such as /p-b-m/ or /t-d-n/, show a clear indication of rhythm and timing. Auditory feedback is useful for patients who have some residual hearing, and is even used in some cases for auditory training: one may record sounds such as a door closing, a dog barking, etc, and ask the patient to discriminate them without looking at the screen.

In some cases, in spite of the limited frequency band used by SpeechViewer, some contrasts between fricative consonants can be clearly seen on graphs, such as the opposition between /s/ and /sh/ (Maulet, 1990).

In languages where contrast between long and short vowels or consonants is important, graphs also bring useful information to the patient (Öster, 1989).

SpeechViewer in itself does not teach how to produce speech sounds, nor does it attempt to present mouth cross sections or similar diagrams; the teaching task is clearly that of the speech therapist, SpeechViewer acts only as a tool which helps the therapist explain more precisely which exercise he requests from the patient, offers visual and auditory feedback to allow the patient to check for himself how well he performed, and tries to do so in a stimulating and playful way. The system's interactivity allows the therapist and the patient to check immediately how well an exercise was performed, thus reinforcing the advice given by the therapist.

And now, SpeechViewer II...

SpeechViewer and the prototypes which preceded it were the subject of studies in different countries. In particular, reports were made by four US centers (Duke University, Durham, NC; Jackson Mann School, Boston, MA; Lexington School for the Deaf, New York City, NY; Saint Francis Hospital, Poughkeepsie, NY) and published in a IBM brochure ("SpeechViewer, four case studies", number 6024936). In Europe, evaluations were also made at the National Hospitals College of Speech Sciences, London (Heath, 1991), as well as in Sweden (Öster, 1989) and France (Maulet, 1990).

Although those studies were overall positive and concluded to the usefulness of SpeechViewer and its prototypes, they also pointed out domains in which improvements could be made, an area in which much information also became available through informal contacts with private practitioners using the system: since its announcement in 1988, SpeechViewer was used by thousands of speech therapists in many countries, thus expanding very widely the user's base of the initial prototypes; those many new users were thus able to gain more practical experience and to judge what the system could or could not do to help speech therapy. Inevitably, this led to a list of new requirements, which guided the development of a follow-on system, SpeechViewer II, announced at the end of 1991 in the USA and Canada in its English version. Versions in other languages should become available in 1992 in most European countries.

The new features brought by SpeechViewer II over SpeechViewer 1.0 can be summarized briefly as follows:

- expanded frequency range (0-7.3 kHz)
- uses IBM M-Audio card (with TMS320C25 DSP)
- real-time grey scale spectrogram, with a 3D display option
- processing of stable consonants as well as vowels
- new phoneme recognition module to oppose two phonemes or practice a chain of up to four phonemes
- simple word recognition module
- improved graphics with a selection of formats for various age groups
- choice of dual headset microphones or single microphone as input
- user profile and data management facility to set user parameters and manage patient files
- data statistics gathering and reporting in most clinical modules
- low-speed speech playback while preserving pitch frequency
- ability to process and store longer sentences (up to 20 seconds)
- operation on a wider selection of machines, including the PS/1 and micro channel (TM) systems
- etc...

Speech therapists in many countries are now discovering with SpeechViewer and SpeechViewer II that technology can bring them and their patients a useful assistance in their daily practice, and that the system can fit perfectly in their reeducation project. It also helps them to better understand what technology can and cannot do, to express their needs and formulate new requirements for speech training systems, which may pave the way to improved systems in the future.

References

Barth, S. (1975). *Application des procédés de reconnaissance automatique de la parole à l'aide aux déficients auditifs profonds.* ENSP Thesis.

Crichton, R.G. & Fallside, F. (1974). *The development of a deaf speech training aid using linear prediction analysis.* Speech communication seminar, Stockholm, August 1974.

Haton, M.C., Haton, J.P. & Lamotte, M. (1975). Syrène, un système interactif pour la rééducation vocale des non entendants. In: *6th JEP proceedings, GALF,* Toulouse, May 1975.

Haton, M.C. & Haton, J.P. (1979). *SIRENE, a system for speech training of deaf people.* ICASSP 1979, Washington.

Heath, S. (1991). Viewing speech from a different angle. *Speech Therapy in Practice, January 1991.*

Maulet, M. (1990). *Using SpeechViewer with Profoundly Hearing-Impaired Patients.* European Voice Technology Seminar, National Hospitals College of Speech Sciences, London.

Nickerson, R.S. & Stevens, K.N. (1973). Teaching speech to the deaf: can a computer help? *IEEE transactions on Audio and Electroacoustics, AU-21,* 445-455.

Öster, A.M. (1989). *Applications and Experiences of Computer-Based Speech Training.* Quarterly Progress Status report 4, Department of Speech Communication and Music Acoustics, Royal Institute of Technology, Stockholm.

Riesz, R.R. & Schott, L. (1946). Visible speech cathode ray translator. *Journal of the Acoustical Society of America, 18,* 50-61.

Risberg, A. (1968). Visual aids for speech correction. *American Annals of the Deaf, 113,* 178-194.

Sign Language and Manual Communication

Multimedia Dictionary of American Sign Language

Sherman Wilcox[1] and William C. Stokoe[2]
[1]Department of Linguistics, University of New Mexico, Albuquerque, NM 87131, USA
[2]Linstok Press, Inc., 9306 Mintwood Street, Silver Spring, MD 20901, USA

Abstract. Writing is a technology which for many centuries has supported the construction of dictionaries of spoken languages. Recently, writing systems for signed languages have been created, making possible the development of signed language dictionaries. Print media have not been entirely successful in making signed language dictionaries accessible to large numbers of people. Application of current and emerging multimedia computer technology to the construction of signed language dictionaries is reviewed. One application currently under development, the *Multimedia Dictionary of American Sign Language*, is discussed.

Keywords. American Sign Language, deafness, dictionaries, writing, multimedia, computers.

Writing as Technology

Although modern historians of writing are reluctant to admit it, writing is an invention (Harris, 1986). The origins of writing are for the most part lost in prehistory. There is no doubting the fact, however, that writing has made a tremendous impact on civilization. In its turn, writing has spawned generations of technological offspring -writing instruments such as the stylus, papyrus, paper, and pen; the printing press; linotype; the typewriter; computers and keyboards; word processing; desktop publishing; electronic mail; fax.

One type of "application" which writing made possible was the dictionary, and with it the practice of lexicography. Dictionaries developed not as theoretical enterprises but as practical tools, often to assist students learning another language: *"The oldest existing dictionaries were made in Iraq for practical reasons; the Assyrians who came to Babylon about three thou-*

sand years ago had difficulty in understanding the Sumerian signs, and their schoolboys found it useful to prepare "syllabaries" giving the Sumerian signs and their Assyrian translations. Arabic lexicography emerged in the seventh century for religious reasons; dictio-naries were first written to explain the rare words which occurred in the Koran and Hadith. The first English bilingual glossaries evolved to meet educational needs; the schoolmasters compiled those Latin-English glossaries to help their pupils understand the textbooks which were written in Latin." (Al-Kasimi, 1983: 1-2).

Writing depends on two facts:

- the words of a language are composed of minimal units of meaning (morphemes) and minimal units of sound or formation (phonemes)
- a systematic correlation can be established between these linguistic units and graphic marks.

The level of unit chosen (phonemes, syllables, words) determines the type of the resulting writing system: alphabet, syllabary, logography. The universal essence of writing, however, is that the technology can be applied to any language.

For many years, linguists and language scholars claimed that natural signed languages such as American Sign Language (ASL), French Sign Language (FSL), British Sign Language (BSL), and others were fundamentally different than natural spoken languages. Their words -signs- were considered to be unanalyzable. Therefore, the only type of writing system possible for signed languages were logographic systems in which one graphical mark, a grapheme, represented an entire word. Often, such systems were highly pictorial, nothing more than stylized drawings of signs, and thus hardly qualified as writing systems. It was not until 1960 that researchers realized that the words of signed languages, like those of spoken languages, are composed of units (Stokoe, 1960). Signed words are both composed of units of meaning (morphemes) and units of formation (cheremes, the signed equivalent of phonemes).

The discovery that signed languages are composed of cheremes made possible for the first time the creation of an alphabetic writing system for ASL and the publication of a true signed language dictionary, the *Dictionary of American Sign Language on Linguistic Principles* (Stokoe, Casterline, & Croneberg, 1965), often referred to as the DASL. While a pioneering work and an extremely valuable reference tool for linguists and language researchers, the DASL has not in the years since its publication enjoyed widespread success as a practical tool for students and teachers of ASL. We believe that this is because despite the theoretical *ability* to develop a writing system for signed language, in *practice* these systems are unwieldy for the dictionary user. It was this realization which led us to explore the technology of multimedia.

The Multimedia Dictionary of American Sign Language

In 1989, the authors embarked on a project to apply new technological innovations to the construction of a dictionary of ASL. The project consists of three phases:
- feasibility (1);
- research and development (2); and
- commercialization (3).

In order to demonstrate feasibility under Phase I of the project we developed a prototype system. We have called the system the *Multimedia Dictionary of American Sign Language* (MM-DASL).

The MM-DASL Prototype

The prototype MM-DASL consists of a set of videodiscs, a Macintosh IIci computer with standard 13" colour monitor, a RasterOps 364 Colourboard (for real-time digitizing of video images), and a Pioneer LD-V4200 laserdisc player. Under the time and monetary constraints of Phase I we did not attempt to produce our own video material. Rather, we used a set of videodiscs published by Access Network, entitled "ASL in Canada", containing 4500 ASL signs and their English glosses.

The prototype MM-DASL implements most of the features planned for the full working version. Specifically, the prototype MM-DASL:

- Allows users to enter an English word and look up the ASL equivalent.
- Asks the user to specify the meaning of the English word when more than one ASL word is a possible translation. The correct answer to "How do you sign 'part'?" is "It depends on what you mean." The ASL translations for 'part in a play', 'I read part of the book', 'I part my hair on the left', and 'Moses parted the waters' are all different. The MM-DASL does not make the mistake of displaying an ASL word based on an English gloss. Instead, it asks the user to clarify the meaning and only then displays the correct ASL translation
- Allows users to look up an ASL word based on phonological features (e.g., handshape, location, movement).
- Is capable of containing definitions, usage, and grammatical information. Definitions will focus on the semantics of ASL, with special emphasis on meaning differences between ASL and English. Usage information will include currency or frequency (e.g., archaic or rare ASL words); regional variation; technical or specialized words (possibly including manually coded English words gaining acceptance as part of ASL vocabulary); restricted or taboo words; style or register (informal, poetic, humorous,

etc.); status or cultural level (nonstandard, substan-dard). Grammatical information will include traditional categories (noun, verb, adjective) as well as ASL-specific categories (directional/nondirectional verbs, predicate classifiers).
- Allows users to view the sign in slow motion forward or backward, or frame-by-frame.
- Incorporates audio (spoken English and French translations of the ASL word).
- Includes a special feature for ASL researchers which allows users to mark portions of ASL words, obtain precise timing data, and output this data to files which can be imported into spreadsheet or statistical applications.

Features which are planned for the commercial version of the MM-DASL but were not implemented in the prototype include:

- Fuzzy search (ASL to English). We plan to allow two types of "fuzzy" search. One, multiple codings, will allow users to enter acceptable variants (for example, a regional or dialectal variant) of an ASL word and be directed to the standard citation form. The second type will make it easier for novice users to successfully search for and find ASL words. Here, users will input the search criteria (handshape, location, movement, etc.), but will be allowed to vary the degree of confidence. A "fuzzy factor" of one, for example, will direct the MM-DASL to return ASL words which match exactly the search parameters. A factor of five will return all words which merely resemble the specified parameters.
- Fuzzy search (English to ASL). This feature will implement a phonetic ("sounds like") search for English words. It will be based on the soundex algorithm and should pose no problem to implement in the final version.
- Special features for students (notes attached to individual entries, lists of words); teachers (tests or practice materials based on dictionary entries).
- Capability of searching for an ASL word based on grammatical or usage information. For example, a user could search for all size-and-shape-specifiers, all verbs which inflect for person agreement, all archaic words, all regional variants, etc. and combinations of these with each other or with formational (phonological) features.

What We Learned Under Phase I

The most important lesson we learned during Phase I development was not to underestimate the growth in video/computer technology. In the Phase I proposal, we suggested that the final system would display video on an external television monitor; we hoped to explore the future possibility of displaying video on the computer monitor. By the time Phase I development began, computer display of full motion video was a reality.

During the first few months of Phase I we experimented with implementing the MM-DASL in various multimedia authoring environments, such as Hypercard, Macromind Director, and Authorware. Each product is promoted as providing developers with the tools necessary to build multimedia applications. We soon decided that the MM-DASL is multimedia in name only. At the heart of the application we felt we needed a powerful, flexible database engine.

Consequently, during the final months of Phase I development we turned our attention to implementing the MM-DASL in user-programmable, relational database systems. The final prototype demonstrates the success of this approach. It was programmed entirely in a Mac database, 4th Dimension. Modules necessary for controlling the laserdisc player and the video card were added to the program.

Finally, we have struggled with the special challenge of storage and display of video material. One second of full motion, full frame video source requires more than 30 megabytes of storage - more than many home computer hard disks can hold. Laserdiscs are capable of storing one hour (one-half hour per side) of video material. Laserdiscs, however, are analog devices; the video signal must be digitized before it can be displayed on a computer monitor. While real time video digitizing cards are commercially available, they add to the cost and complexity of the computer system required to operate the MM-DASL. Thus, the limitations of video storage and display dramatically impact the implementation of the MM-DASL.

Multimedia and the MM-DASL: Looking to the Future

Multimedia has been called "a zero billion dollar industry" (Said, 1991). While many industry experts believe that once multimedia finds a direction it will experience rapid growth, no one yet seems to have discovered the direction.

Like all technologies, multimedia must succeed as the solution to a unique problem. So far, multimedia projects have been simple reworkings of problems which other technologies have already solved. The multimedia solutions are flashy but ultimately unnecessary.

We believe the MM-DASL points the way to the future of multimedia. Developing a dictionary of a visual language is a problem which print media cannot adequately solve. It is a problem which demands, not merely supports multimedia.

Our research during Phase I made it clear to us that there are two directions in which future development of the MM-DASL can proceed. One direction relies on existing technologies such as laserdiscs and third-party software. Basing the MM-DASL on these technologies, while certainly feasible, will ultimately limit the product both technologically and in its marketability. First, laserdiscs are expensive and single purpose. CD-ROMs and CD-ROM players are less expensive (and becoming more so quite rapidly) and multipurpose. We believe that in the not-too-distant future every computer will be equipped with a CD-ROM player (much as only a few years ago high-capacity harddisks were rare but have now become common equipment). It seems clear to us that CD-ROM will become the preferred storage and distribution medium for digital video, at least in the near- to mid-term. Second, relying on third-party software requires that the user own a copy of the software, or pay a licensing fee built into the cost of the product for a "run-time" version of the program. Also, third-party database programs are by nature general purpose, offering features (and attendant overhead) not needed by the MM-DASL.

Recent and emerging developments in video/computer technology offer the means to implement a technologically innovative MM-DASL. By incorporating these technologies, we hope to develop a MM-DASL which looks forward to the future of multimedia. In the short term this direction will mean rebuilding the MM-DASL to take advantage of these emerging technologies. In the long term we are convinced it will put us in a position to ensure the market success of the MM-DASL; to foster research and development in related areas such as signed language lexicography and sign perception; and, in a small way, to provide direction to the multimedia industry.

We plan to rewrite the MM-DASL as a stand-alone application. This will give us full control over program structure and future enhancements. The next version of the MM-DASL will be constructed using object-oriented programming techniques and will incorporate our own database engine, optimized for the storage and retrieval of only those data types required by the MM-DASL. In addition, programming our own application will allow us to take advantage of current and emerging developments from two sources:

- Apple's operating system extension, QuickTime, and related video storage and display technologies
- The Apple/IBM technology alliance, especially their joint venture, Kaleida.

QuickTime

QuickTime, an extension to the Mac system software released by Apple Corp. is an excellent example of the technological tools which have a direct impact on the development of applications such as the MM-DASL. QuickTime provides the means for consistently incorporating time-based data, such as video and sound, into mainstream application programs.

QuickTime defines a Movie format that standardizes organizing, storing, and exchanging time-related data. A QuickTime movie contains tracks, each with its own timing, sequencing, and data description (the actual video data to be played are stored separately). QuickTime synchronizes the tracks and retrieves the data to be played (Poole, 1991).

QuickTime movies also specify a *poster*, which is a single image that represents the movie. This feature will allow us to improve the interface for the ASL to English search over its implementation in the prototype MM-DASL.

In the prototype, when a user specifies an ASL search, it is possible for the MM-DASL to return several ASL words that meet the criteria of the search. In the prototype MM-DASL, the user must then select from a list of English words in order to display the ASL word. This is not an ideal solution because the user does not know which English word to select - that is why he is doing an ASL to English search. Presumably, he only knows what the ASL word looked like.

The correct design would be to present the user with graphic thumbnails of all the ASL words matching the search criteria. These would be displayed as small still images arranged in rows and columns. The user could then scan the images for the one that looks like the ASL word. Clicking on it would display the ASL word in full motion video.

The trick is knowing which portion of the full movie to display as the thumbnail. For some signs, the first frame will be most representative. For others, it will be a frame in the middle; for still others, a frame near the end. QuickTime's poster allows the developer to specify which frame to display; clicking on it then plays the full movie.

QuickTime movies are digital. This means that they can be stored on hard disks or CD-ROM. In order to overcome the storage limitation problems, QuickTime incorporates an Image Compression Manager. Software-based video compression is currently limited in its abilities - the trade-off is higher compression (more video source can be stored) versus lower frame rates (10-12 rather than the normal 30 frames per second) or a smaller video display. However, hardware compression is currently available, and we expect compression ratios to constantly improve. For example, one compression board currently on the market permits one hour of full motion (30 fps), full screen colour video and stereo sound to be stored on one CD-ROM. The prototype MM-DASL uses only a one-quarter screen video display, which is quite adequate. This would allow four hours of ASL video material to be stored on one CD-ROM.

The hard disks or CD-ROM players which store QuickTime movies can be networked to many workstations. Such a configuration would allow many users to share and access the MM-DASL without needing a CD-ROM player and the MM-DASL disc at each computer. This makes possible computer language labs for students of signed languages. Combined with video input and digitizing capabilities at each workstation, the lab would provide students with full facilities for practicing and monitoring their production and reception.

QuickTime movies can be cut, copied, and pasted just like words or images. A user can select a word from the MM-DASL and copy it to the Mac clipboard. This word can then be pasted into a paper he is writing in a word processor. When the paper is turned in on disk to a teacher, the teacher can click on the movie in the document and see the ASL word signed in full motion. Graphic images (arrows, text) can be overlaid on the movie pointing out characteristics of the sign.

Finally, QuickTime is a system software extension, enabling it to use other system features. One of these is AppleEvents. AppleEvents dynamically link programs. By making the MM-DASL AppleEvent aware, users can open the MM-DASL, conduct searches, and view ASL words from within other applications.

For example, a deaf user might be reading electronic mail and come to a word he does not recognize. He would select the word and issue a key sequence which sends a command to the MM-DASL to conduct an English to ASL word search using the selected word as input. A window containing the ASL QuickTime movie of the word (or a scrolling list of words if there is more than one ASL translation) would appear. By clicking on the movie, the deaf user could see the English word signed in ASL.

Kaleida

Kaleida is the multimedia joint venture resulting from the recent Apple/IBM technology alliance. Kaleida will focus on establishing standards for video, sound, graphics, and animation on computers. In addition, Kaleida will be responsible for encouraging third-party companies to create media content using its technologies (Gore, 1991).

Kaleida consists of three building blocks with important implications for the development of the MM-DASL:

- MediaScript
- Kaleida environment
- Media players.

MediaScript is a platform-independent architecture and language designed to control a wide variety of media objects, such as video, sound, animation, and graphics. MediaScript is expected to include a derivative of Apple's QuickTime. It will remove one of the biggest roadblocks to the broad acceptance of multimedia: the lack of a defined cross-platform standard (Gore, 1991).

Kaleida environment is an object-oriented media operating system. It

Table 1. MM-DASL Overview.

Features	Benefits
English to ASL word and phrase searching	Allows users to find the ASL equivalent for an English word or phrase
English to ASL search by meaning	Avoids incorrect use of ASL words and phrases
Definitions, usage, and grammatical information for each ASL entry	Teaches correct use of ASL Encourages respect for the richness of ASL
ASL to English word searching	Allows users to easily find the meaning of a word which they have seen signed
Fuzzy search capabilities	Ensures that users can easily find ASL signs even when they do not remember exactly what the sign looked like Ensures that users can easily find an ASL translation even if they misspell the English word
Full motion, color video displayed on the computer	Displays native ASL users - not computer generated graphics
CD-ROM technology	CD-ROM is the media of choice for video CD-ROM drivers are reasonable in price and have multiple uses Both video means users do not have to buy additional digitizing cards Video compression allows several thousand ASL words to fit on one CD-ROM
ASL entries based on Apple QuickTime movies	Allows users of any Mac system to use the dictionary Users can scan forward or backward or view the ASL word in slow motion Audio can be synchronized to the QuickTime movie Permits future development on IBM platforms
QuicTime "posters" present representative frames	Makes it easy and intuitive to select from multiple ASL words in an ASL to English search
Apple System 7 and AppleEvent savvy	Users can open the dictionary and conduct searches from within other applications QuickTime movies can be cut and pasted into other documents

will allow media authors to create more-sophisticated multimedia titles faster and more easily than is now possible. By integrating the technologies that are needed to create quality-content titles, Kaleida will help to jump-start the multimedia market (Gore, 1991).

The Kaleida operating system will run on a new class of consumer product called media players. This technology is currently under development at Apple, IBM, and several Japanese companies including Sony, Toshiba, and Sharp Electronics. According to computer trade sources (Gore, 1991), the Kaleida operating system will first appear on handheld CD players that will include colour screens. These media players will have the ability to store two hours' worth of compressed video and sound on a rewriteable CD.

By allying the MM-DASL early on with QuickTime, object-oriented programming techniques, and CD-ROM storage, we will be in an excellent position to take advantage of future technologies such as MediaScript and the Kaleida media operating system. The possibility of making the MM-DASL available across Mac and PC platforms is especially important for its long-term success.

If media players prove to be a successful consumer product, it is even possible to imagine handheld versions of the MM-DASL in the not-too-distant future, taking their place alongside Sharp pocket spelling checkers and language translators.

In summary, an overview of features and benefits of the MM-DASL system appears in Table 1.

Intended Users

The MM-DASL is intended for use by several groups of consumers:

- hearing and deaf students of ASL as a second language
- deaf, ASL-native students learning English as a second language
- ASL linguists and researchers
- parents, teachers, employers, and others who interact with deaf people.

Initially, we expect that the MM-DASL will be of interest primarily to deaf education, university programs that teach ASL or ASL interpreting, and public libraries. We also plan to market the product to businesses, government agencies, hospitals, and other organizations which hire or come into contact with deaf people. As multimedia technology becomes more widely available we expect to see the MM-DASL reach a broader consumer market.

Testing and Evaluation

Testing and evaluation will take place in three phases. Each phase involves a version of the MM-DASL system that is closer to the final release version than the previous phase and evaluators that more closely represent the target audience of the release version.

Developmental Phase

Testing during the developmental phase will be conducted in conjunction with software development. As functions or modules are developed, they will be tested in the laboratory setting by individuals chosen to represent characteristics of the target audience. They will be given verbal instruction on the software and will attempt to exercise the functions of the software being tested.

Data gathering will be by direct observation. Since the software will be in a preliminary state, the observers will be software engineers and other system development personnel. They will freely offer help to the evaluators but will record the questions asked and their answers along with other problems and observations. These data will be used for further development of the software and will form one of the bases of the users documentation.

The purpose of testing in the developmental phase is to provide data necessary to design and execute software development. Therefore, it is informal and episodic, with no set schedule, except that it is concluded when the complete, pre-release version of the system is available.

Pre-release Phase

While the pre-release version will be complete with respect to functions, it can be expected to require fine-tuning with respect to the user interface. Testing of the pre-release version will involve intensive use by individuals chosen to be representative of the target audience described above. The testing will take place in the development laboratory, so that software development personnel can observe the testing.

Evaluators will receive verbal orientation from development personnel and will use the draft version of the users' documentation. Data gathering will be by observation during the tests and by interviews after the tests. Observers will answer questions from evaluators, but they will not offer other assistance unless the evaluators cannot extricate themselves from difficulties with the system.

The pre-release tests will be conducted by a group of eight to ten evaluators. The size of the group is limited to keep the time required for testing to a manageable length, but it is large enough to represent the entire target audience.

Results of the pre-release testing will be used to modify the software to the extent that such modifications are cost-effective. Primarily, test results will provide information on the adequacy of error handling and user interface provisions. Testing will also uncover previously undetected errors.

Equally important, test results will help document writers to revise and refine users' documentation. Aspects of documentation to be revised as a result of testing may include the following:

- Comprehensiveness. Documentation should include information on all functions and detectable errors. Testing will exercise all function and reproduce most user errors.
- Accuracy.
- Ease of use. Needed information should be easily found and understood. Testing will show what information is most important to efficient use of the system.

Final Release Phase

Final release testing will use the releasable version of software and final version of the documentation. Testing will take place at three sites, using standard hardware configurations under conditions of normal use.

Data gathering for this phase of testing is more difficult than in the other phases since development personnel cannot be present during the tests. Several techniques will be used, as follows:

- Trouble notices. Evaluators will fill out a form for each problem they encounter. These forms will be collected and tabulated.
- Interviews with evaluators. Selected evaluators will undergo structured interviews to determine user reaction to software and documentation.
- Focus groups. Groups of users will be interviewed together to project improvements both for the release version and for future upgrades.

Since testing in the final release phase uses software and documentation in its final, ready-to-ship version, changes as a result of this testing will be more difficult and expensive than in previous phases. As a result, changes will be limited to modifications and corrections that are essential to the proper operation of the system. Modifications that have value but are not essential will be considered for subsequent releases of the software.

Further Research and Development Plans

With only a working prototype of the MM-DASL in hand and development of the commercial version awaiting funding, it may appear premature to discuss future research and development plans. We are convinced, however, that it is important even at this stage to plan for the future. Some of the reasons are:

- Multimedia technology is changing rapidly - applications developers must keep their eyes on the future or watch their concepts slide into the past.
- Interest in signed languages is increasing worldwide (Wilcox & Wilcox, 1990).
- The MM-DASL and similar applications can become commercially viable products - if we, as developers, have a vision for how to make them meaningful to the lives of deaf and hearing people.
- Many of the advancements which we envision for the MM-DASL will depend on further basic research in language (signed or spoken) perception, linguistics, computational lexicography, and computer interface design.

Although the MM-DASL is designed to be a cross-linguistic dictionary linking a spoken and a signed language, the technology certainly can support bilingual signed dictionaries. For instance, ASL-BSL, BSL-FSL, and many other international versions of the application could be developed.

Just as the technology supports bilingual signed dictionaries, it also supports the development of dictionaries in which the definitions, usage, and grammatical information for the signed language words are presented entirely in that language. Thus, an ASL-English version of the MM-DASL, designed primarily for ASL natives whose second language is English, would present English usage, definitions, and so forth in ASL. In fact, it is common for bilingual dictionaries to address the specific needs of different users in this way (Al-Kasimi, 1983).

Once the initial investment is made in purchasing the hardware and software necessary to operate the MM-DASL, consumers will want to have more titles available to them. Future development can address the need for specialized dictionaries (medical, legal, etc.) or versions for use in deaf education classrooms. Furthermore, the concept is not limited to dictionary applications, but could be expanded into multimedia materials of all types for signed languages - teaching, reference, entertainment, personal information are just a few.

Finally, we hope to explore innovative technologies for providing input to the MM-DASL. Currently, in order to conduct an ASL to English search the user must enter the phonological information necessary to find an ASL word (handshape, location, movement, etc.) through a series of point-and-click operations. While the graphic user interface of modern home computers makes such a design possible, it is not the most intuitive solution.

Ideally, a user should be able to sign the desired word (or as close an approximation to the word as the person can remember), and the dictionary would respond with the word or a list of possible choices. One way in which this could be accomplished is with computer gesture recognition.

Several systems are currently on the market which allow gestures as input to computer applications. One product, the VPL, Inc. DataGlove, is a device which converts hand gestures and positions into computer-readable form. Sensors mounted on a lightweight lycra glove monitor finger gestures (flexion, extension, opposition, abduction, adduction, etc.). A motion detector on the glove also detects movements of the hand in 3-dimensional space.

Such a system would require a greater understanding of how to parse signed language gestures than we currently possess. The basic research required to implement such a system is closely related to projects currently under way which are developing models of speech perception based on a gestural theory of phonology (Browman & Goldstein, 1990; Hochberg et al., 1991).

Conclusion

"The most profound technologies are those that disappear. They weave themselves into the fabric of everyday life until they are indistinguishable from it. Consider writing, perhaps the first information technology. The ability to represent spoken language symbolically for long-term storage freed information from the limits of individual memory. Today this technology is ubiquitous in industrialized countries.... It is difficult to imagine modern life otherwise" (Weiser, 1991). Unless you happen to be one of the hundreds of thousands of deaf people around the world whose native language is a signed language. As we have seen, spoken languages are not the only languages which can be written. Writing systems can also be devised for signed languages. But the products of "literacy technology" for signed languages are far less ubiquitous than they are for spoken languages. Perhaps, however, as innovations in computer hardware and software lead to "ubiquitous computing" (Weiser, 1991), we will see a parallel development in what may become the 21st century's answer to literacy technology for the deaf - multimedia books, dictionaries, encyclopedias, magazines, newspapers, and journals in signed languages.

Acknowledgments

Development of the *Multimedia Dictionary of American Sign Language* prototype was supported by a Small Business Innovation Research (SBIR) phase I grant from the National Institutes of Health, Institute on Deafness and Other Communication Disorders, to Linstok Press, Inc. The authors would also like to thank Robert Matthews, Dennis Cokely, Doug Wood, and Larry Gorbet for their invaluable assistance throughout this project.

References

Al-Kasimi, A.M. (1983). *Linguistics and Bilingual Dictionaries*. Leiden: E. J. Brill.

Browman, C.P. & Goldstein, L. (1990). Tiers in articulatory phonology, with some implications for casual speech. In: J. Kingston & M. Beckman (eds), *Papers in Laboratory Phonology I: Between the Grammar and the Physics of Speech*. Cambridge: Cambridge University Press.

Gore, A. (1991, November 12). Kaleida scopes out media OS. *MacWeek, 1*, 102.

Harris, R. (1986). *The Origin of Writing*. LaSalle, Illinois: Open Court.

Hochberg, J., Laroche, F., Papcun, G., Thomas, T. & Zacks, J. (1990). *From phonemes to gestures: Non-linear speech recognition at CNLS*. CNLS Newsletter No. 67. Center for Nonlinear Studies, Los Alamos National Lab, Los Alamos, NM.

Poole, L. (1991). QuickTime in motion. *MacWorld, September 1991*, 154-159.

Said, C. (1991, June 11). Multimedia: Industry in search of a market. *MacWeek, 1*, 94.

Stokoe, W. C. (1960). *Sign Language Structure: An Outline of the Visual Communication Systems of the American Deaf*. Studies in Linguistics Occasional Paper 8, revised 1978. Silver Spring, MD: Linstok Press.

Stokoe, W. C., Casterline, D. & Croneberg, C. (1965). *The Dictionary of American Sign Language on Linguistic Principles*. Silver Spring, MD: Linstok Press.

Weiser, M. (1991). The computer for the 21st century. *Scientific American, 265(3)*, 94-104.

Wilcox, S. & Wilcox, P. (1990). *Learning to See: American Sign Language as a Second Language*. Englewood Cliffs, NJ: Prentice-Hall Regents.

A Computer Dictionary for Subject Specific Signs
A contribution to the vocational education of the deaf

Siegmund Prillwitz and Rolf Schulmeister
Zentrum für Deutsche Gebärdensprache und Kommunikation Gehörloser
Universität Hamburg, Rothenbaumchaussee 45, 20148 Hamburg, Germany

Abstract. The computer dictionary responds to different user needs. It represents contextual information for more than 1,500 computer terms, offers a wealth of illustrations, and represents signs in form of digitized video movies. It combines different sorts of information, verbal, symbolic, and visual, thus enabling to be read by teachers, deaf students, sign language interpreters, and linguists interested in sign language research. Dictionaries for specific subjects might win a new dimension if they are, like this one, produced in an electronic form and utilize all features provided by these new media.

The Vocational Education of the Deaf

In former times deaf people were only admitted to 'simple' manual or technical jobs, but during the last decades the range of accessible professions for the deaf, at least in Germany and other western countries, has been widened remarkably, partly due to an improved deaf education, partly due to technological advances in industrial environments. For a long time deaf people preferred to become technical draftsmen or dental technicians; today computer technicians, computer programmers, graphical computer artists are professions within the reach of the educated deaf. More recently deaf students may study at a normal university with the help of sign language interpreters. Hamburg has the leading edge in that the city generously provides interpreter services for deaf students.

The success is overwhelming. Deaf students demonstrate a similar performance and achievement as hearing students, only assisted by sign language interpreters. What hearing students hear, deaf students see in sign language. And what is most striking is that this experiment is welcomed with great enthusiasm by all members of the university and that sign language is accepted througout the campus: faculty, department, and

Academic Senate have unanimously voted to enhance the facilities of the Centre by developing a curriculum for sign language and a curriculum for interpreter training. Moreover, the parliament of the city of Hamburg has submitted a proposal to the Federal Government to support these projects by establishing the project as a model[1].

A necessary condition is, of course, that a proficient interpreter is able to translate the subject specific topics correctly into sign language and that the deaf student has a differentiated competence in sign language.

This approach is not only useful in academic studies, but may be of even more importance for the improvement of the vocational education and further education. So far the major problem in the field of vocational education was that the deaf participants had difficulties in following the exclusively oral communication or written language of their hearing educators, who consequently tried to adapt the level of their teaching to the low level of the oral communication by simplifying the subject matter sometimes beyond recognition. This must have resulted in negative consequences for the motivation and engagement of those involved.

The situation might be improved by introducing qualified sign language interpreters. But there are major obstacles to overcome: At least in Germany there is a lack of interpreters, because there is no professional training of interpreters for sign language comparable to the standards of interpreter trainings for oral languages. And even if you do not put too much emphasis on the qualification of the interpreter, you will not find too many of them. There are so few interpreters that we have to reduce our expectations and have to drop the assumption that the interpreter should have an expertise in the subject, too, in which he or she is trying to translate.

We are trying step by step to improve this unsatisfying situation at the "Hamburg Centre for German Sign Language and Communication of the Deaf" by developing and publishing material for a continuous interpreter training, video lessons, printed material, and computer-based programs. This contribution is a report about the development of a computerized dictionary for a specific subject matter, the computer training of deaf persons, and is supposed to provide a model for the integration of sign language in the vocational education of the deaf.

As a first subject in which to demonstrate the chances and power of using sign language as a communicative medium we have chosen the field of computer technology, because a large amount of deaf persons are in danger to lose their jobs if they are not willing or able to learn how to use computers.

---

[1] see Drucksache 13/7969 "Mitteilung des Senats an die Bürgerschaft"; cf. Das Zeichen. Zeitschrift zum Thema Gebärdensprache und Kommunikation Gehörloser Vol.5 (1991) No.16, p. 182-183

Aim of the Project

The aim of the project is to develop learning material for the vocational education of the deaf. The first example in an intended series of dictionary projects is the development of a dictionary for computer terms or technology. It is expected that the dictionary will be very useful in preventing further disadvantages for the deaf in learning how to use computers at work and by stimulating a sign language communication between teachers and students in further education settings[2].

Our intention is to develop an electronic dictionary which is easy to use and allows users to browse through the terms, definitions, explanations, and examples like leafing in a book and at the same time look up the corresponding signs in form of movies. The purpose of the application is to

- enable teachers of the deaf to learn signs and communicate more easily with the deaf;
- facilitate communication among the deaf about the professional knowledge involved in learning how to use computers;
- to provide sign language interpreters with sign language equivalents for the terms they have to translate.

Sign Language Research

We would like to expand on how the project was conducted. There was a team of 14 deaf people dedicated to the task of collecting signs. Among the members of this team were two deaf colleagues from the Centre of Sign Language and Communication of the Deaf. The members of this group were either computer experts (computer science, electrical engineering, teachers of vocational schools) or experienced computer users. They all have an extensive knowledge of sign language and are using it daily.

From the Centre for German Sign Language the team received a list with more than 1.500 terms, definitions and explanations in German and English. These were discussed in the project group to establish a common understanding of their meaning, and then signs were proposed. If there were concurrent signs the members of the group decided which sign was best or whether several signs should be registered in the dictionary as is normally done with local dialect variants in dictionaries. In those cases in

---

[2] Several German institutions dedicated to the vocational education of the deaf contribute to the project by providing us with information about the needs of their institutions.

which no sign for a certain term existed the group tried to invent a new sign in accordance with the rules of formation in sign language:

- Some signs were imported from American Sign Language (ASL) as long as there was no contradiction concerning the laws of sign formation in German sign language (Deutsche Gebärdensprache = DGS);
- Some new signs were formed as a combination of two or more other existing signs, e.g. hard-disk (Fest-Platte), hard-ware (Hard-ware), software (Soft-ware), which we might call hyphenated signs or compound signs;
- Some other new signs were formed by adapting existing signs to the new term thereby transferring meaning in a more metaphorical fashion, e.g. switching (wechseln), directory (Inhaltsverzeichnis, Katalog);
- Other signs required a combination of a sign with a letter from the fingerspelling alphabet, e.g. array (Matrix) is "A" + sign for "brackets".

We were quite surprised that deaf computer users had already generated regular signs for more than 80 percent of the technical terms covered by our survey. This clearly proves that German sign language has managed, within a very short period of time, to create a large number of new signs for new terms in the field of technology and thus offered evidence of its creativity. We observed that these new technology terms had been formed strictly according to the innate rules of sign language and its morphological principles:

- familiarity: most signs for technical terms, like in oral language, fall back on everyday signs with a very general meaning. They only obtain an additional or supplementary meaning within the specialized technological context, while their original features remain unchanged. The same

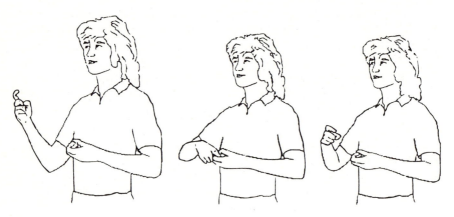

Figure 1. "Log-In" - "Log-Out".

signs are used, for example, for *opening* and *closing* computer programs as for opening and closing doors and windows (see Figure 1).
- incorporation: the grammatical principle of incorporation is frequently applied to technical terms, too. An example for an incorporated object occurs in the sign for *mouse-move*, where *mouse* is incorporated in the sign for *move* (Figure 2).

Figure 2. Mouse-Move.

- iconicity: generally, the external features of the respective conceptual references serve as basic orientation for generating two- or three-dimensional "illustrations" reflecting the essential visual characteristics of a term. The signs for *monitor* [Bildschirm] or *icon* [Abbild], for example, reproduce the display screen surface in a two-handed sign (Figure 3).

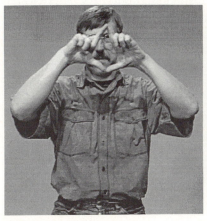 

Figure 3. (Ab)bild.

- functional representation: another frequently occurring principle for generating signs is a shortened reproduction of the functional action characterizing a term. Thus for example, the sign for a computer *mouse* does not use the German sign for *Maus* (the articulation of the English and the German word is identical) (see Figure 4), but makes reference to the handshape which is used to operate the computer device (i.e. clicking).

Figure 4. Mouse.

- translation: quite often technical signs are generated which "translate" the original verbal expression. This normally is the case when compound expressions are reproduced in sign language. For example, the term *hard-disk* (in German "Fest"-"platte") is not formed according to the usual positioning rule for adjectives which in DGS always comes after the reference term (postposition), but rather as a combination ("hyphenation") of the two signs *hard* [*fest*] and *disk* [*Platte*], known from everyday sign language. For the word *fest*, which has two meanings in verbal German, the semantically correct corresponding sign [FEST = HARD] is signed rather than *fest* in the sense of *Feier* [festivity] (Figure 5).

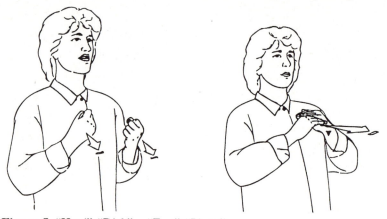

Figure 5. "Hard"-"Disk" = "Fest"-"Platte".

- alphabetization: another form of generating new signs for technological terms which takes into account the written form of the oral term, uses the manual alphabet. Generally available signs receive a special meaning by juxtapositioning a letter from the manual alphabet on the handshape, representing in most cases the first letter of the technical term. An example for this method, which is more common in ASL than in DGS, is the term *array*, signed as a combination of the letter A handshape and the *bracket* movement. Other examples are "A"-"ssembler", "A"-"cronym", "A"-"lphabet", "A"-"rithmetic", "B"-"ackup", "E(n)"-"Code", "D(e)"-"Code" etc. This type of sign is however relatively rare in DGS, because deaf people in Germany are only beginning to accept and use fingerspelling more extensively (Figure 6).

Figure 6. E(n)-code, D(e)-code.

- oralization: on the other hand, in generating signs DGS sometimes features a different form of orientation towards oral language which is less prominent in ASL. Some signs in DGS are formed by differentiating an existing sign - in most cases a generic term - with a special mouth pattern. Thus for example the sign for the term *data* is expressed by combining the mouth pattern *data* and the sign for *program*.
- prefixation: some everyday signs are prepositioned with a prefix-sign in order to distinguish them from their everyday counterpart, e.g. "An"-"frage" (query), "An"-"zeige" (display), "An"-"Zahl" (count).

Although we have not yet been able to focus our attention upon the above-mentioned lexical and morphological aspects, because our work on the sign language dictionary for computer terms has so far been rather practice-oriented, it has become clear that the data acquired may be of considerable value for further linguistic research in this field. But let us return to the more technological aspects in the development of the dictionary. The group of deaf computer users did not only collect and/or develop signs for technology terms, but also checked whether the definitions and the explanations of the terms may be easily understood by deaf students; after all the dictionary was not designed for experts, but for naive users, and was not only intended to transport linguistic information, e.g. for interpreters, but also to present an opportunity to learn more about the meaning of these technical terms.

The Content Structure of the Dictionary

A dictionary for the deaf which is made available on a computer should really try to make use of the technological advantages of the new medium and incorporate multiple dimensions of information, sources of knowledge, and media of representation in its environment which otherwise cannot be combined in one single medium, for instance in a book. These different aspects are e.g.:

- the verbal information in the dictionary not only consists of technical terms and explanations, but its contents is structured hierarchically, it classifies terms according to the group to which they belong; a search for all terms belonging to a certain category (e.g. "hardware", "peripherals", "programming") is possible; the user may switch easily between a list of terms and list of categories (see Figure 7); he may also switch easily, just by pressing radio buttons, between this 'list' view and a 'text' view presenting the definitions and explanations for the chosen term;

Figure 7. The basic card of the stack: two index lists with terms in German and English and a third list containing group or classifier terms. The buttons below offer all essential user functions: play a sign movie, show handshape, show a technical drawing, find a specific term, search for sign components in HamNoSys, go to the card with additional database functions, help.

- the dictionary contains also explanations of terms and sample sentences illustrating the usage of that term in an everyday context (see Figure 8);

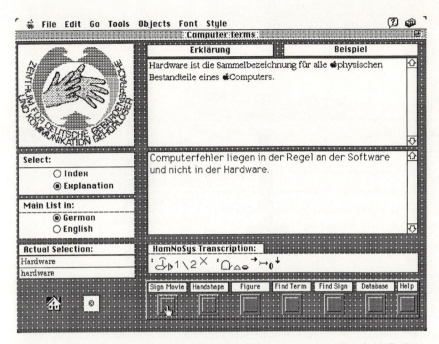

Figure 8. One field shows an explanation of the selected term, here "hardware", the other field offers a sample sentence. A third field contains the HamNoSys transcription string for the selected term.

- besides verbal information the dictionary also contains pictures (figures, diagrams), graphical representations of the objects, video movies either of the objects explained or animations illustrating relations and processes (see Figure 9);
- the dictionary contains transcriptions of all signs in the HamNoSys notation system ("*Ham*burg *No*tation *Sys*tem for sign language"[3]); searching for components of signs like handshapes or movements or combinations of both combined with *and* or *or* in HamNoSys strings is possible; the result is displayed in a list of terms and transcriptions. It may be necessary to explain a bit more in depth what the HamNoSys notation is and what it does: HamNoSys has been developed by the team of the Centre for Sign Language and Communication of the Deaf. The system consists of symbols for handshapes, finger directions, palm orientation, hand locations, and shapes of movements; the symbols are represented by a font on the keyboard of the Macintosh and may be typed in any word processing application or entered with a special editor using pictures for

---

[3] for the Hamburg Notation System compare Prillwitz 1989; Prillwitz & Zienert 1990.

224   S. Prillwitz, R. Schulmeister

selecting components of the sign (for which the Centre has received the German University Software Award 1990) (see Figures 10 and 11);

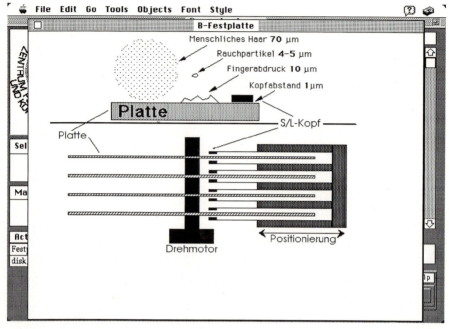

Figure 9. Clicking the "Figure" button opens a technical drawing which illustrates the term, in this case "harddisk" (Festplatte). Instead of drawings there might also appear a video movie or an animation driven by Apple's Quick Time®.

- the dictionary represents signs in form of video movies, and additionally contains enlarged pictures of handshapes. This will be described in the next section in more detail.

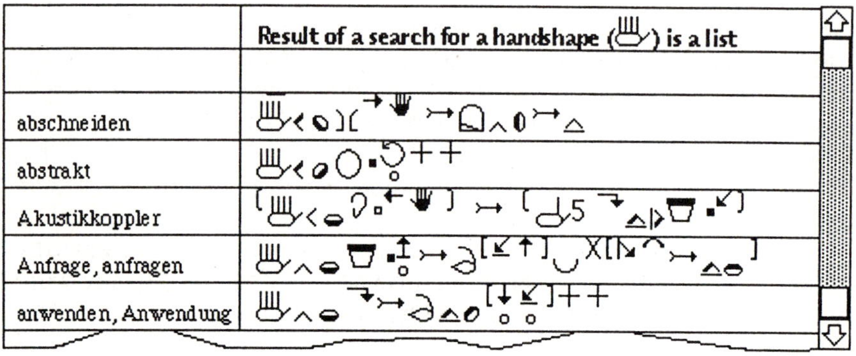

Figure 10. Results of a search for a particular handshape.

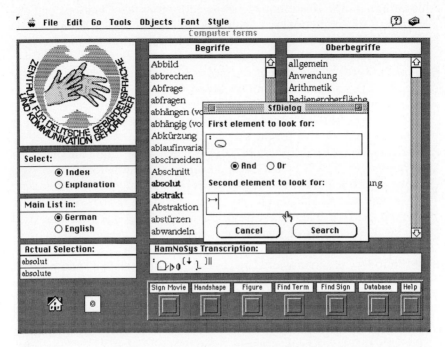

Figure 11. Searching for sign components in the HamNoSys transcription opens a dialog in which the user may enter HamNoSys characters in two fields combined by *and* or *or*. The result of the search process is listed in a scroll field as shown in Figure 10.

Functional Advantages of Computerization

It is not only the mixture of information sources which make a computerized version of a dictionary so powerful. The computer offers at least two advantages over a printed version of a dictionary:

- Especially if the dictionary is not just electronically stored text, but utilizes database techniques for search processes, then indexing provides the user with a quick access to all information available, and Find and Search features are capable of generating user-oriented selections any time.
- As anybody can see from the pictures in this article illustrating signs there is a definite advantage in using movies instead of stills.

Special features of a dictionary, some also covering the sign language aspects of the specific knowledge area, are e.g.:

- multilingual representations of terms, definitions, explanations and examples; thus the dictionary contains all terms in English, French, German, German sign language in HamNoSys transcription, and German Sign Language as video movies;
- it is possible to browse through the information of the stack hierarchically (see above) as well as horizontally; all occurrances of terms contained in the dictionary in definitions or explanations of other terms are treated as hypertext words; the user may click at them and will automatically jump to the explanation part for the selected term;
- since the dictionary uses certain database techniques and contains transcriptions of signs it offers an opportunity to search for certain sign language components and combinations of sign language components, and is thus able to generate for the first time in the history of linguistic research on sign language a descriptive sign language statistics (frequency distributions of handshapes, movements, their occurences in certain parts of the sign space, etc.);
- the dictionary is accompanied by about 1.600 digitized and compressed videotaped movies of the signs explained in the dictionary (see Figure 12). The movies contain between 7 and 20 pictures, they have been videotaped in RGB and grabbed with a 24 bit framegrabber board in colour; the size of the movie window has been reduced in scale by 50%; they may be played back either in 24 bit or 8 bit colour or in 256 greys; movies run at a speed of about 30 pictures a second (on a Macintosh Quadra) or 15 pictures a second (on a Macintosh IIcx); the user does not need a special videocard or other additional hardware, the Apple 8 bit videocard is sufficient; the movie format is Apple's new QuickTime® "movie" format; since QuickTime® has been officially released in January 1992 as part of the Macintosh system software, it is now available for every Macintosh user free of charge; this is one of the reasons why we chose this technique, because QuickTime is expected to become a real cheap and popular multimedia system and platform; as part of the operating system QuickTime offers an integrated multimedia synchronisation and compression for sound, pictures and digitized video movies; the compression scheme is very effective reducing for example the amount of disk storage needed for a movie of one sign from 2,5 MB to 180K;
- the dictionary also contains pictures of the handshape occuring in the sign actually selected; the picture enlarges the handshape in such a way that the user can clearly see the handshape which probably was not large enough to be recognized in the sign movie (see Figure 13).

A Computer Dictionary for Subject Specific Signs 227

Figure 12. Clicking the button Sign Movie opens and plays a movie of that sign in Apple's new movie format. The movie window owns a controller which enables the user to play the movie repeatedly and to step through the movie picture by picture.

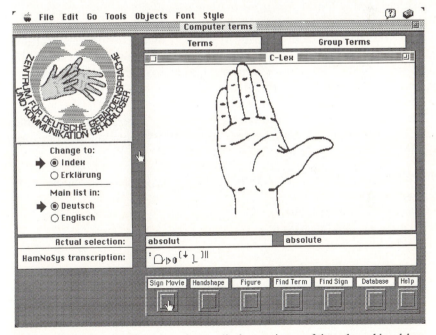

Figure 13. Clicking the Handshape button displays a picture of the enlarged handshape of the selected sign.

This amount of data, texts, compressed video movies, and pictures (about 600 MB), of course, does not fit any longer on the harddisk of a computer; the data are at the moment stored temporarily on an optical CD drive, but will have to be transferred to a CD ROM which, hopefully, will be released in the summer of 1992.

User Functions

The concept of the dictionary also needs to be described in terms of user functions, because the extraordinary composition of signs and written language as well as pictures and movies has to be dealt with in a totally different way compared to a traditional printed language dictionary. User functions therefore are essential for the success of the project. The dictionary should be easy to use and yet offer powerful functions e.g. for Search & Find, for generating lists, for making random selections etc.

We have chosen HyperCard® from Apple as a special object-oriented programming tool and prototyping environment for the dictionary, because it is available for every Macintosh user free of charge. The basic interaction structure of the dictionary is the first card of the HyperCard stack where most of the user interaction takes place: Selecting a term in the index list, chosing to play a sign movie, displaying the picture of a handshape etc. All user functions may be triggered (see Figure 14).

But the hypertext structure of this tool enables the user to browse through the material, to jump from one page to another, switch from text to pictures very easily. It offers the user all language dependent material in form of a huge net of linked texts and terms (see Figure 15). Browsing through the semantic net should be possible both on the same level as well as between different hierarchical levels of information.

The computer provides the dictionary with easy access to files and other sources of information available in text format. By selecting the appropriate button, it is possible to:

- "Make a list" of selected terms in the dictionary for a limited application in a classroom,
- "Save a list" to disk, and
- "Load a list" on the screen.

A Computer Dictionary for Subject Specific Signs 229

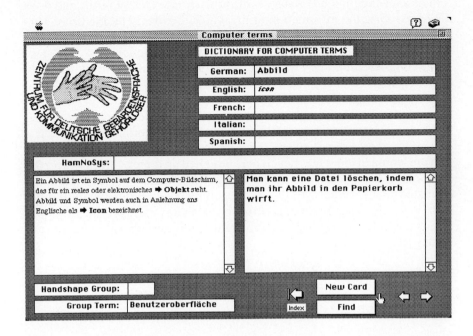

Figure 14. Each term in the directory is described on one HyperCard card. The card lists the term in German, English, French, the HamNoSys transcription, a definition, a sample sentence, the handshape classifier, the group term.

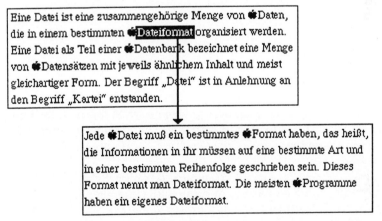

Figure 15. Browsing: Jumping from one definition to another, in this case from an explanation of *Datei* to a definition of *file format* ("Dateiformat"); from there the user may either return to *Datei* or continue to *format* or *program*.

Thus a teacher or student may start from a limited list of terms and does not have to use the information of the whole dictionary all the time. This also provides users with the chance to establish their own hierarchical levels of categories and classifier terms within the dictionary.

The complete dictionary will be released on CD ROM. It will additionally offer access to other applications developed with HyperCard, for instance the technical HyperCard stacks produced by Apple Computer and illustrating the different Macintosh machines, CD ROM technology, networking technology, etc. The choice of HyperCard as a development tool opens a rich realm of other available material for the use, illustrating the information presented in the stack, which may be called up directly from within the dictionary, e.g. pictures of the motherboard, inside the keyboard, an animated movie of networking or telecommunication demonstrating the data flow, other stacks demonstrating the working process of the processor (registers, calculating in Hex), illustrating and describing different machines, etc.

Acknowledgments

The project has been supported by a grant from the Federal Ministry of Labour and Social Affairs.

References

Prillwitz, S. (1989). *HamNoSys Version 2.0. Hamburg Notation System for Sign Language. An Introduction.* (= International Studies on Sign Language and the Communication of the Deaf, vol. 5). Hamburg: SIGNUM (1st ed. 1987).

Prillwitz, S. & Zienert, H. (1990). Hamburg Notation System for Sign Language. Development of a Sign Writing with Computer Application. In: S. Prillwitz & Vollhaber (eds): *Current Trends in European Sign Language Research.* Proceedings of the 3rd International European Congress on Sign Language Research. Hamburg: SIGNUM, 355-379.

Machine Recognition of Human Gestures

Shirley Peters and Richard Foulds
Applied Science and Engineering Laboratories University of Delaware/
A.I. duPont Institute Wilmington, DE 19899, USA

Abstract. Communication by gesture or sign language is used by many for robust and fluent interpersonal conversation. The consistent biomechanical structure of sign languages which allow them to be accurately interpreted by human observers may also make it possible to develop techniques for computer recognition. This paper examines the use of neural networks as the basis for machine recognition of sign language.

As with any language, sign language requires significant training and practice on the part of the user. This practice involves interaction with more experienced signers in order to accommodate the variation in the production of signs. This is also the case when the computer is expected to recognize gestural inputs. The use of neural networks allows kinematic features associated with the gestures to be used to train a network which can generalize and make inferences on subsequent inputs.

Human Recognition of Sign Languages

Human recognition of messages conveyed in sign language is a remarkable process. While the same gesture, exactly repeated, may be easily identified, the signs used in sign language are subject to considerable human variation. This is demonstrated by signers who "whisper" by producing small signs or "shout" by grossly enlarging signs. The actual image viewed by the receiver can vary greatly, yet the interpretation of the intended message remains consistent.

The meaningful information contained in signs is inferred more from biomechanical relationships than the image received by the receiver. Stokoe (1960) discussed sign formation, or "cherology," through the simultaneous parameters of hand shape, place of articulation, and movement.

There appears to be significant information contained in the biomechanical activities which define the sign. It is not important that a sign be produced perfectly in order to be understood. Bornstein and Jordan (1984) discussed this in terms of robust and fragile parameters of signs. They considered 330 signs in terms of their three parameters and rated the ability of each parameter to be distorted while maintaining the intelligibility of the sign. They concluded that many signs were still recognizable even when some of the parameters were distorted.

The ability of a receiver to correctly identify signs viewed from different angles or signs produced by left-handed signers adds to the argument that the intelligibility of signs is due in large part to its biomechanical structure and not either the precise spatial orientation or particular visual representation. Johansson (1973) reported the results of his study on biological movement where the point-light technique was used to track 10 locations on a walking male. Lights were placed on the shoulder, elbows, wrists, ankles, and the hip. A camera recorded only the movements of the lights. The experimental results were quite dramatic. When shown still images (single frames of the film), subjects never identified the pattern of lights as representing a human. When the subjects were shown the moving film, all easily recognized the pattern of moving lights as a person. Johansson explained thatwhile these results may be due in part to previous visual experience, recognition is due to spontaneous grouping based on general principles of human perception.

Similar effects have been shown with sign language (Poizner, Bellugi, & Lutes-Driscoll 1981; Tartter & Knowlton, 1981). While the intelligibility of the signs presented in these studies was less than 100%, the results indicate that the dynamic movements of key anatomical sites are sufficient to convey meaningful sign language.

Machine Recognition of Sign Language

An early attempt to have a computer recognize hand shapes was reported byTamura & Kawasaki (1988). Video images of signs produced by a single signer were matched with signs stored as attributes in an on-line dictionary. The algorithm was designed to recognize a sign by extracting the signer's hand image from the video and determining its trajectory, position and shape. This was done by first extracting the skin area of the signer from the background of the video image. The skin area was then divided into a hand and a face in one of two ways: if there were two separate light coloured areas, the lower right section was the hand; if there was only one skin area, which would happen if the hand passed in front of the face, a face sized oval was blacked out from where the head was last detected and what was left was considered the hand. To determine the hand shape, the extracted skin area was approximated as a single polygon which was then pattern-matched against polygons stored in the system. The trajectory and position of the hand were measured by following the hand from a predefined starting place. These attributes were then used to look up the word in a list of words stored in the dictionary. If only one sign matched the parameters, the corresponding word was returned; if not, the system returned nothing. When this system was tested on 20 carefully picked signs, the recognition rate was only 45%. In addition, this procedure is not scalable. As the number of signs in the data base increases, recognition rate will decrease since the differentiation between signs would become less distinct.

The recognition of sign language by machine requires consideration of the biomechanical structure of the signs as well as the variation in production. The possibilities of employing image processing and image recognition are limited by the tremendous variation in the captured image due to the angle of view, the particular signer, and the distance between the signer and the camera. Similarly, recognition approaches employing templates of biomechanical information fail due to the variability in the production of the signs. These factors demonstrate the need for a flexible algorithm that can learn the signing style of a particular user, but be general enough to overlook any subtle variations in that style. Artificial Neural Networks have these characteristics.

Artificial Neural Networks

Rather than exploiting biomechanical information by requiring parameter templates, or by developing explicit algorithms which define the Stokoe parameters in terms of finger joint angles, limb velocities and positions, it is possible to employ neural networks as a means of recognizing human gestures as meaningful signs.

While this approach does not precisely parallel the human processing capabilities for gesture recognition, it is possible to avoid many of the difficulties which will prevent more conventional computational methods from succeeding in this task.

Employing a data collection device such as the DataGlove from VPL Research (VPL 1989), or the CyberGlove® by Virtual Technologies (based on theTalking Glove (Kramer, 1989)), it is possible to input dynamic information on finger joint angles, wrist orientation, location, trajectory, velocities, and accelerations. Rather than develop an explicit rule base for the recognition of signs, it is possible to train a neural network through repeated interaction to associate input patterns with desired outputs. Once trained, it is expectedthat a neural network will be able to tolerate the variations in biomechanicaldata and make inferences as to the correct sign.

Artificial Neural Networks are computer simulations of the computational style of the biological nervous system (Yuhas, Goldstein, Sejnowski & Jenkins, 1990). Biological neurons are simulated by layers of simple processing elements which are richly connected. Learning is performed by passing the input values through connections between the layers of units where they are amplified or attenuated by the numerical weight or strength of each connection. The outcome is then compared to the correct answer and the weights are adjusted to make the output closer to the correct values on the next pass. This training is continued until the output is minimally different than the actual values. Once the network is trained, thestored weights can be used to quickly classify novel input with the same general characteristics as the training set.

To illustrate the current state of the field of gesture recognition using neural networks, the two most advanced projects will be described here. The Glove-Talk Pilot Study (Fels, 1990; Fels & Hinton, 1990) resolves the limitations of image processing by using a DataGlove as the input device. The DataGlove is a nylon glove with fiber optic sensors attached to read the finger angles and a 3SPACE Polhemus to read the hand location and orientation. To best utilize the sensors provided with the DataGlove, and to best measure the results of the recognition, a sign system was created solely for Glove-Talk. In this system the hand shape was a root word, the direction of hand movement indicated the tense of the word, and the speed and distance of the movement indicated rate and stress, respectively. The system was designed with a 203 word vocabulary made up of 66 root words, each having as many as six different endings and/or tenses.

The recognition process was broken into five subproblems: the recognition of the hand shape, and the determination of the direction, speed, distance, and cadence of the hand movement. Each subproblem had its own neural network recognition process that used only DataGlove measurements relevant to that particular process. All five processes were then run concurrently to speed up the final outcome. The results of this system are encouraging. With the 203 word vocabulary, they report an error rate of only 8%. The system produces no word in 7% of the trials, and the wrong word only 1% of the time.

The contrived sign system is the main user interface limitation. Because this system is designed for the purpose of research, it requires the user to learn a new, non-intuitive language in order to use this system to communicate. For this system to be used as a viable communication tool, a minimum of the 850 words of Basic English (Ogden, 1968) would have to be included. The authors concede that to increase the vocabulary and make the system easily learnable by signers, the entire word definition system might have to be changed. The DataGlove itself also makes using the system more cumbersome because it covers the users dominant hand, making it difficult to type at a keyboard, pick things up, or use the hand for anything other than signing.

Despite these limitations, this research has made some important contributions to this new, expanding field of study. The system proves that real time recognition of hand shapes is possible using today's computer systems. It also shows how neural networks can be used for real-world problems with very promising results. Another very important contribution is the idea of using more than one recognition algorithm for the total recognition process. Fels (1990) noted that smaller problems train faster and better with neural networks and, therefore, the total process will train more quickly and more accurately.

Kramer (Kramer & Leifer, 1987; Kramer & Leifer, 1989) also designed a glove-based hand shape recognition algorithm. He designed the algorithm to recognize the handshapes of the American fingerspelling alphabet. However, because the DataGlove did not measure some angles he thought necessary to recognize those handshapes, Kramer designed his own glove. The result, the TalkingGlove®, has specially designed strain gauges that ride on the back of each knuckle to measure joint angle. In addition to measuring all of the angles measured by the DataGlove, the TalkingGlove also measures abduction for all of the fingers and rotation of the pink and thumb. These extra sensors allow all of the hand shapes of American Sign Language to be distinguishable. Kramer's system also uses neural networks for recognition. He describes the network, which was specially designed for the purpose, as *"a Tree-Structured Neural Net Classifier (TSNNC), (which) divides joint space into regions that can be hierarchically tested and eliminated in a decision tree like fashion."* (Kramer, 1991). He explained that even though the generalization of a regular feed forward neural network (FFNN) is slightly better than the TSNNC, the greatly reduced training and recognition times of the TSNNC relative to the FFNN seem to far outweigh the slight reduction in generalization performance. No accuracy data have been published.

There are a few limitations to the recognition algorithm in Kramer's system. It is designed to recognize static hand shapes only, so each letter must be produced in a static, canonical form. Further, the algorithm looks for a stop in the hand motion after each letter to trigger the recognition process. However, fluent fingerspellers actually use nearly continuous movement which is a combination of the intended letters and the transitions between letters. Also, there is still the problem that the user is required to wear a glove which is attached to the computer system. Kramer is working on making the communication system portable, with infrared interfaces between the glove and the recognition computer.

Like the Glove-Talk system, Kramer's system has also made many contributions to this field. The 'talking glove' is part of a complete communication system for the deaf and deaf-blind. In his complete system, a non-signing person can converse with a deaf or deaf-blind person by typing his message on a portable keyboard, which is then displayed on a two-line LCD wristwatch-like display worn by a sighted deaf person, or a Walkman® size eight cell braille display hooked to the belt of a deaf-blind person. Throughout his research, Kramer has worked closely with the deaf and deaf-blind communities to solicit their feedback and suggestions for making the system better suited to their needs. The design of the TalkingGlove was greatly influenced by the suggestions from his deaf-blind colleagues, who pointed out, among other things, that since their main form of communication is tactile, a glove would greatly reduce their ability to read signs. As a result, the TalkingGlove has been designed with an open palm and fingertips.

Conclusion

Gesture recognition is a field that is expanding as we speak. Many research groups are starting to look into hand shape recognition as it deals with sign language recognition, manual communication, user interfaces, and other uses that we can not even conceive of yet. There are many graduate level research projects in addition to Fels and Kramer at the time of this writing (Hogrestad, 1991; Vamplew, 1991; Dalley, 1991; Shankar, 1991; Indurkhya, 1991; Bernstein, 1991; Murakami, 1991). There are also commercial product designs in development based on the use of gesture recognition for augmentative communication for handicapped people (Greenleaf, 1991). The future looks bright for the prospect of technology based communication aids for real-time conversations between non-signing hearing people and the non-oral deaf.

References

Bernstein, L. (1991). Personal communication via electronic mail.
Bornstein, H., & Jordan, I.K. (1984). *Functional signs a new approach from simple to complex.* Pro-Ed, Austin, TX.
Dalley, C. (1991). Personal communication via electronic mail.
Fels S. (1990). *Building adaptive interfaces with neural networks: The Glove-Talk Pilot study.* Technical Report CRG-TR-90-1, University of Toronto, Toronto, Canada.

Fels, S., & Hinton, G. (1990). Building adaptive interfaces with neural networks: The Glove-Talk Pilot Study. *Human-Computer Interaction - INTERACT `90*, 683-688.

Greenleaf, W. (1991). Personal communication.

Hogrestad, T. (1991). *Klassifikasjon Med Nevraie Nett.* Unpublished masters thesis, Univ. Oslo.

Indurkhya, N. (1991). Personal communication via electronic mail.

Johansson, G. (1973). Visual Perception of Biological Motion and model for its Analysis. *Perception and Psychophysics, 14, 2*, 201-211.

Kramer, J. & Leifer, L. (1987). The Talking Glove: An expressive and receptive "verbal" communication aid for the deaf, deaf-blind, and nonvocal. In: Proceedings of the Third Annual Conference *"Computer technology/Special education/Rehabilitataion"* California State University, Northridge, 335-340.

Kramer, J. & Leifer, L. (1989). The Talking Glove: A speaking aid for nonvocal deaf and deaf-blind individuals. In: *Proceedings of RESNA 12th AnnualConference, Louisiana, USA,* 471-472.

Kramer, J. (1991). Personal communication via electronic mail.

Murakami, K. (1991). Personal communication via electronic mail.

Ogden, C.K. (1968). *Basic English: International Second Language,* prepared by Graham,Harcourt Brace and World Inc, NY USA.

Poizner, H., Bellugi, U., & Lutes-Driscoll, V. (1918). Perception of American Sign Language in dynamic point-light displays. *Journal of Experimental Psychology: Human Perception and Performance, 7*, 430-440.

Shankar, R. (1991). Personal communication via electronic mail.

Stokoe, W. (1960). *Sign Language Structure: An Outline of the visual communication system for the American deaf.* Studies in Linguistics Occasional Papers No 8.

Tamura, S. & Kawasaki, S. (1988). Recognition of sign language motion images. *Pattern Recognition 21*, 343-353.

Tartter, V. & Knowlton, K. (1981). Perception of sign language from an array of 27 moving spots. *Nature, 289*, 676-678.

VPL Research Inc (1989). *DataGlove Model 2 Operating Manual.* CA, USA.

Vamplew, P. (1991). Personal communication via electronic mail.

Yuhas, B., Goldstein, Jr. M., Sejnowski, T., & Jenkins, R. (1990). Neural network models of sensory integration for improved vowel recognition. In: *Proceedings IEEE, 78*, 1657-1668.

A Multi-Media System for the Teaching of Sign Language

Bencie Woll[1] and Peter Smith[2]
[1]Centre for Deaf Studies, University of Bristol, Bristol, England
[2]Attica Cybernetics, Oxford, England

Abstract. This paper describes the development of a training system using Digital-Video Interactive Technology on CD-ROM to support the teaching of British Sign Language. The system supports a variety of courses from introductory to advanced level. Interactive technology has been chosen because it enables the tutor or students to construct lessons targetted on specific linguistic areas. Of available interactive technologies, the DVI technology has been chosen because it enables a student's attempts at signing to be captured and displayed side by side on the computer screen with the correct model displayed digitally from compact disk. The importance of such feedback to the student will be discussed together with an outline of system uses.

Keywords. British Sign Language, Digital-Video Interactive, Visual Feedback.

Background

The Centre for Deaf Studies has been engaged in teaching and researching British Sign Language (BSL) since 1978. There has been an enormous increase in the past 15 years in the number of students of British Sign Language and a number of standard curricula and examinations are available for students. Because of the absence of a written form of BSL, opportunities for study outside the classroom are limited. Unlike learners of spoken languages, who may be expected to spend substantial time in language labs, such facilities are unavailable to learners of sign languages.

One striking observation, dating from our earliest research on hearing people's learning of BSL (Kyle, Woll & Llewellyn-Jones 1981), is that it is often reported that the production skills in sign language of hearing learners exceed their receptive skills. This is in striking contrast to learners of spoken languages, where normally better comprehension skills than production skills are reported, except at the earliest stages of language learning, when the learner only has access to a limited number of phrases in the language. Learners' views on the superiority of their production skills extend even to interpreting-level students, who claim to interpret better into Sign than into English. This is equally unexpected, as spoken interpreters generally prefer to interpret into their first language.

Explanations

Because it seems unlikely that adult learners of any language could actually produce that language better than their first language, it is most likely that learners overrate their production skills. This is supported by the views of deaf signers, who prefer deaf translators to hearing translators (Woll, 1991). It is therefore necessary to seek explanations for this apparent effect. Models of feedback in language are of particular use here. One striking difference between speaking and signing is the role of feedback. The speaker essentially hears himself as others do, and thus has available a means of monitoring his own output. This ability to monitor speech and compare it with a more fluent speaker is the essence of the use of speech production practice using self-teaching tapes and language lab work in foreign language learning. In production exercises in the language lab, the learner uses his own ability to monitor his speech to judge the accuracy of his repetitions or answers to questions provided by the tutor on the tape.

In contrast, the signer does not see himself as others see him: his view of his own signing is very different from that of an observer. In other words, there is an asymmetry in the feedback mechanism for regulating sign language production. Learners often gaze at their hands during signing, in contrast to fluent signers, who use gaze at hands only intermittently, and then for specific linguistic functions (Baker & Padden 1978).

The Role of Feedback

Despite this asymmetry, feedback is essential for maintaining normal signing in those already fluent. This can be seen in the alterations in signing which take place in those suffering from Usher's Syndrome, in which congenital deafness is combined with retinitis pigmentosa, leading to a progressive restriction of the visual field (tunnel vision, together with poor nighttime vision and loss of depth perception). Signers suffering from Usher's Syndrome show consistent alterations in their signing which result in the restriction of signing to their remaining visual field with signing confined to a small area immediately in front of the face (Hassinen, 1989). Thus for fluent signers, the ability to see, although not gaze at, one's own hands appears to be essential in maintaining fluent and normal signing.

Sign Language Acquisition

Research on the acquisition of Sign as a first language has indicated that deaf mothers use many devices to provide the deaf child with feedback during early language learning. These devices include the mother manipulating the child's arms to articulate signs, and signing in front of the child's signing space, either by leaning into the area in front of the child, or by actually placing the child on her lap, facing away from her, and signing with her arms in front of the child's body (Maestas y Moores 1980).

The importance of the opportunity to see models of signing from the same point of view as the learner has, can be seen in the frequency with which adult learners make placement errors with inconsistent reversal of right and left in arrangements of referents in topographical space (i.e. failure to maintain the required mirror imaging); in frequent shifts between dominant and non-dominant hands in asymmetric signs, for example, in "centre" (Figure 1) and "shoe"; in incorrect front-back relationship of hands, for example in "new"; and in errors in the two-handed fingerspelling used by British signers. While fluent signers maintain one hand as the dominant hand throughout signing, learners frequently alternate hand dominance from letter to letter and from sign to sign. Such dominance shifts have also been noted in non-native deaf child signers and in non-native deaf adult signers (Frishberg, 1983).

Figure 1. Correct form of BSL "centre".
Errors produced by learners include:
1) transposing the locations, so that the left hand is above the right hand, with the right hand moving up to touch the left palm.
2) transposing the handshapes, so that the right hand is flat, and below the left hand; the left hand moves down to touch the right palm.
3) transposing the handshapes and location, so that the right hand is flat and palm down; the left hand moves up to touch the right palm.

Since adult learners cannot sit on their tutors' laps and are never provided with the opportunity to monitor someone signing in their signing space, it was felt that it was necessary to improve learners' opportunities for monitoring their own sign production in the same spatial field as that of a fluent signer. Clearly, signing in front of a mirror only compounds the problem of left-right reversals, and while it is possible to make video-recordings of a learner signing, it has been impossible to allow the learner to compare his own signing with that of a tutor, in a way parallel to that provided by deaf mothers to their children.

Early System Development

Accordingly, in 1989, the Centre requested a small internal University grant to explore the possibilities of developing a system which would enable the setting-up of a video language lab for sign language learning. The technology available at the time, however, did not satisfactorily meet the three functions required. These were:

- to provide the learner with the possibility of practicing signs and phrases from memory and comparing them with a model
- to provide the learner with the facility of imitating sentences presented on-screen, and then viewing them alongside the target sentence
- the ability to take part in 'pseudo-dialogues' with pre-recorded materials.

Therefore, the Centre welcomed the opportunity of collaboration on the development of a CD-ROM system which was able to meet these criteria. The system described below represents an application of technology which has wider potential uses than that of teaching sign language and offers a real advance in any situation where the ability of the user to monitor his or her own motor skills would be an advantage.

Technology and BSL Learning

The Authoring System

The authoring system functions at several levels: for the system designers, for BSL tutors, and for students. The system may be used in a pre-set fashion or with varying amounts of interactivity built in. Tutors have the option of choosing a preplanned series of lessons which takes a student through a normal introductory course in BSL. Each lesson offers several interactive functions (see below) combined with background text information and opportunities for assessment. Tutors may also choose to design their own lessons, using the data base and as much of the pre-planned lesson material as they wish. For example, a tutor may want to design a lesson around a special topic, such as regional variation in signing, which does not form part of the pre-planned lessons. The system therefore provides the tutor with instructions on designing customised lessons. Students may also wish to use the system for self-directed practice, or may be asked by the tutor to work on a particular linguistic topic. Finally, the data base can be accessed for linguistic research purposes, rather than for language learning. An important consideration, because of the wide variety of users, ranging from deaf tutors to advanced linguistics students, was to make the authoring system as accessible as possible.

The Data Base

The data base consists of 60 two-person conversations in BSL, each of which consists of up to 10 turns. The conversations have been designed following research into the main contexts for BSL conversation both between deaf people and in deaf-hearing interaction (for example, educational or medical settings). For example, while the weather is a common conversational topic among the hearing British community, this is rare amongst the Deaf community. The conversations were recorded using a variety of signers of different ages, and include a vocabulary of about 3000 signs. Each conversation is assigned a coding for context and participants, and each turn is further analyzed to include English translations, English glosses, and a series of labels relating to the linguistic categories of which the turn and the signs in it are exemplars. The data base includes the categories listed below.

The material in the system covers the following areas:

- a range of conversations on different topics, with different signers of different ages and from different regions
- a dictionary from Sign to English and from English to Sign
- a dictionary of fingerspelled forms
- a dictionary of numerals
- a dictionary of facial expressions
- linguistic information on:
  - interrogatives
  - numerals and numeral incorporation
  - time reference
  - size and shape specifiers
  - spatial verbs

- agreement verbs
- affirmation and negation
- intensification and degree
- complex signs (multi-channel signs)
- sign order
- pro-forms
- aspect.

The Equipment

The DVI based BSL training system is based on an IBM-compatible PC. The minimum level PC system is:

- 80286 level processor (80386 preferred)
- 2 Mbyte RAM
- 40 Mbyte hard disk
- keyboard
- mouse
- VGA display adapter and monitor.

The additional equipment required for the DVI training system is:

- an INTEL DVI Action Media Playback interface card. This has a minimum of 2 Mbytes of VRAM and two INTEL developed custom Pixel processors;
- an INTEL DVI Action Media Capture interface card;
- a video camera with suitable (RGB) connections for the Action Media Capture Card;
- a SCSI interface CD ROM drive; either internally or externally mountable.

DVI Technology

Briefly, the INTEL DVI Action Media system is a PC based sub-system which has the capability to playback full motion, full screen video and audio using digital data from a CD ROM. The CD ROM data rate is 153 Kbytes per second. This is achieved by using a variety of compression techniques which are encoded into the DVI pixel processors contained on the Action Media playback card.

The algorithms to encode and playback the video sequences are currently INTEL proprietary; INTEL have committed to supporting MPEG algorithms.

An additional subsystem - the Action Media Capture card - supports the real time capture and digitization of both video and audio sequences.

Feedback Technology - Implementation Issues

As mentioned above, the capture and feedback component of the training system is one of the key innovative features of the product. The capture of the student's video practice is done through the Action Media capture card. Once digitized, this is stored on the hard disk of the PC.

The visual feedback is achieved using the playback card; the two digital video sources - the original signed utterance from the CD ROM and the student's signed practice from the hard disk of the PC, are accessed alternately. A single video frame is created in the VRAM of the playback card from these two sources; this is then output using a modification of the standard DVI playback software.

A frame rate of approximately 15 frames per second for the two incoming sequences allows just sufficient timing gaps in the video display to allow for the processing necessary to create the single composite video output frame.

Database Implementation and Access

As mentioned in an earlier part of this paper, the training system is supported by a database which, in addition to the frame identification information about each signing sequence, also stores a translation of the sequence and a linguistic analysis of the sequence.

An inverted index is created for each word or linguistic symbol in the database. A search and retrieval routine translates the users input into a field based Boolean query which identifies the frame boundaries for the video sequences which meet the users requirements. The video sequences are then made available to the user.

The CD ROM Component

CD ROM is used as the publishing medium for the signing course. The 660 Mbyte capacity translates into 72 minutes of full screen, full motion video. However, as the signing system uses only quarter frames, a significantly increased capacity is available.

Using the System

As described above under the Authoring System section, the system is designed so that it can support any BSL course. Just as language lab work supports work with a language teacher, the student uses this system for individual practice between lessons. The course teacher can either choose a pre-selected lesson sequence, or specify a linguistic topic for particular study. The student, in turn, can follow the teacher's selection, browse through the data base, or mix among these. Three main user functions are available: *View*, *Learn* and *Conversation*.

View Mode

The *View* mode offers the student the opportunity to watch signs, sentences or conversations, selected by linguistic category, conversational content, vocabulary or lesson title (see Figure 2). All material can be viewed with or without an English translation, enabling the student to practice comprehension. There is also a set of support reading materials available within the "view" mode. With this mode, as with all functions, the system offers the student normal, slow motion or freeze-frame viewing, and any section of the screen can be selected by the student for enlargement to show such detail as facial expression or hand configuration.

Learn Mode

In the *Learn* mode, the student can mix any material from disc with his own signing (see Figure 3). This mode is used for the practice of sign production. The student selects the material for practice, which is displayed on the screen. He then copies (in the case of a video example) or translates (in the case of a written example). This is recorded via the camera, for immediate replay. On replay, the student can view his practice side-by-side with the model, running them from the same starting point. The enlargement facility is also available for detailed analysis of errors. A VHS copy of the signing produced by the student in the "learn" mode can be kept for later examination and discussion with the tutor.

A Multi-Media System for the Teaching of Sign Language   247

Figure 2. Interactive system in *view mode*. Symbols on screen represent features as follows: 1) Illuminated text box above question mark controls appearance of glosses or translations. 2) Symbols at lower left control image functions. From left to right these are: *play/stop, pause, frame step, return to beginning of sign, zoom, full screen display.*

Figure 3. System in *learn mode*. Symbols on screen represent features as follows: 1) below left hand image (from CD) symbols control *play/stop, pause, frame step, return to beginning of sign.* 2) Below right hand image (from camera) symbols control *play/stop, pause, frame step, return to beginning of sign.* Buttons below these control *record* (from camera), *sync* (synchronising with the student's recording from camera), *lock* (locking the two together so that they can be played using the left hand controls).

Field Trials

Field trials of the system have been undertaken. There were two major components to the field trials. The first was the testing of features of the prototype system to determine students' and tutors' preferences for access to the data base and for those functions of the system thought to be most useful. The main component of the field trials, however, has been the testing of the students' progress in sign production and comprehension, compared with students using more traditional methods of practice.

The applications of new technology to a new field of work are exciting in themselves. The creation of a new technology with its first application in the deafness field is especially exciting.

References

Baker, C. & Padden, C. (1978). Focusing on the nonmanual components of American Sign Language. In: L.A. Friedman (ed.) *On the other hand: new perspectives on American Sign Language.* New York: Academic Press, 215-236.

Frishberg, N. (1983). Dominance relations and discourse structures. In: W. Stokoe & V. Volterra (eds), *SLR 83: Proceedings of the IIIrd international symposium on sign language research.* Silver Spring MD: Linstok Press.

Hassinen, L. (1989). *A preliminary study of the signing of Usher's signers.* Unpublished paper. Bristol: Centre for Deaf Studies.

Kyle, J.G., Woll, B. & Llewellyn-Jones, P. (1981). Learning and Using BSL. *Sign Language Studies 31*, 155-178.

Maestas y Moores, J. (1980) Early linguistic environment: interactions of deaf parents with their infants. *Sign Language Studies 26*, 1-13.

Woll, B. (1991) *Sign Language and Television.* Report to Channel 4. London: Channel 4 Television.

Glossary for the Deaf
A Laservision Sign Language Dictionary

Olle Eriksen
Trondheim Døveskole, Sobstadveien 65, 7080 Heimdal, Norway

Abstract. The primary language for deaf students is Norwegian Sign Language, and they learn written Norwegian as their second language. When the students have reached a certain reading level (i.e. they understand the basic structures and grammatical rules of the written language), they still need a lot of lexical information. In order to give the students an understanding of the meaning of words in the written language, we provide access to a translation of words and phrases into Norwegian Sign Language.

We have produced a Laservision disc containing 1500 signs covering the words from a book ("Fairy Tales from 17 Countries"). The student types a word on the computer keyboard, and one or more signs for this word are presented in full-motion video on the computer monitor.

Keywords. Deafness, language learning, interactive video.

Introduction

This paper is about a project called "Glossary for the Deaf". The first preparations started at the Trondheim School for the Deaf in 1984. Seven people have been involved in the project, of whom two were deaf and five were hearing. None of these have worked on a full-time basis on the project, which is why it has taken such a long time. We received some financial support from the Norwegian Department of Education and Research. In this way we have covered the cost of equipment, programming and the technical production of a Laservision disc.

Background

The primary language of Norwegian deaf students is Norwegian Sign Language, and they learn written Norwegian as their second language. This bilingual approach to teaching deaf children is fairly new, and we have yet to develop appropriate teaching aids and teaching materials. When the students have reached a certain reading level (i.e. they understand the basic structures and grammatical rules of the written language), they still need a lot of lexical information. In order to give the students an understanding of the meaning of words in the written language, we provide access to a translation of words and phrases into Norwegian Sign Language.

Figure 1.

When they have access to a dictionary the students can study Norwegian texts on their own without having to ask their teacher for help all the time. Another reason for making the dictionary is that, unfortunately, some teachers of the deaf still have quite limited competence in sign language, and have problems explaining the meaning of words to the students.

Goal

What we wanted to achieve was to make a glossary where it would be possible to type a Norwegian word on the computer keyboard and then immediately get a translation into Norwegian Sign Language (NSL) on the monitor. It would have been fairly easy to make this glossary with still photos or drawings, but our experience with this type of dictionary (in book form) is that they are only used by hearing people as a reminder when learning sign language. The most obvious reason for this is the lack of motion which is of vital importance in sign language. One often tries to compensate for this by adding arrows to indicate the direction of movement, or by supplying more than one picture for a single sign. Still, this is obviously not good enough for our purpose.

The use of notation systems was also considered, but there is no single system commonly used in Norway, and we were certainly not competent to choose between the existing systems or make up a new one. In order to use a dictionary based on a notation system the students would first have to learn the system. This was not considered to be practical, and would severely limit the use of the dictionary.

Another possible solution was computer animation for the NSL presentation, but at the time it was not possible to get the speed and resolution, combined with the adequate storage capacity needed, for the quality we wanted. It also would imply a lot of computer animation work - probably more than we could afford.

We found that the use of interactive video was the best solution taking into consideration our limited budget, ease of production and desired picture quality. We wanted to make a Laservision disc, but because of the relatively high production costs and the lack of possibility to make changes on the disc, we decided to do some tests with interactive videotape before producing the disc. We called this "Phase I" of the project, and the production of the Laservision disc was called "Phase II".

Phase I (VHS Test System)

When making a general dictionary independent of any specific text, translations have to be made on a word/phrase level and not on a sentence level. But even if we make a dictionary tied up to a specific text, translations of whole sentences would consume a lot of space and severely limit the amount of material that can be stored on a Laservision disc. There was some serious scepticism as to the effectiveness of making such a translation between a spoken/written language and a sign language. Some people questioned whether such translations would be of any value to the students. To test this we made a set-up with a VHS videocassette player controlled by a computer through an interface. In this way we were able to produce the videomaterial, make changes and make new versions when we needed to, - and all without great expense. We translated two texts both on a word/phrase level and on a sentence level, and designed a test to find the answer to the following questions:

- Will the use of a dictionary have any effect on the reading comprehension of the students?
- Will there be any difference in the comprehension when the students get a translation on a word/phrase level only, as opposed to a translation on a sentence level?

Due to the relatively long random access time of a videocassette player compared to a videodisc player, we had to optimise the program for speed. The translation of each word was taped on the videocassette in the same order as in the text, and the sign language translation of the whole sentence was taped after the last single word translation in that same sentence. In this way we managed to get acceptable access times if the student who was reading the text used the dictionary once in a while.

The system was tested on 30 deaf students in our school. This work was done by a teacher of the deaf as part of a masters degree in Special Education. There is a written report in Norwegian describing the design and the results. (Lund, 1989). The results were promising:

- The students had a significantly better comprehension of the written text when using the dictionary.
- The test showed only a small (not significant) difference between the word/phrase level only and the sentence level.

The conclusion of the experiment is that it can be of great help to deaf students to have access to translations from written Norwegian to NSL even if only on a word/phrase level. This is also what we normally get when using an ordinary dictionary.

Phase II (Laservision Disc)

Target Group

The dictionary is primarily made for deaf students ten years of age and older. When trying out the dictionary on all our students, however, we found that even children from seven years on up who were able to read and write a little, really enjoyed using the dictionary. (Children start school at seven years of age in Norway). I might also add that the dictionary is a useful aid to hearing people wanting to learn NSL.

The Laservision Disc

The Laservision disc contains only the sign language material. Random access time for a sign is approximately 1.5 second (depending on type of player). One sign needs anywhere from one to three seconds to be presented. The average sign lasts a little less than 1.5 seconds (36 frames), which means that one side of the disc can hold approximately 1500 signs. The Laservision disc is the limiting factor for the size of the dictionary. To save valuable space on the disc, the first frame in each sign is presented as a still for one second before the full motion video starts, and then the last frame is a still for one second. In this way we manage to save at least two seconds disc space per sign. The first frame is one frame before the presenter raises his hands to start signing, and the last frame is what we judged to be the end of the sign. Usually one frame before the signer starts to put his hands down or closes his eyes.

We also wanted to get some experience on other possible ways of saving disc space. On the disc there are a few signs with reduced frame rate (five frames per second). When these signs are presented at the correct speed they look very jerky. This method of presenting the signs was not judged to be good enough, though it might be acceptable if the frame rate were reduced a little less than we did.

Another possible way of saving space on the disc might be to reduce the size of the picture. It is possible to have four different quarter-screen-sized pictures simultaneously, and zoom in on one of the pictures at a time with a video overlay card. This was not done because we wanted to make it possible to use the disc without a video overlay card as well. We did frame doubling on the whole disc in order to be able to present stable still pictures.

The use of a high speed shutter on the camera was also considered, as this would give clear, clean still pictures even of hands in fast motion. However the use of a high speed shutter is clearly visible (as a strobe effect) in normal play, and was rejected because of this.

Choice of Material

The above mentioned problems with limited space on the videodisc clearly limits the size of a dictionary based on this technology. Fifteen hundred signs certainly is a very small dictionary. To make a useful general dictionary we would probably want the size to be at least ten times as large.

Facing the problem of how to choose which signs to put on the disc we made the following considerations: We wanted to make it possible to supplement this first videodisc with other ones later on to make up a (more or less) complete dictionary. Following this line of reasoning, it seemed logical to choose the most frequently used words in the written language for the first disc. This strategy was abandoned because - as one might guess - the experience from Phase I of the project clearly told us that frequently used words were never looked up by the students. With a dictionary like that the students would probably not find what they were looking for, and hence stop using it. We wanted the student to get an answer on (nearly) all inquiries.

We finally decided to choose the words from a limited text, preferably a complete book. In this way we could guarantee that the student always would get a translation when looking up a word from this book. The book "Fairytales from 17 countries" was chosen because:

- children at different ages find fairytales interesting and exciting
- this particular book was already in use at a number of schools for the deaf
- the amount of material in the book seemed sufficient.

Translation

A group of four people (two deaf persons and two hearing persons - of whom one is a teacher of the deaf and the other a sign language interpreter) did the translation work. For any specific word, the signs that deaf people use was given first priority. In some cases the signs that parents learn at sign language courses were included as well. The reason for this is that some children learn these signs from their parents.

Even if it is possible to type in an inflection of a word, only the uninflected form of the word is translated. When the same word has more than one meaning in the book, signs for the different meanings are presented, and the student has to choose the one that fits in the context. This is similar to an ordinary dictionary. When the sign translation of a word such as "size" or "carry" is completely dependent on the context (i.e. what has "size", or what is being carried/who carries), different variants are shown. Some commonly used expressions were also translated (example: "once upon a time"). Some words were not translated because they are not used in sign language (example: "that" used as a conjunction).

When all the signs had been taped we found that there was not enough room for all the material on the videodisc. We had to reject 30% of the original material, and the diversity of signs that we desired on the disc suffered.

Glossary for the Deaf: A Laservision Sign Language Dictionary

Computer Program

A vocabulary list and a computer program are stored on the computer harddisc. At the moment this program will run on a IBM compatible PC only, but the program will also be converted to Apple Macintosh.

User Interface

We wanted to keep the user interface as simple as possible. Even computer illiterates should be able to use the dictionary. We did not want to use a touch screen because the preferred viewing distance for full screen sign language presentation is too far away for the hands to reach the screen. The program autostarts from a menu, and on the first screen there are two fields (boxes).

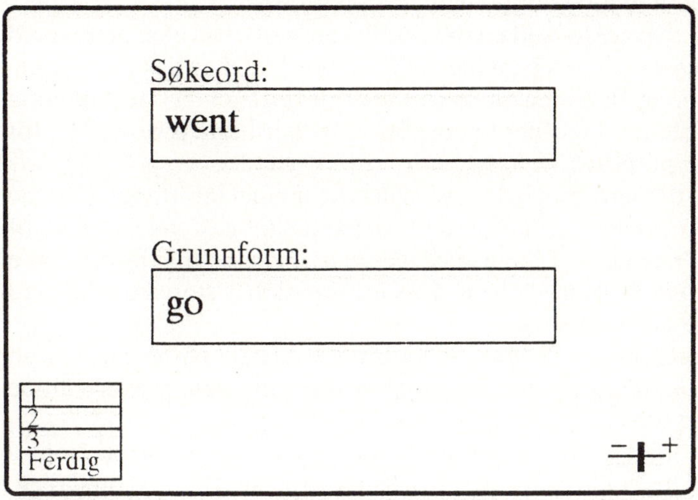

Figure 2.

"Søkeord" means word to search for, and "grunnform" means the uninflected form of the word. The student types the word he wants to look up on the computer keyboard and finishes with a "Return". The typed word shows up in the box at the top, and the uninflected form of the word is shown in the box at the bottom. The student can type in an inflection of a word, but the sign shown is always the uninflected form of the word. In addition the number of signs for this word is shown in the left bottom corner. The first sign is highlighted, and when the student hits the "Return" key once again, the first sign is presented on the screen in full motion video. When the presentation is finished, the next sign is highlighted, and will be presented when the student hits "Return" again. When all the signs for this word are presented "Ferdig" (which means finished) is highlighted, and if the student hits "Return", the screen is cleared for the next input.

This is the simple way to use the dictionary, but we also have some options: The student can move the highlighting in the left bottom corner up or down with the cursor keys (arrow up/arrow down) and repeat or skip signs. It is possible to alter the speed of the presentation with the cursor keys (arrow left/arrow right). One gets an indication of the chosen speed in the right bottom corner of the screen. If you hit the space bar while a sign is presented, the video goes into still mode. With the letters B and N on the keyboard it is possible to step one frame at a time backwards or forwards. This is a useful option if you wish to study a sign in detail (handshapes etc.). To have access to the vocabulary list you hit a function key (F2). With the cursor keys and the page up/page down keys you can look through the list alphabetically. To see the sign for a specific word you hit "Return" and the sign for the highlighted word in the list is presented.

All the words that are looked up in a session are stored on a separate word list . This makes it easy to repeat the difficult words at the end of a session. These word lists can be stored on a disc and retrieved later on. This function makes it possible for a teacher to construct smaller limited word lists for special training purposes.

In addition to the sign translation, we can have textual information for the words in the vocabulary. This could be an explanation of the meaning of the word or an example of the use of the word. The textual information appears in the middle of the screen. This information is stored on the hard disc and can be altered easily.

By hitting function key F6 you can look at the content of the disc as you would look at a video. All the functions of the videodisc player can be controlled from the computer keyboard.

As mentioned above the words in the dictionary are all taken from a specific book. This could have made it possible to present the text on screen, and then highlight the words for translation into sign language (with a mouse or the cursor keys). This would in many ways make the translation work easier, we could avoid the problems with words that have different meanings in different contexts. Still this approach was not utilized because we wanted:

• our dictionary to function more like an ordinary dictionary,
and we wanted the students to
• read in a book and not on the screen and
• learn to spell the words right by typing them.

The program can be used either with a video overlay card and one screen or without a video overlay card and with two screens. The single screen setup is clearly preferable, but the dual screen setup is cheaper. A vocabulary list with a barcode printed after each word will be produced in the near future. It will then be possible to use the videodisc with a videodisc player connected to a barcode reader. For small children the written words can be replaced with pictures or drawings.

Conclusions

The students have a significantly higher reading comprehension when they have access to a sign language dictionary. The students have shown great pleasure in using the dictionary. Having access to translations of Norwegian words and phrases into their own language NSL has greatly enhanced their motivation for reading. The students have also been able to work more independently with Norwegian texts.

This is a very small and limited dictionary, and what we need is a general dictionary between the two languages written Norwegian and Norwegian Sign Language. For the time being the size of the dictionary is limited by the technology available to us, but this is rapidly changing. When technology makes a large sign language dictionary feasible it would be nice if we had the basic research and knowledge needed to develop such a dictionary. This requires a great deal of sign language research which should be given the highest priority in the years to come.

References

Hvenekilde, A. (1979). *Eventyr fra 17 land.* (Fairy Tales from 17 Countries) J.W. Cappelens Forlag a.s.
Lund, B. (1989). *Tegnspråkordbok for døve.* Vikhovtrykk.

Interactive Introduction of the Logical Bases of a Communication System

F. Lowenthal
Sciences Cognitives, Université de Mons-Hainaut,
Place du Parc 20, B-7000 Mons, Belgium

Abstract. As mathematician and researcher in cognitive psychology, we had the opportunity to work with children having communication problems. We thus discovered the advantages of a nearly non-verbal approach inspired by logico-mathematical techniques: the use of this approach favours the development of a structured communication system in children who suffer from language disorders. In this paper, we want first to explain why we chose to let the subjects manipulate *concrete representations of formal systems*. We will then use a paradigmatic example and show how this technique has been succesfully used with an aphasic child: we will describe in details two of the devices we used. We will also explain why this approach is relevant for deaf children. Finally, we will show that the computer can play a useful role, during nonverbal interactive sessions, in this rehabilitation process.

Preliminary: What is a Language ?

Linguists, psychologists and psycho-linguists have tried to formulate a satisfactory definition of the concept *language* in order to be able to discuss our usual language. They asked themselves the following question: *what is a language?* but were not able to produce a generally accepted answer. Osgood (1980) suggested to change the question and to try to describe how we would identify something as a *language* if we encountered what *might* be one in an obviously nonhuman species. This lead him to describe a language as a communication system which must satisfy specific criteria: a language, for him, is a communication system *governed by precise rules*. Moreover, for Osgood, a natural human language is necessarily based on the vocal-auditory channel: he justifies this choice by man's integration in a spatio-temporal universe, but he thus excludes *the signing of deaf-mutes, as far as being a **natural** human language*. This justification corresponds to observations made by Jakobson and is of great relevance for the rest of this paper as will be shown later. The major conclusion we can draw from

Osgood's definition, is that any language is essentially a *structured communication device used by individuals who can both understand and produce communicative elements*. The special characteristics of a human language enable its users, among other facts, to discuss objects which are not present, or even facts which are impossible; it gives them a possibility to manipulate the reality without having to actually manipulate it.

This possibility appeared useful for mathematicians and logicians. At the very beginning, they used everyday language to create their proofs and theorems. Plato, Aristotle and others used the verbal language to describe what a reasoning might be, and what kind of rules reasonings had to obey. Nevertheless, there were problems: the sentence "Paris is a five letter word" seems to be true; should we deduce *naturally* that "The capital town of France is a five letter word"? The situation became even worse when mathematicians and logicians started to manipulate complex and abstract universes. It is nearly impossible to use everyday language to describe and discuss e.g. "5-dimensional objects immerged in a 7-dimensional universe": the usual language is misleading since it is linked to a cognitive background which is not adapted to the mathematical situation! These scientists, inspired by Leinitz, decided to create special sets of symbols, special rules to connect such symbols in order to create formulae which enabled them to manipulate the universe they were studying. As these symbols are *by definition* meaningless, they also agreed that they could arbitrarily select some of these formulae, which they *chose* to consider as basic formulae, and rules enabling them to transform one formula into another in a 'legal' fashion: this gave them the possibility to describe meaningful reasonings about their universes. But these universes are different and might thus require different basic rules: we do not use the same basic rules for chess and for backgammon! This justifies the existence of various formal systems adapted to various mathematical universes; in each case the choice of the basic formulae and of the transformation rules will define the *mathematical meaning* of the formulae used. These sets of symbols and of non-ambiguous rules concerning them are called "formal systems": in fact each formal system defines its own rules of reasonings, and thus its own logic. The use of these formal systems appeared very useful to study and create mathematics and logic; they are even more useful now that we are confronted with a growing number of 'computer languages' which are also formal systems.

It has been shown that our usual language, as Osgood defines it, is nothing else than a very complex formal system provided with ambiguities; but that the *fundamental principles* governing its use are *identical* to those governing the use of real formal systems. Nevertheless, formal systems, as used in logic, do not seem appropriate to start a communication about everyday life, especially since they are technically very complex. We have shown (Lowenthal, 1986a) that small sets of objects, provided with technical constraints, are nothing else than tiny formal systems which enable us to create reasonings concerning a restricted domain. Lego bricks form such a very simple set of objects: it is possible to place them horizontally or vertically on the base bord, but never in diagonal; this is sufficient to provoke the emergence of simple but precise reasonings in 4-year olds. We call such small sets of actual objects "Concrete representations of formal systems". As they are simple but real formal systems, the *fundamental principles* governing their use must be the same as those used for complex formal systems, such as those in arithmetics. But this implies that these fundamental principles are also those governing the use of our usual language. Moreover, these concrete representations are easy to handle, can be presented in an interactive way by means of a computer, and can be used in nearly *non-verbal* way. It appears thus reasonable to train children with communication problems to use these concrete representations of formal systems: our main purpose then is not to let these subjects play with the concrete devices for the sake of playing with them, but instead to let them acquire *in a non-verbal* way the fundamental principles governing the usual human languages.

Introduction

Linguists have clearly distinguished two essential components of the verbal language: semantics (or "meaning") and syntax (or "grammar"). These two components must be mastered by the child who is learning to speak. Researchers such as Bruner (1966, 1972) claim that the meaning of words or sentences is easily learned by the child who is exposed to an adult world where object-name associations are made easy by adults functioning as educators. The situation is rather different for syntax. This component is associated to a set of formal rules, and as we have seen in the preliminary, such a set of rules is *a* logic. One can speak of the logic of English, but it seems easier to understand the concept "logic" in the frame of games. The starting positions and the nature of chess pieces, combined with the rules governing their moves defines the standard logic of chess; nevertheless, Lewis Carrol, in *"Alice through the looking glass"* let Alice go through a strange country which is defined in such a way that it is in fact a chess board where the starting position and the number of pieces is not the standard one: this author is using a non classical logic for his game of chess. As long as an author warns us explicitly of the changes he has adopted, he is free to do so. The problem with a natural language is that this language has an existence independent of our fantasy and our whimsy! It is thus important for the young learner to master as quickly as possible enough of this standard language-logic in order to communicate easily with others; it becomes thus relevant for an educator to wonder how young ones acquire this complex knowledge in order to be able to help them. Many psychologists claim that the verbal and natural language can only develop in a child, if this child has previously acquired the essential elements of *a* logic. Independently and simultaneously, other researchers have shown evidence that a child, while developing *a* logic, is mostly using the most common vector of this logic: the verbal language. Taken separately, these two statements are not contradictory; but taken together, they give rise to what seems to be a paradox, a dreadful vicious circle: the acquisition of a verbal language seems to be based on the acquisition of a logical structure which cannot be acquired without a previous mastery of the same verbal language! Nevertheless, children learn to speak: there must thus be ways to break this vicious circle. This problem has been studied by many researchers (e.g. Siegel, 1978; Rondal, 1983).

The development of the usual verbal language in *normal* children depends on the acquisition of a logical structure. All the oppositions (day-night, left-right, in-out, ...) encountered by the child appear to be essential elements enabling him to break the vicious circle mentioned above: they enable the young child to acquire a *basic* logical structure which will serve as a trigger for the complex process of language acquisition (Piaget & Inhelder, 1959). Jakobson (1939) described how children elaborate their *phonological* system: they play with sounds, firstly they oppose *the* consonant to *the* vowel, by doing so, they discover different categories of consonants which they can articulate on a main common vowel, and finally they articulate different vowels on known consonants and they learn to distinguish different classes of vowels. From this description it is obvious that the phonetic oppositions, the child's babbling and his construction of a phonological system by *sorting* (putting things in given classes) and *categorizing* (creating classes to put given things into them) seem to be some of the most important elements in the elaboration of a first tiny logical structure. This first logical structure appears to be the "*trigger*", the unavoidable starting point for the rest of the procedure. This is probably one of the reasons for which Osgood claimed that all *natural* human languages must be based on the vocal channel. Normal hearing children seem to use the tiny and basic structure established through all these oppositions for a first structuration of a communication system, this system will then give birth to a first form of verbal communication. This communication will favour the development of the logical structure, and this in turn will favour the development of language.

Deaf children are in a more difficult situation: as they cannot hear, they cannot use the oppositions which could be offered by the verbal expressions formulated by adults in their families. One might believe that sign language could replace the verbal language, but this signed mode of communication is not associated to the permanent "noise" of everyday life;

moreover this "language" is the result of an adult construction and not the consequence of a natural ontogenetical and phylogenetical evolution: Osgood (1980) refuses to accept it as a true human language; anyway this non-verbal mode of communication does *not* offer to deaf subjects oppositions which could replace those of the lacking verbal language. The normal process described above is thus impossible, these children start their lives by having problems in building their basic logical structure. It is thus not astonishing if they suffer from severe communication troubles; most of the techniques used to help them seem to be *surface-like* patching-up processes with little or no *structural* influence. We believe that it is more important to create conditions which will enable the therapist to develop the missing basic structure, and thus to have a *structure-like* influence. We are convinced that such an influence is essential since it will enable the deaf child to develop his *own* approach to the usually accepted communication system. We will show that the best therapy is not necessarily based on the develop-ment of a verbal communication: deaf children cannot oppose sounds, but luckily they are able to manipulate and oppose objects. It seems thus useful to use sets of objects which make opposing and sorting activities easily accessible. Concrete representations of formal systems are such sets of objects.

The paradigmatic example described in this paper shows that manipulations of *concrete representations of formal systems* can be used as a "trigger" for children who do not master a structured system of communication: these manipulations might be compared (among other things) with those which enable *normal* children to elaborate a structured phonological system.

Definition of Concrete Representations of Formal Systems

A teaching experiment with socio-economically disadvantaged children (Cordier & Lowenthal, 1973; Cordier, Lowenthal & Héraux, 1975) showed that the problems observed in their verbal language (Bernstein et al., 1969; Cordier, 1975) could be bypassed using an approach inspired by that described by Frédérique and Georges Papy (1968, 1970, 1971, 1972). This fact suggested us to try and use other devices (Lowenthal, 1985a, 1987). The experiments realised with them led to a new approach for the rehabilitation of several categories of children having structural communication problems. This approach is based on manipulations of concrete representations of formal systems. Such a representation is in fact a set of tools provided with technical constraints. These constraints make certain actions technically possible and other actions impossible. This in turn suggests a logical structure. Manipulations of these concrete representations do not involve verbal interactions, and logical problems can easily be introduced in a nonverbal way. Two of these devices are mentioned in this paper: Dienes' Attribute Blocks and Cohors-Fresenborg's Dynamical Mazes. The first device can be used to develop sorting and categorising processes in children who did not have the opportunity to use phonetic oppositions; in fact such children can play with the blocks as they would have done with phonemes. The second device makes it possible to introduce the concept of finite automaton in a nearly nonverbal way; this enables the therapist to let the child *construct* solutions for nonverbally presented problems, and *discover* the problem for which a solution has been presented. In both cases, the manipulations of these devices favour the development of a logical structure in the child. This entails several transfers towards other domains: the verbal language when it is possible; a better mastery of reading, writing and computing in certain cases; but always the develop-ment of a more structured communication system.

A Paradigmatic Example: Saïd, an Aphasic Child

Saïd is a right-handed child. He is the fourth child in a family of six children. All his brothers and sisters are normal. His psychomotor development was normal and the boy started to utter one-word sentences and to walk at the age of 13 months. At that age he lost the ability to understand and speak natural language, as a result of a herpetic meningo-encephalitis followed by a right hemiplegia. He recovered from the hemiplegia, but there was still a slight right apraxia at the age of 5 years 6 months when we examined him for the first time. There were no overt signs of debility. Formal hearing tests and EEG were normal, but the CT-scan showed two symmetrically localised brain lesions. Neurologists do not agree about their exact localisation: some say these are rolandic lesions, other prefer to speak about temporo-parietal or even temporo-parietal and partially frontal lesions. The only points about which these neurologists agree is that the regions of the brains which are usually associated with vision are intact while the lesions are obviously localised in the regions of the brain which are traditionally associated with language comprehension and language production. Neurologists say now that Saïd is an aphasic child, or *since he never had the opportunity to learn completely the syntax* a child having an auditory agnosia. Anyway, all of them agree: the child did not understand or speak any natural language at the age of 5,6 years.

One can assume that, to a certain extent, this child behaved then as profoundly deaf children do. Although this child is neither deaf nor mute, he treated all commu-nicative stimulae, and especially the verbal ones, as deaf-mutes do. Since the age of 13 months, Saïd has been treated by several speech therapists and examined by several psychologists. The child was not able to understand the psychologists' *verbal* questions; his cognitive background was such that he could not solve the *nonverbal* exercises they proposed: the psychologists concluded that this child was *severely mentally retarded*. The speech therapists tried to teach him to use Bliss-symbols (Silverman, 1982) or the signs used by deaf children: altogether this was a complete failure. At the age of 5,6 years, the child understood only 5 monosyllabic spoken words: "yes", "no", "good", "bad", "more" and his first name: "Saïd". It was assumed that he relied mostly on the intonation and the mimic rather than on the sounds themselves. He also used two special signs: one (right thumb upward) to mean "good" and the other (right thumb pointing towards his own chest) to mean "me". Besides that, he communicated only by pointing (Lowenthal & Saerens, 1986). It must be mentioned that this child lives in a multilingual environment: his parents spoke Arabic with him, but his father insists: his children must learn to use the Belgian language he knows, French, while they live in Flanders and have to use Dutch at school. This case is relevant for our present discussion since it can be assumed that Saïd, after his meningo-encephalitis had lost the basic tiny logical structure he had already constructed and had become unable, because of the neurological lesions, to use phonetic oppositions to start the construction of a new logical structure. Saïd was thus in a situation comparable to that of deaf children: although he could hear, he could no longer sort the sounds he heard. It is assumed that he was not able to construct the concept corresponding to the vowel "a" and that a "short a" and a "long a" were two sounds as different as an "a" and an "i" for a normally hearing child.

We started our treatment by using Dienes' Attribute Blocks (Dienes, 1966; Dienes and Golding, 1970). The set of A-blocks consists of 48 pieces of plastic; each block can be defined by four variables: shape, colour, size and thickness. There are 4 possible shapes (rectangle, square, circle, triangle), 3 possible colours (red, blue, yellow), 2 sizes (big, small) and 2 thicknesses (thick, thin). In order to have all possible combinations one needs 48 blocks. This makes sorting and other logical exercises possible. Saïd had time enough to play freely with the material before he was asked to solve logical problems. These problems were introduced in a nearly totally nonverbal way by giving examples and partial solutions, by rejecting the child's movements which led to a mistake ("no" was understood by the child) and by approving ("yes", "good") the movements which led to a correct solution. We kept doing this until the child adopted a strategy which was adequate to solve the problem we had formulated. We cannot know how the child understood the problem, we can only say that we interfered until the child had adopted *by trial and error* a solving strategy which we hoped he would extend to similar problems. Some of the problems used and the child's results are mentioned here.

Saïd very quickly learned to sort the blocks according to colour or shape. Later he learned to use also the other criteria: he was then able to sort blocks using one, two or three of the characteristics involved. He also learned to associate a real block with a drawing made by the experimenter or to draw (as well as his apraxia made it possible) a figure corresponding by shape and colour to a block which was shown to him by the experimenter. Later, he learned to use symbols representing the different criteria, the logical *connectives* "and", "or", "not" and the *relation* "equal". He also discovered that three small rectangles could be put together in order to cover exactly a big rectangle, and thus replace the latter one in all sorting processes. After that discovery, he started to search for other potential combinations. These results show that, although some psychologists considered him a severely mentally retarded boy, this child had somehow access to a semantic component, to a syntactic component and that he could learn to communicate in a symbolic way, using abstract symbols instead of blocks or drawings. This fact did not become obvious before A-blocks were used to introduce logical exercises. One must distinguish two aspects of our work: the simple manipulations of actual blocks which was quickly learned by the child and might have been acquired by means of other techniques; and the manipulations of pure symbols, which could probably not have been taught without the device and the approach described here, or a similar one. It seems that the manipulations of blocks played for Saïd a role similar to that of manipulating sounds for the young infant, and that the constraints imposed by the blocks triggered in Saïd a basic logical structure similar to that triggered by sounds in young infants.

After one year of work with concrete representations of formal systems, Saïd started to understand spoken words, simultaneously in the three languages which constituted his environment. He learned with us to write the letters of his name: the action of writing had now a meaning for this child; he also learned to use symbols and to read, write and use numbers. He also started to create "ad hoc" gestures to communicate more easily with his parents and with us. These "symbolic" gestures were in fact based on the context and belonged to the enactive representation level (Bruner, 1966). We then tried to use another concrete representation of a formal system with the child.

A Dynamical Maze (Cohors-Fresenborg, 1978) consists of bricks (see Figure 1) which can be placed on a baseboard. These bricks constitute the basic elements needed to create a railway network: straight rails, curves, crossings (by-passes), joints (pieces *joining* two tracks having different origins but a common ending) and switches. These last pieces impose a first technical restriction: these networks must be one-way networks. The material has other built-in constraints which purposely restrict the number and kind of combinations a child can make with the pieces. As with the A-blocks, the therapist does not need to tell the child that there are restrictions, the built-in constraints automatically impose them. They have been described in great details in several papers (Lowenthal & Marcq, 1980; 1982; Lowenthal, 1984).

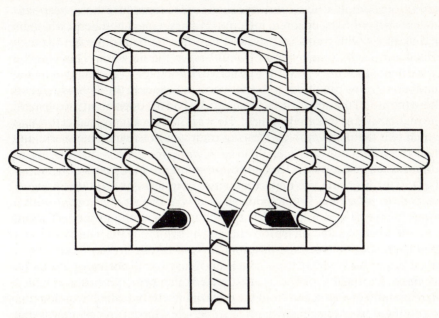

Figure 1. Example of a network made with Dynamical Mazes elements: the entrance leads to an ordinary switch which is open towards the left; the first train will be lead to the left main exit and will then re-enter through the right side entrance, thus changing the orientation of this switch. All odd-numbered trains will leave the network through the right exit and all the even ones through the left exit.

Cohors-Fresenborg uses this material in a direct way: he presents mathematical problems to children and asks them to construct a network which would give the solution of the problem. This is possible since this material also includes a counter and is in fact the mechanical counterpart of the hardware of a computer. We used it rather differently. All this was done in a nearly nonverbal way. As previously, we first let the child play freely with the device and become familiar with some of its constraints. We then asked him to build paths with the given bricks in order to connect a given entrance to a given exit, or several entrances to several exits: the child was then asked to let *trains* (represented by a wooden stock) run through the network. This step implied the use of crossings, joints and switches. At the very start the child failed, although he was very successful with the A-blocks. We decided to wait several months and tried again: we then observed that the child solved all the simple problems very easily. This change might be attributed to ordinary maturation, or to an evolution that started *only after* we introduced the first categorisation exercises by presenting the subject with A-blocks, and thus by providing him with all the oppositions associated to the use of these blocks. We then presented the child with sketches describing complete networks, we asked Saïd to reproduce the corresponding network with the concrete material. We associated numbers (which he had learned) with trains and showed him that he had to predict through which exit each "number-train" would leave the network. This was the equivalent of asking: "What is this network good for?". Saïd had to let the numbered trains run through the network and observe through which exit these trains left the network. By doing so, he had the opportunity to observe the regularities of this environment. He was firstly asked to predict through which exit the *immediately following* train would leave the network, and then the *following one*, and then an *apparently distant* one (as far as numbers are concerned). He had to *formulate an hypothesis* concerning these exits, he could use the actual network to test and *validate it,* and if needed, to *adapt* his first hypothesis. He was in fact confronted with a solution and he was asked: "What is the corresponding problem?". Saïd easily learned to solve such problems and he even used the similarities and the differences between the different sorts of bricks to start to use (or to create?) gestures which were consistently used with the same symbolic meaning. During that period he also created other symbolic gestures which were completely detached from the material itself, but which enabled him to communicate rather easily with other people. His only problem was that he needed to make these people aware of the objects which constituted his universe of discourse. At the very beginning he could only use pointing to mention objects, but after several years he learned to use symbols and written words.

To conclude this section, it seems relevant to state that after 5 years of treatment based on the use of concrete representations of formal systems, Saïd now understands short spoken sentences in three languages (Arabic, his parents mother tongue; French, the Belgian language his father wants to use with his children; Dutch, the language Saïd uses at school and with us). He reads and writes short texts (in Dutch) and performs the basic operations of arithmetics. He is also able to communicate in a structured way, using simultaneously gestures and words he writes to define his universe of discourse.

Concrete Representations of Formal Systems and Deaf Children

Other experiments have taken place, some of them with normal children, others with handicapped children. We want to briefly describe here the results obtained, since these results lead to the same general conclusion: concrete representations of formal systems can be used as structuring elements which favour the development of a structured communication system. These results have convinced us to start new experiments with deaf children and observe how the use of concrete representations of formal systems could help them to learn to read. We used the dynamical mazes with a group of four deaf children, placed in an ordinary school with non-deaf children. These children were not able to follow the teacher's explanations as fast as the other children and were not really integrated in the "normal" group, they were considered as stupid since they did not understand verbal explanations. But these deaf children understood perfectly how to use the Dynamical Mazes; they realised that they were *not* stupid and that they were able to solve complex logical problems. They were able to explain how to use the material to their hearing companions. This was a wonderful way to let these children express themselves and prove to the others that they were able to solve the problems faster than the "normal" children, and to prove also that they were able to understand and organise once they were provided with appropriate material.

The Dynamical Mazes were also used for an experiment concerning children's reading ability. We present here the results concerning 49 children with normal hearing; we used the same approach as that used for Saïd but the subjects were normal 6-year olds. We compared the progresses they made in reading (Lowenthal, 1986b). These children belonged to 2 different school classes (named here class A and class B) and had different teachers. We used two tests devised by Inizan (1983) and concerning reading competences and reading performances: Inizan's "predictive battery" was used as pre-test, and his "evaluation battery" was used as post-test. According to the author of the tests, the scores at the two tests are *highly* correlated. The pre-test enabled us to randomize our samples and to divide each school class in two subgroups: an experimental group and a control group, in such a way that inside a given class the two subgroups were equivalent as far as Inizan's predictions concerning their reading acquisition was concerned. The two teachers did not use the same teaching method as far as reading was concerned. The teacher of class B taught by asking her pupils to formulate hypotheses, to test them and to adapt them; she gave her pupils short sentences written on a piece of paper and consisting of words the children knew already, *except for one word* which belonged to their spoken language but not to their written language, but in such a way that the children had enough information to guess the meaning of the sentence: the children were then asked to discover the word they were not already able to read, they could use information such as the apparent length of the word, the first letters (if they were known), etc. The teacher of class A used a more classical and more conventional method: she used in fact a method based on the acquisition of the different letters, on their groupings into syllables, on the groupings of these units into words; this teacher behaved as if she possessed the knowledge and was ready to teach and *impose* her reading technique onto children who had no opportunity to *discover and apprehend* any reading technique by themselves, onto children who did not have the possibility to *construct logically* their own reading method.

The children of the experimental groups worked by groups of two with the Dynamical Mazes. During a first session, they freely manipulated the material; during the remaining 6 sessions they were asked to use the given material and to build a maze corresponding to a small sketch. They then had to discover its use as described above. They were also asked to express verbally the hypotheses they formulated about the functioning of their network. It was thus possible to observe whether these children learned to make short, medium or long term predictions, i.e. whether they were able to use this material to make hypotheses, to test them and to validate or adapt them. This fact is important since the reading method used by the teacher of class B was based on similar predictions. In fact we all make hypotheses, test them, adapt them and validate them when we are reading. The children of classes A and B never worked together. The teacher of class B used a logically oriented approach to reading and her pupils did as well as the others at the post-test, as far as reading skills are concerned. The results also show that the experimental group performed significantly better at the post-test ($p=.015$). This difference is in fact mainly due to the scores of children of class A ($p=.005$) *where the teacher did not favour the formulation of hypotheses.*

These observations lead us to conclude that either the teacher of class B was unusually good, or that the use of logically structured material with children aged 6 favours their acquisition of reading skills. In fact the teaching technique used in class B associated very early these reading skills with verbal productions in a structuring way. This was not the case in class A, but the approach we used with *all* the subjects of the experimental group was based on a similar principle: we associated manipulations of a relatively highly structured material with verbal utterances concerning this material, as the material is provided with technical constraints, the verbal utterances were also structured. Similar observations were mentioned by Papert (1980) about children using the logo programming language.

The logically structured material we used, these Concrete Representations of Formal Systems, are not really necessary if the teacher is using a logically structured approach *and if a structured communication exists between teacher and pupil*; but our "mathematical" approach is clearly useful in domains very different from mathematics, as soon as there is a perturbation in the communication between adult and child: this is proved by the fact that pupils with lower prediction-scores performed as well as others for the final reading test, by the fact that a non-communicating aphasic learned to communicate in a structured way, by the fact that socio-economically handicapped children with serious behavioural problems, and with a performance IQ significantly better than their verbal IQ (Wechsler, 1972) learned with pleasure difficult mathematical concepts. It is very important to note here that the "good" method used by the teacher of class B does not seem accessible to deaf children who did not have the possibility to play with sounds and build a basic logical structure similar to that built by the hearing children. Their language will thus inevitably be a deaf version of the natural language, and there will be structural differences, even if these children try to communicate verbally. Nevertheless, there is only one version of the written language. It seems thus relevant to provide these children with another approach to the basic logical structure subjacent to this "normal" language. Verbal approaches do not seem useful since they are based on badly perceived *sounds* and on *phonological competences* which these children are lacking. Manipulations of concrete representations such as the A-blocks and the Dynamical Mazes provide a non-verbal approach to the requested basic logical structure. Other observations, with other devices, show that all these manipulations entail several transfers towards other domains: the verbal language when it is possible; a better mastery of reading, writing and computing; but always the development of a more structured communication system (Lowenthal, 1983, 1985b, 1988, 1990; Lowenthal & Marcq, 1981; Lowenthal & Severs, 1980).

Computers Can Provide Useful Simulations

Actual manipulations of real objects are important, but the mystery and magic associated to the computer suggested to introduce its use. The rapidity of changes on the screen is another argument in favour of this device. We have created several programmes. All of them are based on the principle of the "Ob-serving computer" (Harmegnies and Lowenthal, 1984): the computer is *on the one hand* providing the subject with information and thus the machine is a *server of information*, and simultaneously *on the other hand* the computer is recording all the subjects reactions and thus the machine is an objective *observer*. We will describe here some of the logicials created by our team: in all cases the computer is in permanent interaction with the subject, and these interactions are restricted by technical constraints. These uses of ob-serving logicials can thus be assimilated, as far as the child's reactions are concerned, to manipulations of concrete representations of formal systems. These computer manipulations are useful for the child, but they are also very fruitful for the educators: the notes taken by the computer enable him to reconstruct, after the session is over, all the steps through which the child went while constructing a correct solution; the machine thus provides the teacher with a lot of information concerning the child, information which can be used later by a therapist, in order to adapt the exercises used to the progresses made by the child.

Figure 2. This child is using the Ob-serving computer and tries to reconstruct the hidden network.

The first programme created on this principle is based on the use of the computer to provide the subject with the necessary information in order to enable him to reproduce on a base-board, using the actual bricks described by Cohors-Fresenborg (1978), a diagramm which is "hidden" on a television screen controlled by the computer (Lowenthal & Harmegnies, 1986). The computer runs the presentation of pieces of this diagram *at the request of the subject*. In fact, the experimenter provides the subject with a television screen and a box furnished with 25 buttons. On the screen, the subject sees a big rectangle subdivided by a grid into 25 small rectangles. There is a reproduction of this grid on the top of the button box: there is a button in the centre of each small rectangle. In revised versions of this programme, the box was replaced by a simple PC mouse and the number of subdivisions became a variable that can be selected by the educator. In any case, the grid on the screen divides the diagram into a certain number of rectangular zones. Each pressure on a button (or a move of the mouse followed by a pressure) provokes, in the corresponding zone of the screen, the apparition of the part of the diagram which the subject wishes to observe. This image remains present as long as the subject keeps pushing the corresponding button. Two images occupying two different zones cannot appear simultaneously on the screen. Using the partial informations they get, and even *choose to obtain*, the subjects can adopt a strategy, logical or not, useful or not, to reconstruct the network with actual bricks. They are thus in interaction with the computer to *get the specific information they want to obtain*. Subjects activities can be videotaped. In our setting, whenever a zone of the diagram is observed, the computer identifies it and keeps track of the event and of the time counter value when the image appears and when it disappears. A synchronizing signal enables us to have the same time measure in the computer file and on the video tape (with a precision of 40ms). All these data enable us to know more precisely how the subject is exploring his environment and how he learns to get relevant information: this knowledge is useful for further remediation sessions.

The second programme created by our group enables the educator to provide the child with situations where he simulates manipulations on the computer screen of Attribute Blocks, without having to use the actual blocks. A PC mouse is used mainly as simple switch (each pressure on any button is considered as an "I take it"-signal). For practical reasons, the number of colours has been restricted to three (white, red, blue) and the number of shapes has similarly been reduced to three (square, circle and triangle). This programme offers a whole range of exercises. The simplest ones can be considered as tests: a colour identification task comes first, it can be followed (in any order) by a shape identification task and by a coloured shapes identification task. During the first task, the computer colours the right part of the screen in a given colour (say blue), while it colours successively the left part of the screen in the three different colours *in the same order and at the rate of one new colour every 4 seconds*. At any moment, the child can push on one of the mouse buttons: if the two colours visible on the screen are identical, the computer will react by producing a beep and the screen will be flickering, immediately after that the computer will move to another exercise; but if the two colours were not identical the computer will go on with the present exercises. The two other tasks are similar in nature. As for the previous programme, the computer keeps track of all the information he gives to the subject and of all the subject's reactions: these data can be retrieved later and used to decide whether further exercises of this type are needed or whether the subject is ready to move to exercises concerning classification and categorization. Two further exercises can be used: in the first one the screen is devided in three columns; each column has a "label": a small coloured cloud (the colours used are white, red and blue *in an order chosen by the computer*) and the nine coloured shapes pass, one after the other, from one column to the other until the child has succeeded to put it in the correct column. He then gets a positive feedback from the computer, but it must be noted that the child never gets a negative feedback. The other classification exercise is similar, but labels with shapes replace labels with colours. Finally categorization exercises can be presented to the child: in this context the screen is still devided into three columns but there are no labels and *the child has to decide* according to which criteria he will sort the block. He can do so e.g. by waiting till he sees a blue square in the second column and by pushing then on his mouse button: this implies that this column is either "blue" or "square", the decision to place in this column a red square will *implicitly* associate to this column the label "square" and require other shapes as labels for the two other columns. When the child has successfully completed this task, and provided he does not want to start again (*he might wish to change the labels*), the learner can be confronted with a screen divided in columns and rows which can get a label in a similar fashion.

Another set of programmes consists of simple strategy games played by the child against the computer, or played by the computer against himself. In both cases the child has to discover the logical rule defining the strategy (Lowenthal, Meunier & Willaye, 1986). The child can use many different steps but, again, the computer makes notes, and these notes can be analysed later by the therapist: they give detailed information concerning the level of abstraction reached by the child and the complexity of structures he is ready to deal with. This information is essential for those who wish to help him build gradually and by himself the structures which are necessary for the harmonious development of a structured communication system accepted and understandable by all. We give here two examples of such programmes without giving all the details mentioned for the two first ones.

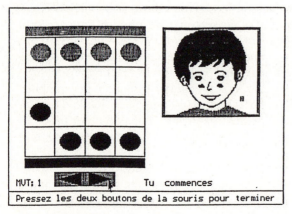

Figure 3. When a subject asks for a replay with feedback, the mini-chess program will show him this image, is this case there is a smiling face: the first move was a good one.

Interactive Introduction of the Logical Bases of a Communication System   275

The mini-chessboard programme (Lowenthal, 1991) is inspired by actual chess. The chessboard is reduced to a 4 by 4 board and the only pieces are pawns. The legal moves are the usual ones: one square forward *or* taking diagonally another pawn. White moves first. There are three possibilities to win: queen a pawn, take all the opponent's pawns *or* block the opponent. This is a finite strategy game and it is easy to discover (after many long computations) that white has a winning strategy, i.e. white can choose to play in such a way that it starts in a winning situation and can come back to a winning situation, whatever black decides to do. The computer can discover the tree of winning moves, but *in order not to discourage* the subject, the computer has been programmed to make wrong choices and thus to make *human like* mistakes. A hierarchy of computer's priorities has been devised: the computer will not make a mistake when a normally constituted human being would automatically select a good move, but otherwise the computer will select bad legal moves at the start of the game and thus give more chances to the human player. This player can try to better his strategy by asking for "replays": replays are presented with comments concerning the child's moves (a smiling face is associated to a good move, a crying face to a bad move and a neutral face to a move made when it is already too late to stop the computer from winning). This interactive programme *simulates* the behaviour of a good but imperfect human player. This enables the educator to analyse the subject's reactions in a precise framework, and to train the learner in the delicate domains of data acquisition and problem solving activities.

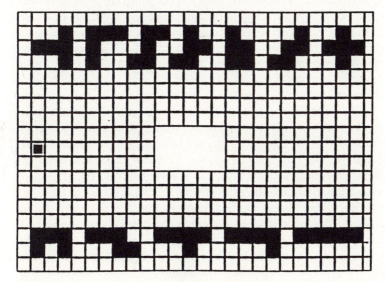

Figure 4. These twelve shapes are the pentaminoes; the child has to select the good ones, he must move them using the direction arrows or a PC mouse, he must turn and flip them using the function keys F1 to F4, and all that in order to fill exactly this small 5 by 3 rectangle.

Pentaminoes are shapes made of 5 adjacent squares. There are in fact 12 basic shapes which give by rotation and symmetry all the possible forms made of 5 such squares. The purpose of the game of pentaminoes is to create, as in a puzzle, given shapes using only the 12 basic shapes, and avoiding any potential overlap. Luc (1990) created a computer programme which enables the child to play this game on a computer screen. He adapted his first programme with our group in order to let the computer keep track of all the child's actions. The pentaminoes game, played with actual pieces, is useful since it lets the player discover physically some of the geometrical properties concerning displacements, translations, rotations and symmetries. One of the major difficulties in geometry arises when, instead of having to construct physically the solution, the learner is requested to invent, to "see" this solution without any *manipulation* of the objects he is studying, and then to represent this solution on a piece of paper, or on a *computer screen*. This is one of the major problems of space geometry. The logicial "Pentaminoes", used after a game with the actual pieces, should make it possible to develop this "vision in a 3-dimensional space" which many of our learners are lacking. Communicating with a computer which accepts certain instructions, rejects others with a negative feedback, and moreover accepts certain instructions but does not produce the expected result, favours the development of a correct spatio-temporal structure which is not completely or harmoniously developed in many deaf children.

As a last example of interactive computerized formal system, it seems relevant to mention the "Logo observer" created by our team in 1991 (Lowenthal, Marcourt & Solimando, 1992). This program is used inside the well-known Logo programming language (Papert, 1980). The purpose of this program is to record all steps used by a child while he is creating or copying a drawing on his computer screen; the program enables us also to record every small procedure created by the subject while he is working: more specifically it enables us to keep track of all attempts a child makes to define a concept. If the subject wants to use the concept of "triangle" as roof for the house he is drawing, it is relevant to note that this child gave to an apparently stupid computer a first definition which the computer cannot understand, that the computer reacted by telling the child in a very simple message that the child's instructions were not clear, and even by specifying what was the type of mistake in a way the child could understand; it is also relevant to note that the child then changed his definition, tried it again; etc. The important fact here is that the standard Logo computer language favours the development in children of anticipation, of "planning ahead" attitudes; this computer language helps them to learn to make hypotheses, to test them and to adapt them *if needed*. These attitudes are generally not present in children with communication problems; but these children also have other problems when they try to use the standard version of the Logo language, since they usually have spatio-temporal problems and since their communication troubles hinder them when they are confronted with the usual Logo error messages. This is why we chose to simplify these messages (while restricting some of the possibilities offered by the standard Logo) and why we decided to keep track of all the child's reactions: once again this is very useful for a detailed analysis of the strategies this child naturally adopts to solve logical problems, and it helps us in the organisation of remedial sessions.

Conclusion and Further Research Projects

The short description we gave here of our work with concrete representations of formal systems adapted to children suffering from communication troubles is certainly not sufficient to prove that concrete representations of formal systems are indeed as useful as we claim they are. In fact we have many other data which lead to this conclusion: concrete representations of formal systems are useful during the observation phase and during the treatment, they can be used with normal and with handicapped children (but the approaches must be rather different), they seem especially useful for children who are not able to communicate in a structured way and for subjects who are not able to understand the verbal language we use. These representations constitute structuring elements which can be used to favour the acquisition of reading skills and communicative behaviour. Finally, concrete representations of formal systems appear most useful when they are used with children who do not master a structured communication system. The interested reader will find more details in the bibliography.

Concrete representations of formal systems have been used successfully with Saïd. Some kind of communication structure has been "implanted" in his mind. One might think that this is due to other causes, but it must be stressed that all other approaches had failed, that no progress had been observed before we started to use concrete representations of formal systems. This seems to be another argument in favour of the use of the logico-mathematical technique described here. This is why we decided to use this approach with deaf children, using Cohors-Fresenborg's dynamical mazes: these children were in a situation similar to Saïd's situation since they too could not play with sounds, they could not discover any structure in them and it thus seemed useful to provide them *externally* with such a structure. Moreover, these children formed a group of deaf children, aged 7, sitting in the same classroom and having the same teacher as children with normal hearing, children who could discover structures in the music of linguistic sounds. At first the deaf children seemed to be left out of the main group. The first observations we made using the Dynamical Mazes were encouraging: the deaf children progressed rapidly and mastered in a few sessions the technique used; they understood the logical problems and solved them. Then, they started to explain non-verbally *their* structural discoveries to the learners with normal hearing (who had been distracted by the absence of verbal exchanges in our exercises). By proving that they were able to give relevant and complex explanations, the deaf children became active members of the complete group. This gave them more self confidence and helped them to develop a structured communication system adapted to their new relations with hearing people. Further experiments in that direction are needed before we can conclude; the use of interactive computer programmes enabling us to observe in a non-verbal way children's *answering strategies* and the processes they use to *retrieve the data they need* will help us to reach a final conclusion.

Acknowledgments

This paper has been partially supported by an ANAH-Rotary grant.

References

Bernstein, B., Brandeis, B. & Henderson, D. (1969). Speech of lower-class children (Letter to the Editor). *Developmental Medicine and Child Neurology, 11*, 113-116.

Bruner, J.S. (1966). On cognitive growth I and II. In: Bruner, Olver & Greenfield (eds), *Studies in cognitive growth*. New York: John Wiley, 1-67.

Bruner, J.S. (1972). Nature and uses of immaturity. *American Psychologist, 27*, 8.

Cohors-Fresenborg, E. (1978). Learning problem solving by developing automata networks. *Revue de Phonétique Appliquée, 46/47*, 93-99.

Cordier, J. (1975). U*ne anthropologie de l'inadaptation - La dynamique de l'exclusion sociale*. Bruxelles: Editions de l'Université de Bruxelles.

Cordier, J. & Lowenthal, F. (1973). Can new maths help disturbed children? (Letter to the Editor). *The Lancet, August 18*, 383-384.

Cordier, J., Lowenthal, F. & Héraux, C. (1975). Enseignement de la mathématique et exercices de verbalisation chez les enfants caractériels. *Enfance, 1*, 111-124.

Dienes, Z.P. (1966). *Construction des mathématiques*. Paris: Presses Universitaires de France.
Dienes, Z.P. & Golding, E.M. (1970). *Les premiers pas en mathématique : logique et jeux logiques*. Paris: OCDL.
Harmegnies, B. & Lowenthal, F. (1984). Dispositifs de communication non verbale et ordinateurs. *Humankybernetik, 25, 3*, 115-124.
Inizan, A. (1983). *Le temps d'apprendre à lire*. Paris: Librairie Armand Colin.
Jakobson, R. (1964). Les lois phoniques du langage enfantin et leur place dans la phonologie générale. Quoted in Troubetzkoy *Principes de phonologie*, translated by Cantineau J. Paris: Klincksieck.
Lowenthal, F. (1983). Strategy games, winning strategies, and Non-Verbal Communication devices (at the age of 8). *PME 7*, 364-368.
Lowenthal, F. (1984). Productions langagières d'enfants manipulant un dispositif non verbal de communication. *Revue de Phonétique Appliquée, 69*, 11-46.
Lowenthal, F. (1985a). Non-Verbal Communication Devices in language acquisition. *Revue de Phonétique Appliquée, 73-74-75*, 155-166.
Lowenthal, F. (1985b). Pegboard as basis for programmation -in 5- and 6-year olds. *PME 9, Vol. I*, 47-52.
Lowenthal, F. (1986a). Relevance of typically logico-mathematical formalisms for research in psychology. *Logique et Analyse*, 501-508.
Lowenthal, F. (1986b). NVCDs are srtucturing elements. In: *Proceedings of PME 10*, 363-368.
Lowenthal, F. (1987). Représentation concrète de systèmes formels et structuration d'une communication. R*evue de Phonétique Appliquée, 82-83-84*, 231-245.
Lowenthal, F. (1988). Concrete introduction to programming languages and observation of Piagetian stages - Clinical interviews -. *PME 12, Vol. II*, 479-486.
Lowenthal, F. (1990a). Pegboard as structuring element for the verbal language. *RPA, 95/97*, 255-262.
Lowenthal, F. (1990b). *The stupid automaton*. Poster for the 6th International PEG Meeting, Genova/Rapallo.
Lowenthal, F. & Harmegnies, B. (1986). The ob-serving computer. In: F. Lowenthal & F. Vandamme (eds), *Pragmatics and education*. New York: Plenum Press, 239-250.
Lowenthal, F., Marcourt, C. & Solimando, C. (1992). *Evolution of problem solving strategies in some handicapped children using Logo*. Abstracts of the 25th International Congress of Psychology, Bruxelles.
Lowenthal, F. & Marcq, J. (1980). Dynamical mazes used to favour communication among 7- and 8-year olds. *PME 4*, 370-376.
Lowenthal, F. & Marcq, J. (1981). Logic, auxiliary formalism and geometry by telephone call. *PME 5, Vol. I.*, 265-270.

Lowenthal, F. & Marcq, J. (1982). How do children discover strategies (at the age of 7)? *PME 6,* 287-292.
Lowenthal, F., Meunier, M. & Willaye, E. (1986). Jeu de Nim informatisé : recherche d'une stratégie gagnante. *Les Sciences de l'Education pour l'Ere Nouvelle, Actes du 30ème colloque de l'A.I.P.E.L.F.*, 329-342.
Lowenthal, F. & Saerens, J. (1986). Evolution of an aphasic child after the introduction of NVCDs. In: F. Lowenthal & F. Vandamme (eds), *Pragmatics and education.* New York: Plenum Press, 301-330.
Lowenthal, F. & Servers, R. (1980). Inductive and axiomatic reasoning at elementary school level. *PME 3,* 148-154.
Lowenthal, F. & Vandamme, F. (1986). *Pragmatics and education.* New York: Plenum Press.
Luc, V. (1990). *Les pentaminos.* Travail de fin d'études, Institut Supérieur d'Enseignement, Flénu.
Osgood, C. (1980). *Lectures on language performance.* New York: Springer Verlag.
Papert, S. (1980). *Mindstorms : Computers, Children and Powerful Ideas.* New York: Basic Books.
Papy, F. (1972). *Les enfants et la mathématique.* Bruxelles: Didier, vol 1., 1970 ; vol 2., 1971 ; vol 3., 1972.
Papy, F. & Papy, Ge. (1968). *L'enfant et les graphes.* Bruxelles: Didier.
Papy, Ga. (1956). Epreuves de niveau d'instruction du passage de classe. *Revue pédagogique, 25,* 1989-2010.
Piaget, J. & Inhelder, B. (1959). *La genèse des structures logiques élémentaires - Classifications et sériations.* Neuchâtel: Delachaux et Niestlé.
Rondal, J.-A. (1983). *L'interaction adulte-enfant et la construction du langage.* Bruxelles: Pierre Mardaga.
Siegel, L.S. (1978). The relationship of language and thought in the preoperational child: a reconsideration of nonverbal alternatives to Piagetian tasks. In: Siegel & Brainerd (eds), *Alternatives to Piaget - Critical essays on the theory.* New York: Academic Press, 43-67.
Silverman, H., McNaughton, S. & Kates, B. (1982). *Le manuel du système Bliss.* Québec: Association de Paralysie Cérébrale du Québec.
Wechsler, D. (1972). *Labyrinthes et Similitudes.* Paris: W.P.P.S.I., Editions du Centre de Psychologie Appliquée.

Contributors

Abberton, E., 137
Arends, N., 165
Ball, V., 137
Bouwhuis, D., 3
Caselli, C., 43
Corazza, S., 43
Dempsey, J., 95
Destombes, F., 187
Elsendoorn, B., 105
Engels, L., 71
Eriksen, O., 249
Esser, G., 175
Foulds, R., 231
Fourcin, A., 137
Geysels, G., 55
Guilliams, I., 121
IJsseldijk, F., 105
Levitt, H., 95
Lombardi, G., 43
Loncke, F., 31, 55

Lowenthal, F., 259
Meiracker, M. van den, 21
Nelson, K., 55
Nolte, P., 175
Pennacchi, B., 43
Peters, S., 231
Povel, D., 165
Prillwitz, S., 215
Printzen, R., 175
Prinz, P., 55
Rampelli, S., 43
Schulmeister, R., 215
Smith, P., 239
Spaai, G., 151
Stokoe, W., 199
Veenker, H., 81
Volterra, V., 43
Wilcox, S., 199
Willems, C., 55
Woll, B., 239
Youdelman, K., 95

Subject Index

acquisition
  language 21
  vocabulary 21
acquisition period 129. *See also*
    discovery period
American Sign Language 199–213
asymmetry in feedback 240
auditory feedback 187–196

Belgian Sign Language 61
bilingual
  education 44
  learning environment 43
bimodal communication 33
British Sign Language 239

cognitive language learning 77
communication disorders 187–196
communication processes 3
communication skills 60, 95, 105
  evaluation 95
  training 95, 105
communication system
  structured 269
communicative principles 3
communicative skills 11
complementarity principle 8
complementary information 130
compound signs 218. *See also*
    hyphenated signs
computer dictionary 215–230
continuous discourse tracking 99, 107

dialogue 3
  content 6
  protocol 6
dialogue control acts 6
dictionary
  computer 215-230
  sign language 251
  signed 199–213
discourse 55–70
discourse development 55
discovery period 129. *See also*
    acquisition period
disorders
  communication 187–196
  voice 187, 187–196

evaluation 113–117

feedback 138
  asymmetry in - 240
  auditory 151, 187–196
  visual 138, 187–196
finite sets 72
formal system 260
frequency 72
  objective 72
  subjective 72
friction 138

German Sign Language 218
grammar 81

hearing aid
  pattern element 137
hyphenated signs 218. *See also* compound signs

Interactive instruction 3, 14–16
interactive video 250
interactive videodisc 44, 105–119, 121–136
intonation pattern 139, 151
Italian Sign Language 44

Klang-Vektor-Analyse 175–186

language
  processing strategies 38
  sign 3
  spoken 3
language acquisition 21, 81
language acquisition process 21
Language Connecting Information (LCI) 39, 41
Language Distinctive Information (LDI) 39, 41
language learning 250
language skills 11, 60, 108
linguistic comprehension 177
linguistic information
  decoding 31
  encoding 33
linguistic manipulations 76
linguistic systems 39
lipreading 121–136. *See also* speechreading
literacy development 55
logic 261
logographic systems 200
loudness 138

maternal reflective method 21, 77
modality 31
  auditory 32
  representational 32
  switching 31
  visual 32

multimedia technology 55
multimodality 31, 55–70

neural networks 231
non-verbal communication 260
Norwegian Sign Language 250

objective frequency 72

parrots 4
pattern element hearing aid 137
phonology 23
pitch 138, 151–163, 188, 191
processing information 32
prototype 22, 170, 188

reading skills 60
reading strategies 82
recognition scores 107

self-monitoring 160
semantics 23
sensory interchangeability 175
Sign Language
  American 199-213
  Belgian 61
  British 241
  German 218
  Italian 44
  Norwegian 251
sign language 3
  computer recognition of - 231
  dialect 217
  formation 218
Signed Dutch 61
signs
  biomechanical structure of - 231
SiVo 143
skills 11
  communication 60
  communicative 11
  language 11, 60
  reading 60
  text 60

speech perception 107, 138
speech production 138, 152
speech therapy 187–196
speech training system 97, 195
speechreading 105–119. *See also* lipreading
spoken language 3
strategies
  language processing 38
  top-down 36
structure
  sentence- 81
  word- 81
structured communication system 269
subjective frequency 72
syntax 23

text skills 60
top-down strategies 36

transformation of speech to colour 175–186

uncertainty principle 5
  recursive 5

video compression 205
viseme 107
visual aid 165–174
visual channel 175
visual feedback 138, 187–196, 239
visual feedback of intonation 151
visual grammar 81–91
vocabulary acquisition 21
voice disorders 187–196
voicing 138, 152, 191
vowel onset 151
vowel timbre 138

writing 199–213

NATO ASI Series F

Including Special Programmes on Sensory Systems for Robotic Control (ROB) and on Advanced Educational Technology (AET)

Vol. 42: Real-Time Object Measurement and Classification. Edited by A. K. Jain. VIII, 407 pages. 1988. *(ROB)*

Vol. 43: Sensors and Sensory Systems for Advanced Robots. Edited by P. Dario. XI, 597 pages. 1988. *(ROB)*

Vol. 44: Signal Processing and Pattern Recognition in Nondestructive Evaluation of Materials. Edited by C. H. Chen. VIII, 344 pages. 1988. *(ROB)*

Vol. 45: Syntactic and Structural Pattern Recognition. Edited by G. Ferraté, T. Pavlidis, A. Sanfeliu and H. Bunke. XVI, 467 pages. 1988. *(ROB)*

Vol. 46: Recent Advances in Speech Understanding and Dialog Systems. Edited by H. Niemann, M. Lang and G. Sagerer. X, 521 pages. 1988.

Vol. 47: Advanced Computing Concepts and Techniques in Control Engineering. Edited by M. J. Denham and A. J. Laub. XI, 518 pages. 1988.

Vol. 48: Mathematical Models for Decision Support. Edited by G. Mitra. IX, 762 pages. 1988.

Vol. 49: Computer Integrated Manufacturing. Edited by I. B. Turksen. VIII, 568 pages. 1988.

Vol. 50: CAD Based Programming for Sensory Robots. Edited by B. Ravani. IX, 565 pages. 1988. *(ROB)*

Vol. 51: Algorithms and Model Formulations in Mathematical Programming. Edited by S. W. Wallace. IX, 190 pages. 1989.

Vol. 52: Sensor Devices and Systems for Robotics. Edited by A. Casals. IX, 362 pages. 1989. *(ROB)*

Vol. 53: Advanced Information Technologies for Industrial Material Flow Systems. Edited by S. Y. Nof and C. L. Moodie. IX, 710 pages. 1989.

Vol. 54: A Reappraisal of the Efficiency of Financial Markets. Edited by R. M. C. Guimarães, B. G. Kingsman and S. J. Taylor. X, 804 pages. 1989.

Vol. 55: Constructive Methods in Computing Science. Edited by M. Broy. VII, 478 pages. 1989.

Vol. 56: Multiple Criteria Decision Making and Risk Analysis Using Microcomputers. Edited by B. Karpak and S. Zionts. VII, 399 pages. 1989.

Vol. 57: Kinematics and Dynamic Issues in Sensor Based Control. Edited by G. E. Taylor. XI, 456 pages. 1990. *(ROB)*

Vol. 58: Highly Redundant Sensing in Robotic Systems. Edited by J. T. Tou and J. G. Balchen. X, 322 pages. 1990. *(ROB)*

Vol. 59: Superconducting Electronics. Edited by H. Weinstock and M. Nisenoff. X, 441 pages. 1989.

Vol. 60: 3D Imaging in Medicine. Algorithms, Systems, Applications. Edited by K. H. Höhne, H. Fuchs and S. M. Pizer. IX, 460 pages. 1990.

Vol. 61: Knowledge, Data and Computer-Assisted Decisions. Edited by M. Schader and W. Gaul. VIII, 421 pages. 1990.

NATO ASI Series F

Including Special Programmes on Sensory Systems for Robotic Control (ROB) and on Advanced Educational Technology (AET)

Vol. 62: Supercomputing. Edited by J. S. Kowalik. X, 425 pages. 1990.

Vol. 63: Traditional and Non-Traditional Robotic Sensors. Edited by T. C. Henderson. VIII, 468 pages. 1990. *(ROB)*

Vol. 64: Sensory Robotics for the Handling of Limp Materials. Edited by P. M. Taylor. IX, 343 pages. 1990. *(ROB)*

Vol. 65: Mapping and Spatial Modelling for Navigation. Edited by L. F. Pau. VIII, 357 pages. 1990. *(ROB)*

Vol. 66: Sensor-Based Robots: Algorithms and Architectures. Edited by C. S. G. Lee. X, 285 pages. 1991. *(ROB)*

Vol. 67: Designing Hypermedia for Learning. Edited by D. H. Jonassen and H. Mandl. XXV, 457 pages. 1990. *(AET)*

Vol. 68: Neurocomputing. Algorithms, Architectures and Applications. Edited by F. Fogelman Soulié and J. Hérault. XI, 455 pages. 1990.

Vol. 69: Real-Time Integration Methods for Mechanical System Simulation. Edited by E. J. Haug and R. C. Deyo. VIII, 352 pages. 1991.

Vol. 70: Numerical Linear Algebra, Digital Signal Processing and Parallel Algorithms. Edited by G. H. Golub and P. Van Dooren. XIII, 729 pages. 1991.

Vol. 71: Expert Systems and Robotics. Edited by T. Jordanides and B. Torby. XII, 744 pages. 1991.

Vol. 72: High-Capacity Local and Metropolitan Area Networks. Architecture and Performance Issues. Edited by G. Pujolle. X, 536 pages. 1991.

Vol. 73: Automation and Systems Issues in Air Traffic Control. Edited by J. A. Wise, V. D. Hopkin and M. L. Smith. XIX, 594 pages. 1991.

Vol. 74: Picture Archiving and Communication Systems (PACS) in Medicine. Edited by H. K. Huang, O. Ratib, A. R. Bakker and G. Witte. XI, 438 pages. 1991.

Vol. 75: Speech Recognition and Understanding. Recent Advances, Trends and Applications. Edited by P. Laface and Renato De Mori. XI, 559 pages. 1991.

Vol. 76: Multimedia Interface Design in Education. Edited by A. D. N. Edwards and S. Holland. XIV, 216 pages. 1992. *(AET)*

Vol. 77: Computer Algorithms for Solving Linear Algebraic Equations. The State of the Art. Edited by E. Spedicato. VIII, 352 pages. 1991.

Vol. 78: Integrating Advanced Technology into Technology Education. Edited by M. Hacker, A. Gordon and M. de Vries. VIII, 185 pages. 1991. *(AET)*

Vol. 79: Logic, Algebra, and Computation. Edited by F. L. Bauer. VII, 485 pages. 1991.

Vol. 80: Intelligent Tutoring Systems for Foreign Language Learning. Edited by M. L. Swartz and M. Yazdani. IX, 347 pages. 1992. *(AET)*

Vol. 81: Cognitive Tools for Learning. Edited by P. A. M. Kommers, D. H. Jonassen, and J. T. Mayes. X, 278 pages. 1992. *(AET)*

Vol. 82: Combinatorial Optimization. New Frontiers in Theory and Practice. Edited by M. Akgül, H. W. Hamacher, and S. Tüfekçi. XI, 334 pages. 1992.

NATO ASI Series F

Including Special Programmes on Sensory Systems for Robotic Control (ROB) and on Advanced Educational Technology (AET)

Vol. 83: Active Perception and Robot Vision. Edited by A. K. Sood and H. Wechsler. IX, 756 pages. 1992.

Vol. 84: Computer-Based Learning Environments and Problem Solving. Edited by E. De Corte, M. C. Linn, H. Mandl, and L. Verschaffel. XVI, 488 pages. 1992. *(AET)*

Vol. 85: Adaptive Learning Environments. Foundations and Frontiers. Edited by M. Jones and P. H. Winne. VIII, 408 pages. 1992. *(AET)*

Vol. 86: Intelligent Learning Environments and Knowledge Acquisition in Physics. Edited by A. Tiberghien and H. Mandl. VIII, 285 pages. 1992. *(AET)*

Vol. 87: Cognitive Modelling and Interactive Environments. With demo diskettes (Apple and IBM compatible). Edited by F. L. Engel, D. G. Bouwhuis, T. Bösser, and G. d'Ydewalle. IX, 311 pages. 1992. *(AET)*

Vol. 88: Programming and Mathematical Method. Edited by M. Broy. VIII, 428 pages. 1992.

Vol. 89: Mathematical Problem Solving and New Information Technologies. Edited by J. P. Ponte, J. F. Matos, J. M. Matos, and D. Fernandes. XV, 346 pages. 1992. *(AET)*

Vol. 90: Collaborative Learning Through Computer Conferencing. Edited by A. R. Kaye. X, 260 pages. 1992. *(AET)*

Vol. 91: New Directions for Intelligent Tutoring Systems. Edited by E. Costa. X, 296 pages. 1992. *(AET)*

Vol. 92: Hypermedia Courseware: Structures of Communication and Intelligent Help. Edited by A. Oliveira. X, 241 pages. 1992. *(AET)*

Vol. 93: Interactive Multimedia Learning Environments. Human Factors and Technical Considerations on Design Issues. Edited by M. Giardina. VIII, 254 pages. 1992. *(AET)*

Vol. 94: Logic and Algebra of Specification. Edited by F. L. Bauer, W. Brauer, and H. Schwichtenberg. VII, 442 pages. 1993.

Vol. 95: Comprehensive Systems Design: A New Educational Technology. Edited by C. M. Reigeluth, B. H. Banathy, and J. R. Olson. IX, 437 pages. 1993. *(AET)*

Vol. 96: New Directions in Educational Technology. Edited by E. Scanlon and T. O'Shea. VIII, 251 pages. 1992. *(AET)*

Vol. 97: Advanced Models of Cognition for Medical Training and Practice. Edited by D. A. Evans and V. L. Patel. XI, 372 pages. 1992. *(AET)*

Vol. 98: Medical Images: Formation, Handling and Evaluation. Edited by A. E. Todd-Pokropek and M. A. Viergever. IX, 700 pages. 1992.

Vol. 99: Multisensor Fusion for Computer Vision. Edited by J. K. Aggarwal. XI, 456 pages. 1993. *(ROB)*

Vol. 100: Communication from an Artificial Intelligence Perspective. Theoretical and Applied Issues. Edited by A. Ortony, J. Slack and O. Stock. XII, 260 pages. 1992.

Vol. 101: Recent Developments in Decision Support Systems. Edited by C. W. Holsapple and A. B. Whinston. XI, 618 pages. 1993.

NATO ASI Series F

Including Special Programmes on Sensory Systems for Robotic Control (ROB) and on Advanced Educational Technology (AET)

Vol. 102: Robots and Biological Systems: Towards a New Bionics? Edited by P. Dario, G. Sandini and P. Aebischer. XII, 786 pages. 1993.

Vol. 103: Parallel Computing on Distributed Memory Multiprocessors. Edited by F. Özgüner and F. Erçal. VIII, 332 pages. 1993.

Vol. 104: Instructional Models in Computer-Based Learning Environments. Edited by S. Dijkstra, H. P. M. Krammer and J. J. G. van Merriënboer. X, 510 pages. 1993. *(AET)*

Vol. 105: Designing Environments for Constructive Learning. Edited by T. M. Duffy, J. Lowyck and D. H. Jonassen. VIII, 374 pages. 1993. *(AET)*

Vol. 106: Software for Parallel Computation. Edited by J. S. Kowalik and L. Grandinetti. IX, 363 pages. 1993.

Vol. 107: Advanced Educational Technologies for Mathematics and Science. Edited by D. L. Ferguson. XII, 749 pages. 1993. *(AET)*

Vol. 108: Concurrent Engineering: Tools and Technologies for Mechanical System Design. Edited by E. J. Haug. XIII, 998 pages. 1993.

Vol. 109: Advanced Educational Technology in Technology Education. Edited by A. Gordon, M. Hacker and M. de Vries. VIII, 253 pages. 1993. *(AET)*

Vol. 110: Verification and Validation of Complex Systems: Human Factors Issues. Edited by J. A. Wise, V. D. Hopkin and P. Stager. XIII, 704 pages. 1993.

Vol. 111: Cognitive Models and Intelligent Environments for Learning Programming. Edited by E. Lemut, B. du Boulay and G. Dettori. VIII, 305 pages. 1993. *(AET)*

Vol. 112: Item Banking: Interactive Testing and Self-Assessment. Edited by D. A. Leclercq and J. E. Bruno. VIII, 261 pages. 1993. *(AET)*

Vol. 113: Interactive Learning Technology for the Deaf. Edited by B. A. G. Elsendoorn and F. Coninx. XIII, 285 pages. 1993. *(AET)*

Vol. 114: Intelligent Systems: Safety, Reliability and Maintainability Issues. Edited by O. Kaynak, G. Honderd and E. Grant. XI, 340 pages. 1993.

Vol. 115: Learning Electricity and Electronics with Advanced Educational Technology. Edited by M. Caillot. VII, 329 pages. 1993. *(AET)*

Vol. 116: Control Technology in Elementary Education. Edited by B. Denis. IX, 311 pages. 1993 *(AET)*

Vol. 118: Program Design Calculi. Edited by M. Broy. VIII, 409 pages. 1993.

Vol. 121: Learning from Computers: Mathematics Education and Technology. Edited by C. Keitel and K. Ruthven. XIII, 332 pages. 1993. *(AET)*